Chris Waddle
the authorised biography

Chris Waddle

the authorised biography

MEL STEIN

SIMON & SCHUSTER
A VIACOM COMPANY

First published in Great Britain by Simon & Schuster Ltd, 1997
A Viacom Company

Simon & Schuster Ltd
West Garden Place
Kendal Street
London W2 2AQ

Simon & Schuster Australia
Sydney

A CIP catalogue record for this book is available from the British Library

ISBN 0-684-81926-0

Typeset in Stempel Garamond 11/16pt by
Palimpsest Book Production Limited, Polmont, Stirlingshire
Printed and bound in Great Britain by
Butler & Tanner Ltd, Frome and London

For Jackie Milburn, who inspired us all, for all the fans in the North-East who continue to live in hope, and for Nicky, who kept the faith and Paul, who didn't.

prologue

I never did like taking penalties. I had no more than a sixty per cent record of putting them away, which is not exactly encouraging, considering the spot is only twelve yards away from a gaping goal, there's only a keeper to beat and he can't move until you've actually struck the ball.

The fourth of July 1990 may have been Independence Day for some, but not for those of us who'd been sweating it out for 120 minutes in the heat of Turin. I felt exhausted. The tournament seemed to have taken forever, that first game against the Republic of Ireland a dim and distant memory, a match that seemed to belong to another cup from which we'd already moved on. Even this semi-final against West Germany felt as if it had been going on for hours. My legs were like lead, my body was about half a stone lighter than when I'd started. I just wanted it to be over.

We'd been faced with the possibility of penalties against Belgium, but it hadn't come to that. Gazza and Platt had come to our rescue; but they couldn't do it now. The ninety minutes, the extra half-hour. They'd both run their course. Platt had put his penalty away, Gazza was in no fit state to kick off, let alone take a penalty. Of course, we'd talked about it before, but then it had all been a joke. Now it was for real. Bobby Robson had always thought that when it came down to the wire we had as good a chance as anyone else. We had loads of penalty-takers in the side – Beardsley, Lineker, Platt, Steven and of course, Stuart Pearce. You would have bet your house on Stuart scoring from the spot. He had a way, a philosophy. He knew exactly how the keeper would react to whatever it was he was going to do, and he had an instinctive ability to change his mind before the keeper could work out all over again what it was he was going to do. But most of all, there was the power with which he hit the ball, and if all else failed – even if the ball went straight at the keeper – most times the ball would still go into the net. Only this time it hadn't worked, the keeper could not help but stop it, and none of us could imagine how Stuart felt. I didn't have to wait too long to find out.

I must have thought too much about it. Even if I'd scored, it was still going to take a save to keep us in it. Maybe that was playing on my mind. I wasn't thinking mathematically, though; I was praying. And for somebody who doesn't pray too often, I was praying very hard. I didn't have time to discuss it with the Boss. I didn't even have time to change my mind as I took the run up. I'd already hit the crossbar from the halfway line. This was just a few short yards from the net, but the keeper looked a lot bigger close up. And was it my imagination, or did the goal also look smaller?

When I watched it again on television, I could see my body shape was all wrong. It's one of the basics you learn: get yourself over the ball and it has to keep low. The other thing that surprised me was the noise. You could hear it on the box, but at that moment I felt I was stepping off the edge of the world into silence. I thought that if I blasted it, then I had a better chance of it going in. I put the ball down, turned my back on it, then turned again and ran in a yard and a half. All I could hear was the sound of my own boots on the turf and then the thump as my left foot made contact with the ball. I think the real problem was that I hit it too well. I made proper contact, but if I'd mis-hit it, I felt it might have gone in.

It didn't and I didn't even look up as the ball sailed over the bar. I just threw my head back in despair. Later somebody told me a spectator had caught the ball and was refusing to return it. Good luck to him. I never wanted to see it again. Some newspaper wanted to arrange a presentation, but I wasn't having any of that. For a long time I couldn't even bear to talk about it.

Somebody, Lineker, I think, and maybe the manager as well, came across to console me. Even Gazza had forgotten his own problems. He was still crying, but now he was crying for me, for Pearce, for England, and not just for himself. He wouldn't miss the final because of his yellow card. We'd all miss the final because I'd just struck a penalty over the bar. I slumped to the ground, knowing that my life would never be the same again.

chapter 1

He's never played for Gateshead, at least not yet; but that was where it began. He would play for Newcastle United, for Tottenham Hotspur, for Olympique de Marseille, for Sheffield Wednesday, for Sunderland and for England. He would also play for Tow Law, Falkirk and Bradford City – humble clubs, but then Chris Waddle always was a humble man.

It would be inaccurate to say that the origins of Chris Waddle were also humble. Modest, yes; humble, no. Chris never knew real poverty, although there was never money to spare. His father, Joseph, was a true Geordie. He'd left school at the age of fourteen and immediately gone to work down the pits. It was 1928. The Jarrow March was eight years away, but already there were murmurs of discontent down the mines about pay and conditions. Everybody was looking for a way out, and Joe Waddle hoped that the fact he could play football a bit might be his escape route. But in the 1920s 'a bit' wasn't enough. He had the skill, but he just lacked the cutting edge of ambition and that vital factor of luck. Jackie Milburn, Tyneside's greatest son, said that when Newcastle wanted a new number nine they'd whistle down the mines. When that whistle blew, there were too many more talented players in the queue ahead of Joe. Not that he'd have wanted to play for Newcastle anyway. He was Sunderland through and through.

Joe, in fact, had an advantage over Chris. He was two-footed from the start and played at either inside-right or inside-left as an amateur for his local team, Pelaw. Football today is different. It is all about professionalism and money. The Premier League, television rights, marketing, merchandising, parents spending more on replica kits than Joe Waddle earned in a year, then having to find money for the away kit; and then having to repeat the process every two years.

Back in the twenties it was all functional. One shirt, washed and re-washed until it was almost transparent. Heavy boots, saved up for, studded, leather. A leather ball with laces, thudding against the forehead like a cannon-ball, leaving the players punch-drunk, until they could assemble in the snug of their local pubs or working men's clubs and get drunk for real.

Even if Joe Waddle had fulfilled his dream and turned professional for Sunderland, he could not have expected to have earned very much more than he received in the pits. Working above ground rather than beneath it would have been the main advantage. Fortune would still have eluded him, even if fame did not.

When Joe was a lad, everybody knew the Sunderland players by name and sight. On a Saturday night, particularly when they had won, they would never have to dip into their own wage packets to buy a drink. Everybody would be keen to get them in, so that they could boast at the pit-head or factory on Monday morning that they'd bought a drink for the likes of Connor or one of their other heroes.

Joe's dreams were never to go beyond that vicarious glory. At twenty-five, when he was probably already too old to make it into the professional game, someone blew the whistle for the start of the Second World War, and for the next six years he would play football only when his ship was in port.

He was in his mid-twenties when he met and married Elizabeth Ashton. As far as his family was concerned, it was as if he had married a foreigner. She was not a Geordie, but a Lancastrian, having been born in the village of Ashton itself, quite near to Wigan. Worse than that, she and her sisters moved south to Watford during the war. Those who do not know Chris particularly well believe him to be the archetypal Geordie. Yet the fact that he has been able to slot in so well wherever he has gone within the country, and the world, suggests a more cosmopolitan streak, due in no small way to the influence of his mother. It is odd, in these days of jet travel, to remember that just a generation ago people in the north-east would think of Watford in the south as some glamorous Bali Ha'i, to be visited at some unspecified time in the future, but meanwhile to be regarded with suspicion. Yet that was the way of it.

With the war behind them, Elizabeth and Joseph made their first home in council accommodation in Gateshead. It was where Joe had been born and bred, and he did not see any need to move any further afield. Some twenty years after he had started down the pits, he'd moved onwards and upwards and was now employed by Monckton Coke works. The Navy had shown him another way of life, and although they had been tough and dangerous years, the fresh air and travel meant that he could no longer face the confines of working underground. Coke to today's teenager is a drink, a baseball cap, a T-shirt, a life-style.

For Joe and his work-mates it meant transforming the coal that came out of the pit into a substance that was fast replacing coal in the nation's grates. Yet the years down the mines had taken their toll, and the innumerable cigarettes that were as much a part of pub life as the endless pints had left their mark deep in his lungs.

Joe's dreams of having a professional footballer in the family were rekindled when he reached the relatively advanced age of forty-one. In 1955 the Waddles' first son, Raymond, was born and Elizabeth gave up her job to become a full-time housewife and mother. Even in her choice of employment she had been a little out of step, just that bit more middle-class, having worked first in the physiotherapy department of her local hospital and then for the local Co-operative. In 1958, Joseph junior became a second chance of a Waddle pulling on the red and white striped shirt of his dad's beloved Sunderland, and in his mid-forties Joe didn't really want any more children. He thought he had his footballing dynasty well and truly in place. But Elizabeth was desperate for a daughter, and throughout her third pregnancy in 1960, the infant was constantly referred to as 'her', even to the point of considering only girls' names. It wasn't to be. On 14 December 1960, the third member of the Waddle trio of sons was born.

Christopher Roland Waddle's first cry announced new life in the north-east of England, and also in its way heralded in a new era for a new generation. The sixties, which had been prefaced by Harold Macmillan with his famous wind of change speech, were hardly yet swinging. A beetle was something you crushed under your foot, rolling stones proverbially gathered no moss, and you'd put the surname Thomas to Dylan rather than the first name of Bob. Elvis was still the king with his coif of dark oiled hair and bedroom eyes. 'It's Now or Never' had been number one in the charts for six weeks, and if Chris Waddle had been able to read, he would have breathed a sigh of relief to learn that the last National Servicemen in the United Kingdom received their call-up cards a couple of weeks after his birth. A new president in the States, the youthful and vibrant John F. Kennedy, had been in the White House for just a month, promising a new life to millions of Americans.

As Joe and Elizabeth hid their disappointment and abandoned their plans to call the baby Gail, they could not have envisaged that this new son would cast a spell over the world of football, would travel the world pulling on the white shirt of England with pride, would make the top ten in the music charts and appear on the stage of the London Palladium, mix with prime ministers and royalty, own race-horses, live in villas in the south of France, and for a moment become one of the two most unpopular men in England.

chapter 2

Chris Waddle began his life in Leam Lane in Gateshead, a massive council estate, probably one of the biggest in England. As it climbs up the hill away from the town, it is hard to see where it starts or ends. Most of its occupants were families rehoused from The Felling in Gateshead itself, families used to living in crowded conditions in tightly packed terraced houses, which they still regarded as home and whose demolition they had viewed with mixed emotions.

By 1963, the family moved on to a new council house in Gosforth Terrace. Already at the age of three, Chris was football crazy. He didn't really have a choice. His mother was as committed as the rest of the family and in later years, whenever his father was unable to take the boys to Roker Park, she needed no persuasion to round up her brood and go to the match.

She adored Len Shackleton: Shack the magician; Shack the renegade. How could she have known that her own son would become a folk hero in distant Marseille, become known through-out France as 'Le Magicien' and would, as his own career developed into maturity, also gain a reputation as a maverick and renegade? Whatever was to come, Elizabeth Waddle liked her footballers with style, with panache, with personality, and in time nobody was to enjoy Chris Waddle's performances more than his mother. And nobody was to be more critical.

Five separate playing fields backed on to Gosforth Terrace, and if Chris had been able to have his way he would have played on all five at once. As it was, he was not allowed out of the house on his own, but had to wait for his older brothers to return from school. From mid-afternoon he'd take up his post as a sentinel at the front room window, awaiting their return, and even before they'd had time for tea he would drag them impatiently out to play with him.

Both his brothers could play a bit in their own right. Chris started at Bill Quay Junior Mixed Infants in 1965, by which time Ray had already made the school team. Joseph junior was not quite in his class as a footballer, but was certainly good enough to play for Bill Quay, so that when Chris pulled on the school shirt, the Waddles became the first trio of brothers to represent the side. It was Joe who talked Chris into the team when he was only six. Throughout his career Chris was never one to miss an opportunity and, despite the fact he was playing with boys three or four years older than himself and twice his size, he more than held his own.

He stood out for several reasons, apart from his age. The school could not afford to buy a strip to fit the diminutive Waddle, so the third brother was forced to wear a shirt that covered not only his shorts but his knees as well. It had to be said that Bill Quay JMI did not have a footballing reputation to strike fear into the hearts of its opponents. Joe was the goalkeeper and most of his mathematical studies involved counting the number of times he'd have to pick the ball out of the net in each match.

When he ran out of fingers, he'd generally get bored and lean against the post chatting to a friend, while the score moved towards the necessity of him utilising his toes as well to keep the tally. As shots rained in on him from a distance, sometimes he would heed the warnings of his brothers and sometimes not.

Even then, Chris did not approve of his brothers' and team-mates' approach to the game. Football had to be taken seriously. It was about winning, and if you didn't take it seriously then you didn't win. You might not win even if you did take it seriously, but at least you could say you had tried.

However, as far as Chris was concerned, you certainly didn't need to try when it came to lessons. 'Of course, I regret it a bit now. Particularly when I'm on the radio or television. You're looking for words and you can't find them because you don't know them. In a way I learned much more once I'd left school. I was never a great one for formal teaching. Even in France I learned my French from the other players, from sitting in a restaurant or from going into a shop and having to make myself understood. Sitting across a table from a teacher with a pen, a book and a note-pad was a total waste of time.'

He never had much time for books then or now. It was a classic footballer's education. Lessons were there to fill in the gaps between playing football, doing what you were good at. It may have seemed like foolish optimism, or even sheer laziness, at the time, but Chris Waddle never doubted that football was going to be his life.

Of the three brothers, Chris lagged far behind in academic terms. Ray was always above average, and perhaps it was only a lack of ambition that left him driving a bus for a living. Joe was really bright and although he came to his career relatively late in life, he is now a teacher, bordering on a headmaster's position.

As children Joe and Chris were never close, although as time has passed it is those two who keep in touch rather than Ray. The company that Joe kept in his youth did not particularly attract Chris, nor indeed any member of the Waddle clan. He would roam the streets until all hours with gangs of undesirables – first skinheads, then heavy metal fans – while the young Chris latched on to Ray like a limpet. For one thing, Ray took his football more seriously, and their father really believed that of his three sons it was Ray who would make it in the professional game. He followed Ray all over the north-east, encouraging scouts to watch him whenever the opportunity arose, but the offers he hoped for from the league clubs never arrived. From the age of twelve Ray got stuck in a groove – a fate familiar to so many youngsters who may well have been outstanding at their primary schools. He was eventually to find his own level playing for local clubs, quite happy in his own way, just as he was quite content to leave school at fifteen and join the Co-op making pots and pans.

In 1967, the seven-year-old Chris had received a pair of George Best Stylo boots as a present, bought from Elizabeth's hard-earned money. Just as was the case with the Milburn, the Charlton and the Gascoigne mothers, Elizabeth Waddle was determined to ensure her children did not go without anything that might further their careers, whatever sacrifice she might have to make.

Chris idolised Best. He was not interested in his life-style off the pitch. That meant nothing to a child of his age. What fascinated him was the magic he could conjure up with the ball at his feet. Best was not just a magician; he was *the* magician.

Chris lived in Best's image. The long, flowing, dark hair, the posture, the longish shorts, all were copied to as near perfection as possible, even to the point of Chris only buying bubble-gum that was endorsed by the Manchester United star. If any one player was going to entice him away from his support of Sunderland, it was going to be the Belfast Boy.

He finally met Best when the Irishman was playing for Hibernian in a testimonial match against Newcastle. Newcastle won 5–1 under Jack Charlton and Best was in the corridor to the players' lounge with his agent Bill McMurdo. Chris asked for his autograph and too embarrassed to say it was for him, requested that it be addressed to his wife Lorna. In return, McMurdo offered to represent Chris. He declined. Years later he met Best again at Scribes nightclub in London, when his hero sat with him, John Harkes and their wives and simply chatted about football. Best had put on weight and the drink flowed, but the thrill was still the same.

The young Chris Waddle had not even seen Sunderland play in real life – nor any professional team for that matter. At the start of the 1967–68 season, his father put that right by taking Chris and his brothers to Roker Park to see a Youth Cup match between Sunderland and their local rivals Middlesbrough. Taking advantage of the reduced prices, the family sat in the grandstand, only to see the home team lose 1–2. In a way the result was irrelevant. If Chris had been football mad before, now the fantasy had become reality and a true obsession began.

As his long-suffering wife Lorna says of his passion for watching football nowadays, linked with an inability to get worked up

■ Chris Waddle

about anything else: 'He should have been a deck-chair, he's that laid back.'

Yet with a ball at his feet Chris becomes a different personality. He needed a ball at school virtually to be able to communicate, for he was painfully shy and teachers recall whole days passing at school without him saying a single word. Unless his mother or one of his brothers actually took him to the school gates, he would refuse to go, and became truly alert and alive only when it was time to go home.

A geography teacher wrote on his report: 'If his brains were in his feet he'd win Mastermind.'

chapter 3

Chris did not make friends easily at school, or even now. There is a suspicion of strangers, an aura he gives off that puts them on their mettle, challenging them to prove that they are not there just for the ride, not merely to be able to say they know Chris Waddle, but are there for the real person.

He was not unpopular, just shy and distant. Chris's taciturnity and solitude at a time when Clint Eastwood's popularity was riding high gave him a certain hard-man reputation that had no foundation in reality. His one real friend was Peter Allen. Peter was a neighbour from the same road in Pelaw, who loved to play in goal as much as Chris loved to play on the pitch. Always one to create mischief, Peter promoted a fight between Chris and the unofficial school champion. There were no rules, no time limits: it was a fight to the death – or at least until the school bell rang to summon them in to lessons. Both boys ended bloodied but unbowed and Chris was never again to be challenged. Only Elizabeth was unimpressed by the state of his clothes.

First football strips never leave the mind and Chris cannot forget the green and yellow of Bill Quay, a shirt in which he reached his first final and won his first medal, in his penultimate year, when he was ten years old. He can still relive the moment today. The setting for the Under-11 Charity Shield final the setting was Hawthorn Lesley's ground, a magnificent pitch compared to the school playing fields. The opposition was St Matthews. Nil–nil with only a few moments to go. A long ball out of defence, Chris Waddle on his spindly legs chasing it, catching it, running from the halfway line, his apparently dubious stamina extended to the full by the big playing surface. He sees the keeper approaching, looking massive, draws him on, rounds him and hits the ball cleanly into the net. It was a goal he would replay a thousand times in his sleep, although that night sleep would not come because of the excitement. So it always is after a match, as anybody will know who has ever met Chris in the player's lounge after a game. He is like an actor after a performance, on a high whatever the result, unable to relax, the words coming out in a torrent, even if they are words of self-criticism. Nothing that has occurred in the match is forgotten, no lesson learned is ever forgotten. Even in his mid-thirties he is still learning all the time with every game.

At schoolboy level, Chris became the target for every hard man of infant football. One defender kicked him so hard he actually broke his shin-guard, and every match ended with Chris counting the scrapes and bruises. There were some who mistook his dribbling ability for frailty, for a reluctance to compete. Later critics would suggest he was a luxury, even a liability, because he would not tackle back. He was accused of disappearing to the by-line when the going got tough, but a detailed analytical approach to his game suggests otherwise. Just because he has always excelled at one aspect of the game – namely control – does not necessarily mean he is poor at defence. Just because he does not automatically find his way into the referee's note-book and has never been sent off in his professional career does not signify a lack of steel. Who would dare suggest that Vinny Jones is a better player than, say, Gary Lineker, simply because his disciplinary record might suggest he is more committed?

Chris's athletic prowess from an early age more than demonstrates his staying power. He'd be asked to run the last leg of the relay for Bill Quay in the knowledge that he'd tough it out down the straight, either by holding out in front or by pressurising those ahead of him right to the line. He won the school cross-country run as well, although it wasn't really across country but a couple of times around the playground. This was, after all, the industrial north-east.

As he grew older, he began to hate the boredom of long-distance running. He wanted to train with the ball at his feet – that was how you played the game. This antipathy added fuel to the suggestion that he always lacked fitness. The poor posture that years later so nearly cost him his move to Spurs, the hunched shoulders that make it seem as if just running out of the tunnel is too much of an effort – they are misleading. Chris loves to train, refuses to play if he is anything less than at peak fitness and when retirement is suggested says: 'I'll know it's time to retire when my legs tell me as I'm getting out of bed in the morning.'

The teachers at Bill Quay realised they were on to something special with the youngest Waddle. Before he was seven, he had a trial for the area district team who were, for the most part, some three years his seniors. What was more important was that he was by no means outclassed or disgraced. Yet, unlike so many other schools in the nighbourhood, Bill Quay itself had no real sporting tradition. By the time Chris reached his final year, there was not even a teacher willing to take on the football team and, with due encouragement from the one son he had left at the school, Joseph Waddle assumed the responsibilities of school team coach, unpaid and ultimately unappreciated.

Under his expert, if at times unorthodox, guidance, the team rose to the top of the league, but just as at every level of the game, success led to jealousy. A teacher saw how well Joe was doing and decided to take over the team. For the first time in his life, Chris Waddle decided to take on authority in the cause of justice. With a rush of blood to his head, he stormed into the headmaster's study – an unprecedented act, even for a lad in his final year with some standing in the school.

'You can't replace my dad.'

'We can't?' the head responded, in a tone that suggested Chris would be ill-advised to proceed further with the dialogue.

'If my dad's not the manager, then I don't play.'

The headmaster was singularly unimpressed by the threat. 'Fine. Then don't play.'

Chris had tried his hand for the first time at negotiation, at confrontation and appeared to have failed miserably. As it was, for reasons that may or may not have been connected with his son's stand, Joe Waddle kept the job and his son kept in the public eye.

He was a regular in the Jarrow, Hepburn and Felling District team and ended his school season and his junior school career with 66 goals to his credit. There was only one match in which he failed to score, and it is typical of the man that he can remember every miss of that match some thirty years on.

As Chris left Bill Quay there was another move for the family.

For a life-long socialist to move to a road called Keir Hardie Avenue in Wardley was a dream come true for Joe. Number one was a three-bedroomed semi-detached house which Hardie himself would have designated a palace. His father was still working at the Monkton Coke Works, and the high spot of Chris's week during the holidays was to accompany his father to collect his wages. They'd travel on the red chopper bike that his brother Ray had bought from his own wage packet for £32. For a long time the Waddle parents had supported the children; now that a son had the wherewithal to help the parents, it was typical of the close-knit Waddle family that he should choose to do so. Of the five family members, Joe junior was the outsider, treading the tightrope of a life that could have gone anywhere. In the end he didn't fall, only stumbled a little.

By the time they moved to Keir Hardie Avenue, Chris had 'grappled to his soul with hoops of steel' those friends he had who were tried and trusted. There was Peter Allen, of course, Keith Mullen – Sunderland and David Bowie daft, interested in very little else – there were the Renick brothers, Keith, Brian and Colin, and last, but by no means least, there was Gary Durham.

Every child has a Gary Durham in his life, a friend in whom he can see no wrong but who is intensely disapproved of by the child's parents. Chris may have chosen Gary as his best friend, but Elizabeth conceived an immediate, irrational and enduring loathing for him. She had only reluctantly come to terms with the fact that Chris was already on the academic scrap-heap. Bill Quay's failures usually went to Highfield School, but even they were unenthusiastic about taking Chris and Gary, who were therefore farmed out to an establishment called Heworth

Grange. Heworth regarded itself as succeeding if it kept a lad out of court while he was with them. GCEs were an unlooked-for bonus.

Gary and Chris approached school as a sentence to be endured, rather than a time to be enjoyed. They rarely made it to the nine o'clock assembly, and even when they got there at nine-thirty they'd make separate entrances with their ties removed, knowing they'd be sent back home to fetch them. That would take another half an hour (an hour if they could convince the teacher they'd also forgotten their keys and had to go via their mothers' works) and meant a lesson missed, another few heart-beats nearer to the end of the day.

Gary was not stupid – far from it – but he would rather expend his energy in directions that were not academic. Starting off in the top set, he deliberately did no work to ensure relegation and a seat alongside Chris in the bottom set. Gary, having been a butcher for most of his life, is now a catering officer within the Prison Service, based at the remand centre at Durham, of all places.

'I think I got some bad press without any real justification,' Gary recalls. 'Mrs Waddle was very protective and only wanted the best for her children.' Obviously, at the time, she didn't think that Gary Durham was the best, but now they get on extremely well.

At least Heworth took its football seriously. Chris's contemporary, Peter Allen, was in goal and there were several lads who would make it to the fringes of the professional game. Chris went immediately into the Under-12 side and within a year was attracting the attention of a whole host of league clubs.

He was always just marking time at school. It was a tough

environment. In his first year he was shaken down for his dinner money every day, a problem he solved by the simple expedient of holding the money in his hand while the gang leader and his junior lieutenants fished through Chris's empty pockets. The young thugs were not exactly Machiavellian when it came to plotting. He endured it all patiently, with persistent stoicism – a trait that was to stand him in good stead in the difficult times ahead. He let his feet do the talking on the field of play. If there was a path out of the blackboard jungle, he would tread it in his football boots.

chapter 4

Teachers can be inspirational, fearsome or just plain functional. When it came to sport at Heworth Grange, Chris was fortunate to come under the influence and patronage of a Mr Fawcett. He entered the school team into the full Durham League, where they distinguished themselves not only by their playing ability but by their kit: yellow shirts with two blue hoops, red numbering topping off blue shorts and yellow socks. Chris had never seen the like before or since. Like most children, he had a fascination for replica kits – and this before they became the multi-million-pound industry that they are today. His mother bought him some ten kits over the years, including Sunderland inevitably (both home and away), Wolves, Rangers, West Ham and Queen's Park Rangers. He was impressed by the mercurial skills of Rodney Marsh in those famous blue and white hoops, and when Chris was linked with the managerial post at the club in 1996, Rodney's name and image were the first things that sprang to his mind.

He once made the fatal error of lending his beloved Sunderland kit to Gary Durham, who promptly left it in an unlocked locker and then expressed surprise rather than regret when it disappeared equally promptly. Chris was too scared to tell his mother how he had come to lose it and took the blame himself, with the inevitable verbal onslaught, rather than mention Gary's name in the house.

Fawcett encouraged his team in their colourful strip with a mixture of enthusiasm and humour. He'd had some ability himself in the past, but a bad knee injury had seen the end of all that. He sparked something off in his lads and in Chris in particular.

At thirteen, Chris was very much the star of the team. In one particular match, recorded by his father for posterity on a cine-camera, he scored twice and made two more in a memorable game that still ended in a 5–4 defeat. The professional club scouts regularly trawled the north-east, which for so long had been regarded as a hotbed of talent. The local clubs, such as Newcastle, Sunderland and Middlesbrough, were allowing the talented youngsters to slip through their nets and it was to be Sheffield United, Blackpool and Leeds, rather than the giants who were on his door-step, who were to approach Joe Waddle concerning his prodigy of a boy. Curiously enough, all those clubs were to show an interest in Chris later in his career. Sheffield United had a few conversations with his advisers just before they appointed Howard Kendall as manager; Leeds competed with Sheffield Wednesday for his signature when he returned from France; and Blackpool wanted him as player-coach when he was in his final year at Wednesday. That is the way of things in professional football in England – a giant merry-go-round with players stepping on and off at regular intervals.

Chris's academic career was certainly not going round, but

merely stuttering along. When it came to making a selection of subjects at the end of the third year, which should really have been influenced by his career ambitions, none of the science teachers wanted him in their classes. He enjoyed history and geography, but his results in those subjects did not bear close scrutiny. Ruled out of some of the arts along with physics, chemistry and biology, Chris was left with physical education and community service to add to the compulsory trio of English, maths and foreign studies. He never did discover what the last of these was about and had already eliminated himself from any serious approach to a foreign language by regularly day-dreaming his way through French. 'I couldn't understand at the time why anybody except the French should want to speak it.' And this from a man who left Marseille with some degree of colloquial fluency.

When the headmaster saw the proposed combination of subjects that would take him up to his inevitable departure from the school at the age of sixteen, he summoned Chris to see him. He brushed aside Chris's explanation that the combination had been imposed on him because none of the teachers wanted him in their classes. The science masters were asked to reconsider, did so, and refused again. It was to be community service or nothing.

As it transpired, there was very little difference between community service and nothing. The community he was supposed to serve were not overly impressed by Chris's efforts to cut their hedges into obscene shapes, mow lawns in the middle of winter or offer to do the shopping for pensioners whose high spot of the week was their own visit to the supermarket. Eventually even his mother could see the futility of it all and signed off his work book under various pseudonyms.

Chris enjoyed the ability to leave school with permission after lunch on a Friday afternoon, abandoning his class-mates to their lessons. He'd go straight home, pick up the paper and look to see what film was showing on Tyne-Tees television. There was always some golden oldie on at two o'clock, starring the likes of Bogart, Cagney or even Norman Wisdom, whom Chris adored. He'd stretch himself out on the settee with a drink and a packet of sweets and wouldn't move until it was time to meet Gary Durham, who'd be making his way home from school at about 4.15.

Generally speaking, his life revolved around football, either playing on a Sunday morning or watching on a Saturday or Sunday afternoon. There was a division amongst the ranks of his friends. Gary Durham, Peter Allen and the Renicks wore the famous black and white of Newcastle, which is perhaps why Gary had taken such a cavalier attitude to the loan of Chris's Sunderland shirt. Chris, himself, and Keith Mullen still supported the Roker Reds, where Allan Brown was the manager. It is hardly surprising that the player from that side who made the most lasting impression on Chris was Billy Hughes – totally right-footed, inventive, inconsistent, a match-winner on his day, frustrating and infuriating when it was not.

In the early seventies, football was having a resurgence in the north-east, although it was a revival that would flatter to deceive. Not until twenty years later would Newcastle chase the Premiership title all the way to the wire in 1995–96, while Sunderland rose out of the First Division to join them in the top flight, and Middlesbrough, under Bryan Robson, played before packed houses in their new all-seater Riverside Stadium with the likes of Brazilians Emerson and Juninho in their side.

In 1973 Sunderland triumphed at Wembley against all the odds, with keeper Jimmy Montgomery guaranteeing the return of the cup to Wearside with a magnificent double save against Leeds United. In 1974 Newcastle were less successful against Liverpool but their disastrous showing on the day could not eliminate the memory of their thrilling cup run, led by the goal-scoring feats of Malcolm 'Super Mac' Macdonald.

Playing their football in the streets, Chris and his friends recreated their heroes' goals time and time again. His mother, and his father to a lesser degree, encouraged him to study, but it was hopeless. He had not even inherited his father's ability to use his hands, and would lie awake at night, trembling at the thought of woodwork lessons the next day and the lashing tongue of the teacher, telling him and the rest of the class just how useless he was. In three years he never managed to complete a project, and even today if a nail needs to be knocked into the wall it will be Lorna reaching for the hammer.

His brothers would help him with his homework, although the intellectual gap between him and his brothers was steadily widening. Joe was the intellectual, the innovator, the rebel. He drank, he smoked, he rode a motor-bike, yet Chris did not look up to him. It was Ray he idolised, because Ray was a footballer.

'I remember Joe taking me to see Status Quo at Newcastle City Hall. I must have been about fourteen years old. His dress-sense was always a bit odd, but that night, for reasons I can't remember, he was wearing a monk's cassock of all things. A pigeon dropped its load on him and he simply looked up, smiled and said, "Ee, I thought I was on your side tonight!"'

It was supposed to be lucky to be the recipient of a pigeon's droppings and Chris certainly felt some surrogate luck when, shortly afterwards, Newcastle asked him to train with them, even though he was too young to sign schoolboy terms until December 1974. The icing on the cake was that Peter Allen was also invited along.

Scouts, in the shapes of Les Cummins and Tommy Jordan, had visited Elizabeth and Joe at home. They were experienced men and the talent drain from the area was not of their making. They simply could not be in all places at once. Blackpool and Leeds were still displaying an interest and had been joined in the race by Coventry. Chris, however, then as now, was a home-loving lad; he was still very young and Newcastle even arranged a car to pick him up from home at the end of his school-day. He'd arrive at 5.30, be changed in half an hour, and then the reality began as he and the other hopefuls had to walk a mile up the road in rain, wind or snow.

Peter Allen had to face reality even sooner when he was told that Newcastle were not pursuing their interest. There is no kind way of telling a young boy that he's not going to make it as a pro-fessional footballer, but back in the seventies the clubs tended to be even more brutal than they are today. Peter was heartbroken, and it would not be long before Chris, too, would experience exactly how he felt. The disillusion was already beginning to set in. Newcastle did not think it worth while sending transport just for Chris, and to get to training he was left with an hour and a half's journey on his own by bus and foot, often in the dark. The romance of professional football was fading with every moment.

'I have to confess I wasn't impressed by the training. There was no shape to it, no consistent pattern. Whoever was taking it would shout a lot, but often we'd not have the same coach two weeks running. It was a shambles, and as Newcastle slid downhill in the late seventies and early eighties, I think the fact they had no organised youth system was a real factor.'

In fact it was not until 1984, when they won the Youth Cup with a team containing a chubby, cherubic lad called Paul Gascoigne, that the system seemed finally to be back on track. If Chris had been Magpie crazy, he could and would in all probability have ignored all the problems. But he wasn't. Sunderland were still his team and, although he would not admit it, there was a psychological problem about playing for the old enemy. He was not contractually bound to sign for the Geordies in December, although it was generally assumed that he would, perhaps even taken for granted. Who knows how life might have turned out had he decided to do so? But life isn't about ifs and buts; life is about opportunities taken or lost.

It was the simultaneous approach of Coventry City and Sheffield United that made him turn his back, albeit temporarily, on his local team. Coventry had searched for talent successfully in the north-east before, and their local scout Jack Nicholls took a certain delight in spiriting away talent from the clubs which were actually on the spot. The Coventry youth director was a Mr Walton, a huge, avuncular man who impressed Chris both by his size and the blue Mk I Escort in which he and Nicholls transported Chris to the Midlands.

He was now away from home for the first time, in digs with other would-be apprentices, training with them, playing with them and coming to terms with the fact that at this level he was not particularly outstanding.

■ Chris Waddle

There is that fatal moment in a young footballer's career when he gets together with his true peers for the first time. At school he's been head and shoulders above his class-mates, he's been the star of his youth club, his father has never stopped lauding him to the heavens at every opportunity and now, suddenly, there are twenty or thirty other youngsters who are as good as him, if not better. For some boys that's the moment of truth and they run home terrified, tails between their legs, ambition in tatters, seeking their own level; for others it simply inspires them to reach greater heights; and for some nervous types like Chris it causes them just to freeze.

Sheffield United were nearer home and demonstrated a more sympathetic approach. Chris was invited down by train with his parents and was shown around the ground by the assistant manager. The club was buzzing. They'd just been promoted, had won their first four games off the reel and were top of the old First Division. Tony Currie was their star, their playmaking inspiration, and his skills appealed to Chris.

But once again the reality differed from the dreams. He was on his own and simply could not cope with the loneliness. He was still painfully shy and would never start a conversation. The others probably regarded him as a loner, when all he wanted was for someone to talk to him. Of the two clubs, Joe and Elizabeth still favoured the Yorkshire team. They'd been impressed that the club had taken them down personally, rather than just have Chris down on his own, and they had been given the right answers to all their questions.

Chris, himself, preferred Coventry City. Having conquered his initial nerves, he was playing a little better and had actually struck up a couple of friendships. He did not have to travel far from the digs to the ground, the food was good and all the schoolboys were housed together, while the apprentices' digs were just across the road. There was a community spirit which he felt gave it the edge over Sheffield United. The Waddles were tolerant parents and Chris got his way.

The Coventry staff, delighted they had got their boy, returned to the Waddle house for the formal signing of schoolboy terms. The *Gateshead Post* were invited to witness the ceremony and the first official press photograph of Chris Waddle was duly taken. At that time he had no idea, no suspicion, of how cruel and destructive the media could be. It all began in innocence; it began with the highest of hopes. The professional career of Chris Waddle was under way.

chapter 5

Without denying the abilities or reputations of either Coventry City or Sheffield United, neither of them was regarded as amongst the elite clubs of the seventies. Yet Chris, who was by now just fourteen, was impressed. Looking back, he realises he should have had sufficient confidence in his own ability to hold out and wait for the club of his choice to come along. To pull on the red and white striped shirt of Sunderland was still his dream – not the replica that Gary Durham had lost, but the real thing. But what fourteen-year-old would not jump at the chance of playing professional football for a Premier League side, or First Division as it then was? By signing on the line for a league club, in his mind at least, he had signed off at school. He could sense a little jealousy amongst his friends that grew with his success. It was hard to pinpoint, but certainly when they'd be sitting in the pub and it was someone else's round, the jibe to Chris would be, 'You're making good money, why can't you get them in?' Gary Durham was never jealous. The fact that Gary was not the most gifted of players did not stop him claiming to Chris's dad, amongst others, that the managers of league clubs were lining up outside his house to meet his parents.

Telling Peter Allen he had signed was the hardest thing of all for Chris. It sounded like boasting, but then he didn't want Peter to hear it from anybody else. Peter took it extremely well. He wasn't a bad player, but he knew in his heart of hearts that he probably wasn't quite good enough. At least he could say he had been there. Years later Chris learned that while Mr Allen realised the limitations of his own son, without Chris knowing, even when he'd been at Tow Law, he'd bombarded managers like Joe Harvey at Newcastle with letters, urging them to give young Waddle another chance.

Chris could not wait for the school holidays to begin so that he could travel to Coventry and get down to serious training. For the midland club, however, Chris was just another schoolboy with potential, a youngster with everything to prove. Indeed, they had so many other lads that they could accommodate him only on alternate weeks. Yet as much as he looked forward to going, as much as the choice over Sheffield United had been his, he needed to be at Coventry for only one night to feel so homesick that he could hardly sleep. It wasn't that the club weren't thoughtful – it was all in Chris's head.

They'd send a car, which would collect him first, then go to Durham for another lad, and from there to collect Ray Godden, who appeared a few times for Coventry before moving on to Hartlepool and then to non-league football after a serious injury. The final passenger was to suffer an even more serious injury. A delightful person, always cheerful, always friendly, Danny Thomas was virtually the first black person Chris had ever met, and he was devastated when Danny's promising career was brought to an untimely end in such a brutal fashion.

Coventry regarded Chris as a straightforward left winger; but whereas at school level he could leave right backs stranded, here they were more experienced, so that he found himself dispossessed time after time, forever running into blind alleys. His confidence sank to its lowest ebb, to the point where he almost dreaded the ball coming to him, where he avoided doing the things at which he was best. He would not dribble, would not run at defences. He just wanted to be back home – and it showed.

As he withdrew into himself, as he saw the other dozen schoolboys with whom he shared a house blossom and flourish, so it got worse. When they went off into town, to the cinema or for an illicit drink, he just stayed in and watched television, before retiring in tears to bed with thoughts of home.

He'd not yet grown enough, and at five feet four and nine stone he was a boy playing with men – and seemingly going nowhere. One Saturday he'd arrived with a slight thigh strain, but Bob Dennison, who was in charge, brushed aside Chris's protests that he shouldn't play, without even offering or suggesting any treatment at the club. Chris found himself back home by tea time. When he was in the north-east he wanted to be off playing football, yet when he was away he wanted to be at home. There was no happy medium, and added to all the confusion that was going on in the mind and body of the adolescent, it made for one very unhappy young man.

Mr Walton, at least, had the courtesy and thoughtfulness to ring him, although the news was not good. The list of apprenticeships on offer had been filled, but if he wanted to come up again at Christmas then he was welcome. Alternatively the club would release him. Taking that as a desire to let him go, Chris accepted. It was May 1975, he was only fourteen years old, but he felt he had gone as far as he was ever likely to go with Coventry. If that meant the end of his career before it had truly begun, then so be it. For a lad who was painfully shy and totally lacking in confidence, the rejection was mind-shattering. But he wasn't the sort of person who would talk his troubles through, bottling them up inside and becoming even more introspective. Again his parents were very supportive. They only wanted the best for him, and although they were pleased to see him home, they recognised the pain and disappointment he must be feeling and shared every moment of it.

He had to think of a job, if he was not going to be getting even an apprentice's wage packet. He was given the chance to work-shadow a motor electrician for a few weeks, but watching the man change light-bulbs in cars in the surroundings of a freezing garage taught him only one thing: despite his love of cars he was not going to follow this particular line of work.

He still had football in his life, and even though the standard in which he was playing was nothing like the level he had experienced at Newcastle, Coventry or Sheffield United, he never allowed his own professional standards to drop. He has followed that creed throughout his career. When he joined Falkirk for a month in the Scottish First Division in September 1996, he would not play until he was physically fit, and then played to the utmost of his ability, even though he, the manager and the players alongside him all knew that he belonged on a different footballing planet.

Back in 1975, Chris was playing on Saturday afternoons for Pelaw Juniors and on Sunday alongside his brother Ray for Whitehouse Social Club. His performances on the field finally attracted the attention of Sunderland, although they needed a little encouragement. Charlie Ferguson was the Sunderland scout who had uncovered the embryonic talents of Bobby Kerr, who in turn had rewarded him and the club by leading Sunderland to their 1973 FA Cup final victory. A neighbour knew Charlie and suggested he invite Chris down to train at Roker, which he duly did.

Hope was born anew as Chris went off to four consecutive Tuesday and Thursday evenings at the end of the 1975–76 season. Again those hopes were to be cruelly dashed. There was little more shape than there had been at Newcastle, and it seemed to Chris that unless you knew somebody, or had a senior member of staff take a special interest in you, then you had no real chance of progress. At the end of the month of sessions he was not asked back. The next time Sunderland showed any interest in him was more than twenty years later, when Peter Reid tried to buy him from Sheffield Wednesday to help in his push for promotion from the First Division into the Premier. Wednesday asked for £750,000 – nearly three-quarters of the sum they had paid for Waddle four years earlier from Marseille – and Reid, not surprisingly, refused to meet their price. Sunderland made it out of the division without the talents of Chris Waddle.

Rejected yet again, there was nothing left for the teenager but to keep plugging away, keep hoping he'd strike lucky and that somebody would see a magic performance or a stunning goal. Many years later, it was to be one goal viewed by Irving Scholar that would leave a lasting impression on his mind and guarantee Chris's move to Tottenham Hotspur. But in 1977 neither the performance nor the goal would come. By Easter the miracle had not happened. He was sixteen. There were no end-of-term exams. There was, however, not only the end of term, but the end of school, the end of what Chris had never perceived to be the safety net. There were a dozen or so other lads in the same position, turned loose like refugees released from a camp with nowhere to go, totally directionless.

'Race you out of school,' Chris said. They set off for the gate, Chris in the lead and maintaining the lead all the way to the local unemployment office on Holly Hill, where he signed on the dole.

chapter 6

Chris had always liked his bed, still likes it today. But in the summer of 1977 it had become a malaise, an illness. At first he'd sign on every Thursday, collect his cheque on Saturday and cash it at the Post Office. That, in itself, filled an hour or so during the week and gave him the chance to meet up with a few of his friends who were in a similar position. But then for £10.30 it hardly seemed worth getting up, so that often he would stay in his room all day long, sometimes all week long.

When he could be bothered he would go to Heworth Youth Club, pay his tenpence admission, one per cent of his weekly money, and play snooker, darts or table tennis. There he would meet Gary Durham, who already had an apprenticeship at Dewhurst the butchers. As was to be the case so often in his life, fate took Chris out of bed and to the club one night when it was filled for a special dance with two hundred or more youngsters. With his by now gangling, thin figure and his penchant for wearing a green and white hooped rugby shirt, with a Rangers badge sewn on, all topped off with a wrangler jacket covered with Sunderland patches, he did rather tend to stand out in the crowd. He certainly stood out for a fourteen-year-old called Lorna Bruce when on this particular night, with a Groundhogs album under his arm, he wore a new crombie overcoat with a red handkerchief on top of his usual layers of mismatched clothing.

'My mum had bought me the overcoat in the summer and it was about three sizes too big. The only way I could get it to look as if it fitted was to wear all the odd clothes underneath,' Chris says.

Jacqui Craven, a girl Chris knew to be a friend of Lorna's, appeared at his side. As was his custom whenever he was approached by a member of the opposite sex, he blushed and became totally tongue-tied. Chris can still remember the music that was playing as the girl asked him if he was seeing anybody – it was a Montrose album. Chris stammered that he wasn't.

'My friend Lorna Bruce would like to see you,' the girl said.

'No, I don't really want to see anybody,' Chris replied with a shake of his head, his low self-esteem convincing him nobody would want to go out with a teenager on the dole and with no foreseeable prospects of a career or even basic employment. Lorna was upset, to say the least.

'I'd been forward and I'd got my hands rapped. I was very shy as it was and I saw this as a massive set-back. It had taken a lot of courage for me to get Jaqui to ask, and I don't think I spoke to another boy for about six months after that.'

With his male friends Chris could continue to be himself. On Guy Fawkes night Gary Durham had an idea. 'Any idea that Gary had in those days should have carried a government health warning and this one involved me being dressed up in a parka as a real live guy to raise a bit of money. I was dumped outside someone's house and generally kicked to pieces whilst we didn't raise a penny and Gary and the rest of them just stood in the shadows killing themselves with laughter.'

Gradually he began to come out of his decline. If he couldn't play football professionally, then the next best thing was watching it. He and his friend Keith Mullen had begun to travel with the Sunderland fans to away matches back in October of 1974, and through 1975–76 they had attended all the home games. However, the growing violence and the cost of travel began to dissuade them from following the side on its travels.

'I could never see the attraction of violence or gangs at football. I didn't even want people to talk to me at a match because I was so intent on watching what was going on, and when a fight broke out near me, I just got annoyed that it was interfering with the game. I can remember one trip to Middlesbrough for a game in the Anglo-Scottish Cup where there were about thirty of us and five hundred of them. They chased us into a park and the gate was just wide enough to let one person through at a time. As you can imagine I was one of the fastest out of the traps and was through the gate virtually first with bottles flying and shattering around my feet. Even when we got on the train at the station there was still a hail of bottles raining down on us. I also recall a game at Blackburn when a couple of our fans had to jump into a canal to avoid serious injury. When they got to the other side they just stood there giving the home fans two fingers.'

The seventies were a free-for-all when it came to violence. It started with scarves being the target, but that, in turn, led to simple theft – watches, wallets, jewellery and clothes. It wasn't unusual for a lad to be left there penniless and shivering in his underwear. Chris has seen a change in the game. 'It's so much safer now, particularly with security cameras both in and around the ground. There's also a lot more female fans watching, many more families.'

It was, in any event, a depressing time to be following Sunderland's fortunes. The team lost the local derby 2–0 to Newcastle and slumped to the bottom of the league. A mini-revival meant their fate went to the wire. They had to travel to Everton for the last match of the season while their relegation rivals Bristol City and his old friends Coventry met each other. Those two sides drew, Sunderland lost 2–0 again and it was the Second Division for them together with, of all teams, Tottenham Hotspur.

Chris felt his life was sliding down the tubes with them. No league clubs were showing the slightest interest in him and no employer was giving him the faintest sniff of a job offer. The future looked remorselessly bleak. Then out of the blue there did come an offer for Chris. Not from Sunderland, Spurs or Newcastle, but from Cheviot Seasoning Limited, a company making spices and seasoning to be used in sausages and pies, whose factory could be seen from the labour exchange. The job being offered was merely labouring, but it was a job nevertheless and Chris was not one to avoid an honest day's work.

His brother Joe took him to the interview on his motor-bike. The first thing that hit Chris as they drove through the industrial estate towards the square building was the smell. It was like entering a giant pepper-pot. Jenny George, the secretary, greeted him and took him through to be interviewed by the manager, Dick Swailes. As Dick explained the job, Chris struggled manfully and ultimately unsuccessfully to remove his crash helmet. Afterwards he thought he'd blown his chance, and waited at home for two days for a call. Apart from the interview having been conducted with him feeling as if he were staring out of a goldfish bowl, even when he'd had the chance to respond to questions he'd answered in monosyllables. But Dick Swailes had both a heart and a sense of humour and saw something in the red-faced, awkward boy seated opposite him that others were to see many years later.

'It was like the first time I appeared on television as an analyst. I just froze thinking about the millions watching, knowing I was wooden, unable to string two words together. And this interview had only been in front of the managing director of a little local seasoning company.'

The phone did eventually ring and Chris was taken on. His first wage packet of £20, reduced by tax and insurance to £13.80, provided little more than he'd received on the dole. From humble acorns oak trees would grow in time, but that forest seemed an awfully long way off.

The company's entire staff consisted of only three others – Jenny, Dick and David Rocks who drove the fork-lift truck. Their core business was the manufacture of flavouring in heavy batches using salt, cayenne, coriander, basil and dye. Although he had been hopeless at memorising the names of ingredients at school, he would never forget these. The job was initially one of mind-boggling boredom. Chris would stand at the foot of the blender and when he thought enough of the mixture had come down to fill a fifty-six pound box, he'd remove the box and replace it with another. Between that thrill he'd sweep up or glue the boxes together, waiting for the odd high spot when David would let him drive the fork-lift. He found himself choking and was forced to wear a mask to try to prevent the dust and dye getting down his throat. 'When I first got home I thought I was

[5]

[5][5][5][5][5]

spitting blood, but it was the red dye getting into my lungs. I think if I'd stayed there long enough I would have been in the same state as those of my dad's generation who worked down the mines.'

Not that the people he worked for were unpleasant. They soon realised that although Chris was quiet and shy, he was honest and industrious. He was also not stupid and eventually he was permitted to share some of the more interesting and responsible jobs with David Rocks. As David supported Newcastle with a passion bordering on dementia, the days would pass in discussion and arguments as to the merits of their respective teams.

Although Chris had raised himself from the depression that had threatened to destroy his whole life, he was in danger of settling into a rut. During the week he was usually too tired to go out in the evenings and would settle for a lunchtime drink with David. At school he'd prided himself on being teetotal, which was a remarkable achievement for someone living in a society where the pub and the working men's clubs were the focal point of social life. He'd regarded himself as a trained athlete – and athletes didn't drink whilst in training. But weekend football didn't require the same level of fitness, and he was certainly no longer averse to the odd pint. Yet he never got to the stage of not knowing what he was doing, until May 1978 when the band Goldie, who were riding high in the UK top ten, appeared at a dance organised by Pelaw Juniors Football Team. An evening dedicated to Special Federation Brew left him so senseless that he could not even get out of bed the next morning to go to work. 'I've said "never again" a few times since then, but the only two occasions I've really meant it were that first time and Gazza's wedding.'

Although he did not appreciate it at the time, the work was as good as proper training. Fetching and carrying fifty-pound bags of salt was weight-training, while hurrying back and forth to the foot of the blender, up and down ladders, was as good as doing circuits. The people at Cheviot nicknamed him 'Grasshopper' after the David Carradine character in the *Kung Fu* series on television. When he'd started, he'd still been only five and a half feet and weighed next to nothing. Now he was in the last stages of his growth spurt, pushing up to six feet and beginning to fill out.

He was becoming more conscious of himself and his appearance and more aware of the opposite sex. This was Newcastle in the seventies, with soul music sweeping the city centre. Chris affected Fred Perry shirts and forty-inch pleated baggy trousers. With a regular wage packet, he felt more affluent than he really was, opened an account at Top Shop and promptly ran up a bill of £100 that he had no chance of repaying.

It was not the Waddle way. Joe and Elizabeth had never been ones for credit. When his father had acquired his first car, he'd saved up for years, and Chris can recall accompanying him with jars of coins and notes to complete the transaction. It's a philosophy Chris has carried with him throughout his life. Nobody could ever accuse the Waddles of being mean, yet they have never flaunted their money, never spent wildly or unnecessarily, and certainly have never bought on credit. If they can't afford it, then they don't buy. In 1978, not yet eighteen, looking at the envelope from Top Shop that had fallen on to the door-mat and which he dared not open, Chris did not envisage a day when he would be able to afford everything to satisfy his heart's desires.

chapter 7

If you've been a triallist for First Division clubs, then turning out for Pelaw Social Club on a Sunday morning sits somewhere at the lower end of the footballing scale. The team had been unbeaten until Chris joined them, but his first match ended in a 5–1 defeat. In the dressing-room after the match, he could see the words written large on the faces of the rest of the side: 'Too good for us, aren't you? Too good to bloody well try.'

If that game was virtually the rock bottom of his career, then the only way to go was up. In the final twelve games of the season Chris received the Man of the Match award eight times.

He was clearly too good for the level at which he was playing, but modesty and lack of confidence, as well as the fact he was playing alongside his mates, had set the benchmark for the lowering of his sights. One goal he did not score, one he made, one result, stands out amongst all the others from his days with Pelaw. In a cup final, with just a few moments to go, the scores were level at 2–2. Chris chipped the keeper to perfection, but Pelaw were playing into a gale force wind and the ball was literally blown back from the goal-line into the field of play. Chris was not to be denied. In extra-time he hit a corner with sweet venom, the Pelaw centre-forward threw himself at it and Pelaw had won. Another medal, another triumph, but where was it all leading? Was Chris Waddle now playing for pleasure or ambition?

The top junior team in the north-east was Clarke Chapman. Having begun life as a works team, it had moved on to a higher plane. They showed the seriousness of their intentions by playing on a Saturday rather than a Sunday, which attracted the sort of dedicated players who were prepared to sacrifice their afternoons on the terraces watching their favoured teams. Peter Allen was already playing for them in goal. Rather surprisingly, Chris was not considered good enough to oust either of the established wingers, and was therefore slotted in on the left side of midfield in a team that was professional in all but name. A father of one of the players was the local scout for Bolton Wanderers, but in his considered opinion Chris had no hope of making it with a league side. Time after time players were invited from the Clarke Chapman squad to Burnden Park for trials, but the invitation was never extended to Chris.

Rather than being disillusioned, he accepted the rejection as a challenge. He had been growing steadily and was now six feet tall, although still painfully thin. He was learning all the time, not arguing about the fact he was virtually being used as a utility player, mid-field, wing, even as a sweeper. Careful and withdrawn in his approach, he was preparing himself for a return to the professional game.

By the end of the 1977–78 season he had already decided that he was now ready for his comeback – not that he had actually really been anywhere from which to return. All he had to do was wait for a team to recognise his talents. When that team came along, it was in the humble shape of Tow Law from the Dryborough Northern League. In the summer of 1978, Billy Bell had just been appointed as their manager and the Clarke Chapman physiotherapist recommended a tall youngster to him as having a bit of potential. It took only a couple of training sessions before he was invited to travel with the first team for an away pre-season friendly at Frickley and told by Billy Bell to 'bring your boots in case we're short'.

As it transpired he needed the boots, making his debut, scoring and creating the other goal in a 2–2 draw. More than one Tow Law player was so impressed by his pace and enthusiasm that they were heard to wonder out loud just where their manager had unearthed this particular golden nugget.

By the start of the 1978–79 season, Chris was actually a part-time professional earning the princely sum of £5 per week from Tow Law to supplement his wages from Cheviot Seasoning. Yet his approach to the game was still far from professional. He had not learned to separate his personal life from his career. Without telling Billy Bell, he'd still been playing for Pelaw on a Sunday, before his brother Ray persuaded him to transfer his talents to Leam Lane Social Club. His erstwhile Pelaw team-mates were less than impressed and somebody must have cast the evil eye on him as his worst nightmare reached fulfilment. Carrying a minor injury he turned out for Leam Lane, aggravated it and found himself ensnared in a web of lies to escape the wrath of Billy Bell; and Chris has never been the best of liars.

Bell, himself, was a bit of a disciplinarian who took his coaching duties with Tow Law as seriously as if he were in charge of Newcastle United. Whatever their daytime working commitments, players were obliged to train on Monday and Wednesday evenings if they wanted to have any chance of selection for the following Saturday. 'I can remember having to drag myself down there after work with every limb in my body aching, but Billy just wasn't one for excuses.'

As his career developed and he played under the likes of Arthur Cox, Jack Charlton, Terry Venables and Bobby Robson, he was to grow accustomed to men who had heard all the excuses in the world and had grown weary of them.

Mondays were devoted to fitness training while the second session concentrated on tactics. Not that these were particularly sophisticated. As Chris became more and more of a fixture in the side, so he became a focal point for Billy's game plans. Basically, whenever Chris was unmarked, the instruction was to give him the ball with the other players coming on to the agenda only if he was being closely attended.

Tow Law, with Chris as their star, developed into a real force in north-east non-league football, living only in the shadow of the famous Blyth Spartans, whose FA Cup adventures were legendary. The game against Blyth was as important to both clubs as the Sunderland–Newcastle derbies, and in 1979 Joe Harvey, Newcastle's famous former captain and manager, was there to watch. Chris did enough in a 0–2 defeat to have him return with Basil Hayward, the chief scout, and in December Joe finally approached Chris directly, asking him to sign for the Magpies.

This time Chris appeared to have some options. Barnsley and Rotherham were known to have been watching him and Sunderland had asked to have him on trial for a friendly. The wheel was beginning to come full circle. Joe Harvey seemed oblivious of the fact that Chris had been about to sign for Newcastle once already, but it appeared to be a cast-iron offer this time and Chris agreed to come to St James' Park on New Year's Day 1980 for what he thought would be the formalities.

He was told he would watch the match against Sunderland (of all teams), then meet the manager Bill McGarry and sign then and there. Yet again he was to be bitterly disappointed. McGarry was too busy to see him and Geoff Allen, the youth team coach, simply told him that perhaps it was best if things were left in abeyance for a little while. It is hard to imagine his thoughts as he returned home, particularly as he had also seen his beloved Sunderland well and truly beaten. Another lad from a similar background might well have given up, but Chris simply bit his lip and returned quietly to Tow Law.

At first it seemed as if another door was going to open for him, when Sunderland's chief scout asked him back for a two-week trial, but there was more torment in store. Having arranged with Cheviot to take his summer holiday in January, Chris was chosen to play in a friendly against Gateshead only to come up against a boy called Stephen Higgins as his marker. Stephen was not the greatest footballer in the world but had played with Chris right through school and knew his game and his tricks inside out. He rattled Chris with a few early and heavy tackles and then began to force him on to his weaker right foot, destroying his confidence and making it difficult for Chris to go on the mazy dribbles that were to become a Waddle hallmark. It became so bad that the rest of the team avoided passing to him, and although he saw the fortnight out, when Frank Clark (now the manager of Manchester City) told him that Ken Knighton, the Sunderland

■ **Chris Waddle**

manager, wanted to see him, he knew it was not going to be good news. They pulled no punches. He was no better than players they already had and there were other younger lads coming through who looked as if they had more potential.

Twenty years old and too old in a young man's game, or so it seemed. Once again he had to return to Tow Law with his tail between his legs. It seemed he was taking one step forward and then half a dozen back. It was all hopeless. His future seemed crystal clear. Third-rate football, a job of utter tedium, with just enough money to live and never enough to break free from the constraints of his background.

The disillusionment showed as soon as he pulled on a Tow Law shirt again. The opposition was Billingham Synthonia, hardly the most fearsome or inspiring of opponents. After ten minutes of watching Chris drift on the periphery of the game, Billy Bell had seen enough. He signalled Chris over to the touch-line and pulled him off. That was it. He wasn't even good enough to play a whole match against the likes of Billingham Synthonia in the Drysborough Northern League. It was all over.

chapter 8

If Chris believed his footballing career had come to a premature end, then at least his personal life was on an upward spiral. In the summer of 1978 Lorna Bruce had re-entered his life. A group of youngsters had stayed for one dance too many at a late-night disco and had missed the last train home. The only option was the all-night bus which did a round trip of the locality, taking an hour and a half to drop off its passengers. As Chris and his friends were walking back up the platform, having seen the lights of the missed train disappear into the distance, they met up with Lorna and a friend who were just arriving. They gave them the bad news and then Chris watched with envy as Lorna confidently hailed a cab to take her home. His companion Keith Mullen noticed him watching a little too closely, a little too keenly.

'Do you fancy her then?' Keith asked.

'No. Definitely not,' was the reply, but it did not have the ring of conviction either to Keith or to Chris himself.

They met up again at a Northern Soul night at the Mayfair night-club in Newcastle, and with the pair of them being so shy, one of Chris's friends decided to play Cupid. Alan Burdis, known as Dylan from *The Magic Roundabout* for his propensity for sleep, owned what could loosely be described as a car. It was a Mk I Escort, with a hole in the bottom through which the ground could be clearly seen. He saw Lorna at Hewarth, offered her a lift and promptly drove her straight to the chip shop where he knew Chris was waiting.

'Why are we going to the chippie?' Lorna asked, between prayers. Despite the frailty of his car, Dylan regarded himself as the Nikki Lauda of the north-east, and drove like a demon. When Chris and Lorna did finally meet, he plucked up courage as she was about to leave – having rehearsed what he was going to say a hundred times in his head – and asked if he could see her again. She had not forgotten the earlier rebuff and was coolly non-committal.

However, Chris did not have to wait too long for another chance. The following Sunday they both went to the Mayfair Club again and, having failed with the direct approach, he used Peter Allen as an intermediary. This time the answer was yes and, as if disbelieving his luck, convinced that if he let her out of his sight she might just change her mind, he sat with her in near-silent heaven for the rest of the evening. From that day on neither of them had another serious boyfriend or girlfriend. There has never been a hint of scandal about the relationship, although Chris did initially have so little confidence in its future that he took Gary Durham with him on their first date in case Lorna did not turn up.

The timing of her entry into his life was perfect. Chris's career prospects were in tatters and the development of his love-affair with Lorna gave him the confidence to begin believing again in his own abilities. Lorna did not appear to commit herself wholly from the start, or at least not so that Chris would notice. She was a bright, intelligent girl who had just starting working at De La Rue's, the currency printers. She had career ambitions herself, and finding a steady boyfriend who was working in a seasoning factory whilst harbouring illusions (or even delusions) of a future as a professional footballer did not fit tidily into her game plan. There was a mischievous streak about her, which would always keep Chris guessing, keep him both interested and anxious, sometimes agreeing to see him, sometimes not. It was in its way a classical courtship.

A combination of Lorna Bruce and Billy Bell began the difficult job of rebuilding Chris Waddle's life. Bell knew the boy had skill and Lorna also knew enough about football to be able to offer him genuine words of encouragement. He began to add a new element to his game – consistency. It was a consistency born from the knowledge that if he'd been able to do it right once, then he could do it time and time again.

Allan Clarke, the former England centre-forward and then the manager of Barnsley, was the first to make an approach to the reborn Chris. He arranged to meet the young player at Scotch Corner, off the A1, in days when there was nothing suspicious about a rendezvous at a motorway service station. Even Clarke had doubts and could offer Chris no more than a two-week trial. However, with no more holiday left to take, he was not prepared to risk losing a job that had been good to him for the mere possibility of yet again chasing rainbows. It was a tough decision to make and one that he might have approached differently just a few months before; but this time he said no and staggered on to the end of the season with Tow Law.

To his astonishment, as if nothing had happened since his visit the previous December, Newcastle suddenly phoned and said they wanted him to sign for them. Tow Law, desperate for new floodlights, asked for a fee of £12,000, while at the same time offering Chris a fresh contract and a rise to £15 per week. Offers were rattling in. Blue Star, in a different league from Tow Law, told him they'd pay £18 per week, but eventually Newcastle and Tow Law agreed a fee of £500 and the deal was concluded.

Chris signed a twelve-month contract at £70 a week with the sleeping north-eastern giants and felt like a millionaire. He walked back to the city centre, taking his time, and eventually bought the final edition of the *Evening Chronicle*. 'United get teenage striker,' he read, as if it were written about somebody else. The article claimed that Newcastle had tried to sign him the previous season but had been unable to complete the deal. For the first, but certainly not the last, time in his career the press had got it wrong.

He had to hand in his notice at Cheviot and curiously, after all the ups and downs, all the false starts, all the disappointments, he was to do it with more than a hint of sadness. Conscientious to the last, he asked Newcastle if he could miss the first two weeks' training of the 1980–81 season so that he could work out his notice.

The Newcastle United that Chris Waddle joined in the summer of 1980 bore no resemblance to the successful money-making machine of the mid-nineties. The squad was a hotch-potch of players past their sell-by date, others coming in from non-league football and just a few who'd made it through the youth system. There were no Czech, French, Belgian, Colombian or even English internationals. The best they could offer was Mick Martin of the Republic of Ireland and John

Connolly of Scotland, whose contract was cancelled in August 1980.

They were predominantly just a group of journeymen whose pedigree was the likes of Blyth Spartan, North Shields and now Tow Law. Chris played in a few of the pre-season friendlies and found it hard to adjust to the pace, even at that level. Alan Oliver, a north-east journalist never slow to criticise Chris early on in his career, wrote after seeing him play against Consett: 'It looks like Newcastle have signed another dud.' Oliver had seen Newcastle already sign Steve Carney, Alan Shoulder and Peter Cartwright from non-league football with mixed results and saw Chris as yet another foot-soldier in that particular procession.

In fact it was unfair to read anything into that night. Chris had already played on a winning side for Tow Law against the same team, but on this occasion, in Chris's own words, he froze and played with all the mobility of a cardboard cut-out.

It was on 16 August 1980 that Chris Waddle drew on a Newcastle shirt for the first time in a competitive professional match – a reserve game in the Central League against Manchester United. United's reserves were stronger than the first team of most sides and when Ray Wilkins nutmegged Chris in the first five seconds, all the doubts as to whether he was ever going to be up to it flooded back into his mind.

In the previous season Newcastle had finished ninth in the Second Division and the fans, the board and manager Bill McGarry had hoped that would prove a platform for a real promotion push. After three games it looked unlikely, with one point, seven goals conceded and one scored – a lone effort from Alan Shoulder (an import from Blyth Spartan) in a 1–1 draw at home to Notts County.

Chris was about to witness the ruthlessness of football at close hand. McGarry had joined the club as a saviour with a wealth of experience. He left as a failure, his contract terminated without notice, and without even the opportunity to say goodbye to his players. Chris was more perplexed than upset. He'd hardly spoken to the man and just decided to wait for the replacement and do his utmost to impress.

For the moment, Joe Harvey acted as caretaker while Geoff Allen continued in charge of the reserves. Chris was now beginning to enjoy himself. He scored twice against Leeds in a 5–2 victory and shone in the five-a-side reserve training sessions. The first team and the reserves were kept scrupulously apart in those days. Chris and the rest of the reserves used the B dressing rooms at Benwell, and if it rained they had to give the first team priority over the gym while they got soaked and muddy out on the fields.

Although there were many fellow-Geordies in the reserves, Chris was still a lad apart, quiet and reserved. He'd arrive on time by bus, would train efficiently and then go home. Pleasant bunch though they were, there was nobody in the reserve squad likely to set the world alight, with the possible exception of defender David Barton, whose career was cut short by injury. Kevin Carr and Kenny Wharton eventually made it through to the first team, but for the most part the others just drifted away into the twilight world of semi-professional football. In that season of 1980–81, if you were half good you were likely to get your chance in the first team.

Gradually Chris did begin to make friends with the likes of Chris Withe, the younger brother of Peter, and a talented Scots boy called Ray Montgomery, who never lived up to his reputation. He was learning all the time, not just from those he was playing with, but also from those he was playing against or had the opportunity to watch. The three most experienced men at the club were Colin Suggett – later to be responsible for the youth team and to be so influential on Gazza – Mick Martin, who'd played for Manchester United and West Bromich Albion as he established himself in the Eire team, and Terry Hibbitt. Hibbitt was in the twilight of his career, in his second spell at the club. He'd enjoyed all the success of the mid-seventies while narrowly missing out on the international recognition that his skills deserved. Malcolm Macdonald and John Tudor may have grabbed the goals and the glory, but so many of their efforts had begun with an incisive pass from Hibbitt's elegant left foot. Sadly he was never to see old age, dying from cancer in 1994. What Chris so admired about him was his ability to break down a defence with one telling pass, inevitably from his left foot. If someone like Hibbitt could go so far in the game with only one efficient foot, surely there was a chance for the similarly limited Chris Waddle.

As the season developed and Newcastle stuttered and faltered on, the rumours heightened as to the identity of the new manager. All the big names who were available were linked with the job. Jack Charlton, Bobby Robson, even Malcolm Macdonald. But then the announcement was made. Arthur Cox. An appointment that was met with a deathly silence on Tyneside. It wasn't so much that he was disliked or distrusted, it was simply that virtually nobody, except the board who had given him the job, had ever heard of him. It was an appointment that was to change the course of history both in respect of Newcastle United and Chris Waddle.

chapter 9

Chris Waddle *had* heard of Arthur Cox and had a firm picture of him in his mind's eye. He had, after all, been the assistant manager of Sunderland when they had won the FA Cup in the previous decade. A stocky, unsmiling figure, with a military crew-cut, he looked anything but a soft touch.

Cox had never been a man associated with the glamorous clubs and his playing career had begun and ended at Coventry when he broke his leg before he was twenty. Desperate to stay in the game, he began by coaching the juniors at Coventry and then, never a man to do anything by halves, took a full FA coaching course. As chief coach at Walsall, he did enough to attract the attention of Tommy Docherty, who appointed him as his assistant at Aston Villa. The big name, the big club did not fit Arthur comfortably at the time and he moved on to lowly Halifax, thence to Sunderland, and then abroad to Turkey before his first managerial opportunity at Chesterfield. Nothing that had come before in his career could have prepared him for what he was to face at Newcastle.

He lived, breathed and probably even dreamed football. Unlike his predecessor, he very quickly knew everybody at every level at Newcastle. He would watch every side personally, from the schoolboys upwards, and when there were no internal games to see, he would drive miles up and down the motorways in an obsessive pursuit of hidden talent.

Just as some years later he would do with Paul Gascoigne, Arthur saw that Chris needed to be pushed to fulfil his potential. Despite the impression of being a dour, humourless midlander with a booming barrack-room voice, the manager always admired flair players such as Chris. He might castigate them on the pitch, his words carrying with embarrassing clarity across the empty stadium at reserve matches, yet there was no malice in him. He was merely expressing his frustration that the players he knew could achieve were not achieving.

'I had to get him out of his *mañana* frame of mind,' Cox recalls. 'I had to shake him up, to get him slick and sharp both in mind and body. I'd kick him up the backside every day. If there wasn't a reason to do so, then I'd make one up. I know I went over the top sometimes, but I had to be cruel to be kind.'

Although Chris was scoring goals regularly for the reserves, Arthur was determined not to push him too fast towards the pressures of league football. 'I've never been one to put myself before my players or my team. I might have needed a goalscorer, but I was determined only to play Chris when he was ready,' Cox says.

Alan Oliver had also revised his opinion. After a 2–0 victory over Sheffield Wednesday reserves he wrote: 'Newcastle manager Arthur Cox played six men with first-team experience in his reserve side at St James' Park last night. But they were all upstaged by nineteen-year-old Chris Waddle . . . . The gangling striker has certainly come on in leaps and bounds since I saw him in a pre-season friendly . . . . Like most tall strikers Waddle appears slow, but looks are certainly deceptive. His control is excellent and he is really confident on the ball. And he has perfected the art of dropping his shoulder to glide around an opponent.'

Dropping his shoulder. It was an art that came naturally to Chris and one that he was to hone and perfect over the next seventeen years of his career. From Newcastle to Spurs, from Marseille to Sheffield, from Falkirk to Bradford and for England on countless occasions around the world, he would leave an opposing defender mesmerised as he dropped his shoulder and either cut inside or drifted by him on the touch-line.

Arthur reacted to the public praise with typical Cox diplomacy and restraint. He talked directly to the press, who were desperate for a new local hero. They'd loved the flamboyance of Malcolm Macdonald, but with his cockney accent he could never hope to replace Jackie Milburn in thousands of Geordie hearts and minds. 'The boy has improved with every game. If he continues to develop at this rate he'll have a good future . . . . He's breathing down the necks of the senior players and that's a good thing. I don't want him to get the wrong ideas. He could read about himself and imagine he is something more than he is.'

It was mid-September when Arthur took up his appointment, and by the end of October he did not seem to have accomplished very much. Defeats at the hands of Bristol City (away) and Swansea (at home) had disappointed both the small, but devoted, band of travelling supporters and the dwindling home fans (just over 16,000 for the Swansea match). The vision of St James' Park filled to the rafters was a million miles away.

It was a reserve game against Derby that convinced Arthur

Cox that Waddle's moment had come. Colin Addison, the Derby manager, punished his entire first-team squad for a poor performance by playing all of them in a Central League game against Newcastle. Chris got a hat-trick in a 5–1 victory and on 22 October 1981 came the moment that Chris had been awaiting ever since he had been old enough to realise that there was such a thing as professional football. Together with his friend Chris Withe, he was named in the squad for a mid-week match against Shrewsbury – hardly the most glamorous of starts. The weather seemed to be in tune with the occasion, raining all day and hardly letting up during the match, which attracted only 11,973 spectators, about the same number who turned up at the training ground to see Alan Shearer's first session with the club in 1996. The numbers in the ground did not bother Chris. He would have been happy to play behind closed doors.

In anticipation of selection some day, he'd bought himself a suit at the start of the season for £15 in a sale. He carefully pressed it and took the 59 bus to the ground. He entered the dressing-room awkwardly, as if he had no right to be there alongside the likes of Terry Hibbitt and Mick Martin.

Despite having played with several members of the team in the reserves or in training, he was still in awe of them, still slightly uncomfortable in their presence. Stuart Boam, the giant centre-half, terrified him. During one practice match Chris had dribbled past him, but did not get much further before finding himself flattened. As he got up unsteadily, Boam whispered: 'If you do that again you'll end up under the pitch rather than on it.'

Yet, as with many seemingly hard men, Boam turned out to be the most gentle of souls off the field and ended up giving Chris a lift to training on a regular basis. Even though he lived less than an hour away, Boam never ventured out without several flasks of tea in his car, which might well have destroyed his reputation if opposing attackers had discovered his secret.

Before the start of the game against Shrewsbury, Chris was pleased to leave the dressing-room to ensure that the tickets were there for his father, his brother Joe and Lorna. As he came out of the players' entrance, a few young autograph hunters begged for his signature. It was all fresh to him, a totally new world, and he took their proffered pens and scraps of paper or programmes with shaking hands.

The match itself was an anticlimax. He realised the responsibility he had in pulling on the mantle of the number nine shirt, the magic number with which the Geordie fans had always had such an empathy, the shirt that Shearer wears. It was a scrappy ninety minutes, disappointing both as a spectacle and a contest. Mel Stein, sitting in the stand, hardly noticed the man who was to become his client. The home team scraped home by a single goal, scored by the ebullient Bobby Shinton, who'd worn the number nine shirt in the previous four matches. Arthur Cox was reasonably encouraging: 'You did all right, son.'

Chris himself was more critical. Again he'd found it difficult to adjust to the pace, but mainly he felt he'd not had the service he needed if he were to play up front successfully. Shinton and Bill Rafferty were taking up positions that he thought might have been his, but he did not have the confidence to tell them so. He did not even feel confident enough to call for the ball when the pair of them had so much responsibility.

By the time he came out of the shower and had finished in the players' lounge, his family party, Lorna included, had already

gone, leaving him to travel home the way he had arrived –
on the bus, alone, unheralded and unrecognised. If Tyneside
were to hail a new hero, it seemed it would have to wait for
another day and, perhaps, another player. During the course
of the season Chris would walk virtually unrecognised through
Newcastle's city centre with Shinton at his side. Heads turned,
fingers pointed time and time again to the Newcastle striker.
After the umpteenth autograph had been signed, Chris asked
Shinton how he could possibly endure it. 'Don't worry, son,
you'll have it all in a few years' time,' Bobby replied with
remarkable foresight.

The pressure didn't seem to bother Shinton, but that same
local pressure, that incredible level of expectation was to be
part of the reason that Chris would depart to the south some
few years later.

chapter 10

London was big, London was glamorous, London seemed an awfully long way away. But London was Chris Waddle's next destination. Not to stay – at least not yet – but to play. Newcastle's next fixture, on 25 October, was a visit to Chelsea. Unlike the Geordies, they were riding high at the top of the league, determined to regain the First Division status that they believed to be theirs as of right. It was a game between two fallen giants and, as the result was to prove, one had fallen far further than the other.

There was no doubt that Chris allowed both the occasion and the atmosphere to get to him. Despite their struggles, the club still stayed at good hotels and their base in Kensington offered the sort of comfort and luxury he had never experienced before. Stamford Bridge as a ground also had amenities that put the old St James' Park to shame.

The crowd was a huge 23,000 and the Newcastle travelling fans were silenced by the volume of noise from the threatening Shed. It was no day for faint hearts on or off the pitch, and when Chris read the programme and saw he was about to be marked by the 6ft 5in giant defender, Micky Droy, he felt almost physically sick. As it was Droy, together with Gary Chivers, had little to do in keeping Chris out of the game. He was still at that slightly naïve stage where he wanted to be friends with everybody, even the opposition.

Peter Rhoades-Brown on the Chelsea wing had impressed him with his pace. 'He's quick,' Chris said admiringly to Chivers as Rhoades-Brown flew by with the somewhat pedestrian Newcastle defenders trailing in his wake. Fast he was indeed, and Chivers ended the one-way conversation by racing away from Chris himself to receive the ball and put it into the net to give the home side a 4–0 lead.

As an act of kindness, Arthur Cox replaced Chris with the Dutchman Franz Koenen and the débâcle ended in a 6–0 defeat in front of the *Match of the Day* cameras, too. Both the Chrises, Waddle and Withe, thought it was the end of their careers and Withe, indeed, was never again to play for Newcastle. He moved on to Bradford City some ten years before Chris, then to Notts County, Bury, Chester, Mansfield and Shrewsbury.

It took fifteen years for him to join the club against whom he made his debut, and nobody wants to record the stories of the Chris Withes who make up the great majority of the professionals in the league today. One match, one performance against an attacker on song and all the hard work can be ruined in ninety minutes. Chris was to do the same many years later to Arsenal's Gus Caesar, but right then, although he did not realise it, what seemed like a disaster was merely part of a learning curve.

'We had quite a few promising youngsters at the time,' Arthur Cox says. 'Apart from Chris and Chris Withe, there was Peter Haddock, Kenny Wharton and Bruce Halliday. I didn't want them to take too many knock-backs as I was worried it might destroy their confidence for ever.'

Chris's education was to continue in the reserves. What must be one of the oddest decisions of the nineties was that of the powers that be at St James' Park to dispense with the reserve side all together. 'Young players need to play proper games, otherwise they end up being put out on loan or simply being sold,' explains Chris. 'Darren Huckerby and Chris Holland who moved from Newcastle to Coventry and Birmingham respectively in 1996 are perfect examples of an unnecessary loss of promising talent.'

While the first team lost at Cambridge, the second team were beating a Liverpool side that contained the young Ian Rush. On that afternoon, it was Chris who scored and Rush who missed an open goal.

Chris waited impatiently for another chance with the first team. After the glamour of big crowds and the first team, afternoon or early-evening matches for the reserves in deserted stadiums had little or no attraction. He had tasted the big-time and was hooked on it. United, meanwhile, were going from bad to worse: a home defeat by Wrexham, a draw at Orient and then a 4–0 hammering at Swansea. Arthur Cox knew he was under pressure, yet he still did not panic. He would play Chris when he thought he was ready and not simply when it was expedient for him so to do. He kept him in touch with the senior side by selecting him for a six-a-side tournament at Wembley, but at the time Chris saw that as small consolation. All he could see was the team scoring only three times in six matches between 8 November and 13 December – all three put away by Bobby Shinton.

Ray Clarke had turned out to be a disastrous signing after his European tour of Bruges, Ajax and Sparta for the then massive fee of £180,000, scoring just once in twelve outings. At least Arthur could point to his signing as being the work of his predecessor. Although his budget was restricted by the financial difficulties the club was beginning to encounter, he realised he had to go out into the market. With relegation, rather than promotion, appearing on the horizon, the future for both Cox and the club was looking bleak.

While Cox sought his man, he brought Chris back for the home match against Bristol City on 20 December, but that game, too, ended in a goalless draw. Arthur still believed that Chris had a future, but not necessarily as an out-and-out striker. He thought, quite correctly, that he needed someone more aggressive playing alongside him, and in buying Mick Harford from Lincoln City, aggression was what he got.

Not even Arthur would have claimed to have known that both components of the twin strike force he deployed for the first time against Grimsby Town on Boxing Day 1980 would still be turning out week in week out some sixteen years later. If Chris was a magnificent servant to club and country, Harford was just as effective in his own way, just as respected amongst those managers and players who really know the game.

He was a quiet young man off the pitch, seemingly lacking in confidence, despite his proven goal-scoring record, albeit at a lower level. The fans certainly did not take to him from the start. For one thing, he had been born in Sunderland – a fact that was never going to endear him to the fanatical Geordie. Malcolm Macdonald had started his career at Newcastle with a hat-trick and concussion. Some wit voiced an opinion that

Harford was actually playing while concussed after he'd kicked off with three blank sheets. Yet Harford's slow start was all to Chris's advantage.

Needing a confidence booster, he would receive it in spades. But first, in the hotel on Boxing Day, all the feelings of loneliness that had so overwhelmed him in his early days threatened to engulf him once again. The telephone was no substitute for the company of Lorna and his friends and family, while the gift of a turkey and bottle of sherry from the club seemed mechanical and cold. Football was a distraction, but the goalless draw with Grimsby proved a boring Christmas hangover, despite the debut of Harford. For Newcastle United, Arthur Cox and Chris Waddle it threatened to be a long, hard winter.

With New Year's Eve out of the way, the FA Cup beckoned – the tournament in which Newcastle had enjoyed so much success in the fifties before enduring so much embarrassment and heartache ever since. Once again, on 3 January 1981, hope sprang eternal in the Geordie breast. They might be languishing in the lower reaches of the Second Division, but the dream of a spring visit to Wembley's twin towers drew 22,500 people to St James' Park for the clash with First Division Sheffield Wednesday, a club managed by none other than Jack Charlton.

Ray Clarke was recalled for the cup-tied Harford, and for once the combination with Waddle actually worked. If there was a turning point in Chris's Newcastle career, then this was it. Newcastle won 2–1 and he scored both the goals. The first was the most memorable, driven home at the Gallowgate end, the faces in the crowd all merging into one as he ran towards them punching the air.

For the first time in his life he was catapaulted into the headlines. 'Waddle's Winners' and 'Waddle's Double Cheers United' were a couple of the more euphoric examples. The media pursued him relentlessly to the point where he fled to what he hoped would be the sanctuary of his brother Ray's house; but they even found him there and photographed him at the kitchen sink, just to prove he was a true working-class hero.

He didn't feel special. He didn't feel heroic. He felt remarkably shy. He'd travelled home on the bus from the match and had sat behind a couple of supporters talking about the disappointing season. 'If anybody's going to turn it around it'll be Waddle.' It never occurred to him to tap them on the shoulder, to say here I am, talk to me, not about me. Tyneside had become accustomed to the glitz and glamour of Super Mac. Chris Waddle was always going to be a different kind of hero.

Back in 1981, all the FA Cup matches were still played on the one day, the first Saturday in January. There were no demands of television to make it otherwise. When the draw for the fourth round was broadcast live on the radio at Monday lunchtime, men would take their transistors to work and those kids who were already back at school would smuggle them into the classrooms. The team itself stopped training early to gather round an old radio to hear the draw. It was home again, this time to a team from the same division, Luton Town, who were riding high under the management of David Pleat. In years to come, Chris would play successfully for him at Spurs until his fall from grace, then fall out with him dramatically at Sheffield Wednesday. On that day he was just another opposing manager.

There was a feeling in the town that, despite their Second

Division status, this could be Newcastle's year for the FA Cup. All too often in the past they had fallen at the first hurdle, and having overcome that, they were convinced nobody would beat them at St James' Park. Their confidence was boosted by a 1–0 league win at Luton in which Mick Harford scored against the club where he was to spend so many happy and successful years. Yet the cup game at home was a far harder struggle, with Newcastle running out 2–1 winners, despite Chris giving away the ball in midfield to enable the visitors to hit the post in the last few minutes. Much of what Arthur said to him in the dressing-room was unprintable, but they were through to the next round and he allowed himself a rare smile.

The whole town was buzzing. They awaited the draw for the next round with eager anticipation, and when they heard it was at home to lowly Exeter of the Third Division, the sixth round and three more matches to Wembley seemed a formality. Chris had yet to experience the team's suicidal tendencies when glory beckoned. He did not have long to wait.

chapter 11

Before the encounter with Exeter, Chris was to play against another manager who would have a significant influence on his career – a man who was to sell him for £4 million and then try to sign him on a free transfer a few years later. That was possibly a typical bit of business for Terry Venables. Venables was in charge of QPR at the time and even before his experience in Barcelona was very tactically aware. His back four were led by Glenn Roeder, he of the famous Roeder Shuffle, who would soon join up with Chris for Newcastle's big push for promotion. Ironically it was Glenn's defensive slip that day that enabled Chris to score the winner and add to his rapidly growing reputation.

'That was the first time I'd had the chance to look at Chris,' Glenn recalls. 'He had good ability, but he was lacking a man's strength. He needed to put five minutes here and there together. Yet, he was a match-winner even then, scoring a far-post header although we had dominated the match.'

Arthur Cox was delighted, particularly as he picked up the January Manager of the Month award, a far cry from the doom and gloom of the previous year. He should have enjoyed it while he could, because February was going to bring little joy.

Exeter City quite clearly had not read the script. Their fifth round visit from one St James' Park to another on 14 February should have been the signal for another St Valentine's Day massacre. But it wasn't. The visitors defended stoutly and could well have won the game at the first attempt. As it was honours ended even at one apiece, and the writing on the wall indicated yet another cup humiliation for the Geordies.

From Chris's point of view, the best thing about the little west country ground was the fact that he flew to a match for the first time. The best thing from a Newcastle supporter's viewpoint was the attractive Exeter physiotherapist who walked to the bench carrying a bucket before the match. As one fan put it, his black and white scarf drooping sadly after his team's 4–0 defeat, 'It was all downhill after the lass with the bucket.'

Arthur Cox was less philosophical: 'You realise what you've done. I'll have to dig the back garden, because I couldn't risk being seen in the front.' He received letters from angry fans, saying he shouldn't be playing Chris and the other kids, that they were contributing nothing, but it was all part of their development as far as he was concerned, and he felt he owed it to them to give them the opportunities.

Once again the BBC cameras had been there to capture Newcastle's embarrassment, and once again John Motson had been the commentator. Motty had been at Stamford Bridge (a 6–0 defeat) at Swansea (4–0) and now this. Fourteen goals conceded and none scored. It was little wonder that there were threats to ban him from all Newcastle matches.

He wasn't to get the chance to comment on Chris again. Chris began a match against West Ham on 7 March, but couldn't finish it.

He was in agony and a viral infection in his groin was diagnosed, so serious that his season was over. Yet his Newcastle career was certainly not. He was offered a new contract on the improved terms of £120 a week plus £70 a game. The pay-as-he-played clause was particularly beneficial, as the following season he was ever-present in all forty-seven matches.

He couldn't wait for the close season to be over, to pick up where he left off. During the break he was invited back to Bill Quay JMI to present the prizes at their annual sports day. He still did not feel like a celebrity, still regarded the teachers who had taught him with awe, even though they were now asking him for his autograph. The playground supervisor was particularly unimpressed by his visit – she was, after all, his mother.

His mother had always been very proud of him, even when he'd been playing for Tow Law. His friends similarly seemed to revel in his success, their initial hesitation fully overcome. Peter Allen, Gary Durham and Stephen Preston, one of Lorna's work-mates at De La Rue's, were ferociously loyal, idolising Chris, while at the same time protecting him. If fame ever threatened to go to his head, Lorna was always on hand to bring him down to earth. 'Chris never really changed, only the attitude of people towards him altered.' That is an assessment made by Lorna herself and echoed by Gary Durham.

'Once in France, I think I did get a bit carried away,' Chris recalls. 'I was doing a fair amount of personal appearances and there'd be hordes of teenage girls there all screaming away as if I were a pop star. Lorna didn't let me develop that aspect of my career for too long, and once I'd pushed it aside I realised it wasn't really me either.'

He would also become a target for troublemakers or so-called fans always ready to make a nuisance of themselves. Lorna recalls that whenever they went out, if she left her seat for a few minutes she'd return to find it occupied by some total stranger giving his views at length on football. 'You can only be polite for so long, but when you make it clear that you've had enough of their company then things can turn nasty,' Chris says.

Things certainly turned nasty one night in Pelaw. Chris and his friends were sitting drinking in a corner, laughing and joking while a darts match was in progress. When they were asked to keep the noise down, they pointed out that they were in a pub rather than a library. It didn't go down too well and all hell broke loose. A glass was smashed in someone's face, and although Chris's friends had tossed him over the counter and out of the back door before things got out of hand, that did not stop the accusation that Chris had in some way been involved in the assault. The police came to his house to interview him the next day, but worse than that was Arthur Cox's investigation into the incident. It was conducted with that steely look that made even the innocent feel guilty and culminated in a dressing-down that left his ears burning and a fine that left his pocket hurting.

He returned to the club in the summer to find changes. Willie McFaul, who was to return later as manager and be responsible for the sale of Paul Gascoigne, had been replaced as first-team coach by Tommy Cavanagh. Cavanagh came fresh from Manchester United, where he'd exploited the two-winger approach with some success. It was by no means so successful at St James'. Mick Harford had already moved on, the money from his sale being used to buy Imre Varadi from Everton. Varadi was a completely different kind of player from Harford, small, quick on the ground, very comfortable on the ball, but unlikely to be able to reach the crosses that had been meat and drink to Harford's battering-ram style. Three defeats in the first four matches saw Newcastle firmly anchored to the foot of the table and Cox feeling it was one step forward and then two back.

As the season developed, things improved slightly but without any consistency. Varadi couldn't find the net in his first seven games, then promptly scored five in the next two. Chris himself was struggling. He'd found it hard to get back after the virus and managed just two goals in thirteen games, a sequence that included another cup defeat at the hands of a team from a lower division – this time Fulham of the Third in the League Cup.

The FA Cup was not to bring them any relief, either. They beat Colchester in a thrilling 4–3 game after a home draw, but Grimsby saw that they got no further. Arthur was experimenting all the time to find a proven goalscorer, convinced that somebody should be able to fire the bullets from the ammunition supplied by Chris. David Mills and Alan Brown were tried alongside Varadi, and although they did not have any immediate success, April saw Newcastle up in fourth position with an outside chance of promotion. But once again it all went wrong as five defeats in the last seven matches saw them slip away to ninth.

It had been a curate's egg of a season for Chris. He was linked with Arsenal, Sheffield Wednesday and Leeds, and Brighton wanted to take him on a month's loan exchange for Neil McNab. He must have been doing something right to attract all that interest, and he was also called into the England Under-21 squad for the two-legged European semi-final against Scotland.

As he worked and trained with Dave Sexton, who led the managerial team, he realised how far he had come, how far he still had to go. On this occasion he got no further than the substitute's bench, but it didn't matter. He was getting recognition outside the north-east, and with one year left of his two-year contract, he knew that for the first time in his professional career that he, and not the club, was in the driving seat. He negotiated (if that was the correct word) a year's extension to his contract, scotching rumours of his imminent departure, and pushed his wages up to £145 a week. If he could have known what the 1982–83 season had in store in the shape of a new team-mate, he might well have been prepared to play for nothing.

chapter 12

Arthur Cox knew that if Newcastle United were to become great again, he would have to build anew from top to bottom. At the bottom he dealt with new contracts for the likes of Chris. At the top he signed Kevin Keegan.

Just as it would be when Sir John Hall brought Keegan in as manager in February 1992, the timing was perfect. Keegan needed a challenge after the years of success at Liverpool and Hamburg, needed to get the adrenalin pumping once more now that he had chosen to end his England career. When the news was announced, nobody believed it. Chris was with the club on a pre-season tour of Madeira. They'd seen the rumours in the papers and, thinking they were just that, were laughing among themselves when Tommy Cavanagh assured them it was true.

'We all thought – why? Just six months before, he'd been captain of England and now he's down in the Second Division with us. It didn't really sink in.'

In many ways it was a dress-rehearsal for the signing of Alan Shearer over a decade later. Thousands assembled outside St James' Park to greet both the news and the player, initially with disbelief and ultimately with jubilation. Newcastle United were back on the footballing map. Two thousand fans came to watch the training sessions on a regular basis. As far as Arthur was concerned, Keegan was the beginning not the end. Terry McDermott was another Liverpool captive and the seeds of the successful managerial partnership were sown. Little David McCreery came from Tulsa in the States after a long spell with Manchester United and Mick Channon added another England international to the pack, although it transpired he was only passing through on his way to a successful career as a racehorse trainer.

Keegan, as ever, was seen to be doing everything just right. He moved up to Morpeth and threw himself into the task of leading from the front with his usual boundless enthusiasm. At first Chris, and the rest of the team, were totally in awe of him. He'd played the game at the very top of his profession, captained his country, and here he was turning out alongside a mixed bag of journeymen in the Second Division. The players at Falkirk and Bradford City must surely have felt the same when Chris joined up with them in 1996.

As far as Chris was concerned, Keegan was never less than encouraging. 'You've got a lot of talent, but you're not working hard enough,' he'd say. 'You're too laid back. Even if you feel you're not playing well, then close your man down, chase him, harass him. Your team-mates will appreciate that as well. Try to be consistent.' It was practical advice from a man who had not been blessed with the natural ability of, say, a Best or a Gascoigne but who had worked tirelessly at self-improvement both on and off the pitch.

The first game of the season simply could not end in defeat. Keegan was writing the script and was determined to direct to perfection the role he had created for himself. It is a match that Chris will never forget.

'The season before, we'd been lucky to get 15,000 people to see us. Now all of a sudden tickets were like gold-dust for the game against QPR. There were 36,185 packed into the ground and you could feel them willing Kevin to score. Then in the second half it happened. John Craggs started the move and played the ball down the line to Imre Varadi. He passed it to Kevin. We were all giving it to Kevin every chance we got. It won't go down as one of the best goals he ever scored at St James', but it's the one everybody will remember. I think it was at the Gallowgate end and, as one journalist put it, as the ball crawled towards the goal the crowd drew in an enormous breath and simply sucked it into the net.'

They won their next match as well, against Blackburn, and although two wins out of two did not mean a lot to the rest of the country, it had been a long time since Newcastle United had taken maximum points from their first two games of a season. Yet Keegan couldn't do it on his own. He found himself constantly man-marked, and it was Chris and the rest of the team who came under pressure. Chris had already been the subject of a tactical substitution against Blackburn, and now with the team running up a sequence of defeats and draws that saw them lying a disappointing twelfth at the end of September, Arthur decided his protégé needed a more extended rest.

Rather than Keeganmania inspiring him, Chris was overwhelmed by it, overawed and subdued by the huge crowds, the constant media circus and the ever-present television cameras. He was starting to think about the game as well, with a deep introspection that temporarily got out of all perspective. His thoughts led him to the conclusion that with Keegan's arrival he was being played out of position, that he was no longer a central striker.

He dropped his guard and spoke of his discontent to a journalist, rather than approaching Arthur privately and directly. At the end of October 1982, the local *Evening Chronicle* carried the headline: 'Give me a new role ... I'm not a winger, says Waddle.'

Not a winger? This from the man who was to gain so many caps for England in just that role. He had got it wrong, very wrong, and he was going to have to pay for his mistake in more ways than one.

Arthur Cox went ballistic. Just before Chris was due to play in the reserves against Coventry, he was summoned to see Arthur, and as he approached his manager, he felt like a man walking towards the gallows. With the expletives deleted, the general message was that if he had anything to say, then it should be said to the manager and not the press. Arthur was right and Chris knew it. It was a lesson he learned early, not to trust a journalist, and it was an expensive lesson, too, because Arthur fined him on the spot.

'If you've got something to say, then knock on the door and talk to me,' Arthur told him. 'I also took the opportunity to tell him some home-truths,' he remembers. 'Shortly after I'd got to the club I'd told him he had all the attributes to be an international winger. He didn't believe me then, but after I'd finished with him then I think he believed me a bit more.'

In a way, it was a turning point in a season that was threatening to turn into disaster for both player and club. Chris ran out on to the pitch angry with himself, furious with the reporter, and promptly scored the first goal. Unlike some managers, Arthur was never one to hold a grudge. Chris was brought back into the team against Crystal Palace and justified the decision by scoring the winning goal. He could feel the confidence flowing back. So much of football is played in the head, rather than with the feet, and against Burnley he turned on the best performance of his career to date in a 3–0 win.

'At the time they were talking about me scoring one of the greatest Newcastle goals ever, but I've no doubt that there's been better since. At the time, though, it did seem a bit special. I got the ball wide, ran straight across the pitch and hit it past Alan Stephenson in their goal from thirty-five yards. Even if I wasn't playing as an out-and-out striker, it *felt* like I was, and that was all part of Arthur's psychology.'

The crowd regarded him as a favourite son, so the rumours of an impending transfer that had followed on his spell in the reserves and his public statement of discontent were not well received locally. Birmingham, Luton, Southampton, Brighton, Barnsley and even Spurs were watching him, while both Portsmouth and Bolton actually offered player exchange deals involving Kevin Dillon and Tony Henry. With hindsight and due respect to their respective talents, it is incredible to think that Newcastle even contemplated it – but they did. It was the board, rather than Arthur Cox, who were always looking to sell and Len Shackleton, for so long a thorn in the side of the Sunderland directors, had turned his waspish attention to north-eastern clubs in general: 'To cash in or not to cash in? That is the question Newcastle face about wonder boy Chris Waddle.'

The fact that there were any questions at all arose from his inconsistency, the fading from a match for long periods. This criticism was to be aimed at him (for the most part unfairly) throughout his career. Within the article Shackleton interviewed Arthur, who said that Keegan was convinced that Chris was not fit enough.

'I can understand it,' Cox added. 'Waddle missed the formative years for a soccer pro between fifteen and nineteen. Consequently he has had too much to catch up with in the professional game . . . he's got to do the business on match days regularly, or get out and let someone else in.'

If Chris could voice his feelings in the papers, then so could Arthur Cox. He didn't want to lose the lad, but there was clearly a problem inside his head. Unless Arthur could get it right, unless Chris could get it right, he would never harness his talents to his true potential. 'I told the lad,' Arthur says, 'that if he couldn't play in front of his own people, I'd put him out on loan somewhere else. He didn't like that. Nor did he like it when I told him if he didn't pull himself together he'd drift into obscurity. I insulted him left, right and centre and he took it all. He had to.'

But Arthur Cox had more problems than just Chris Waddle. In January 1983, Newcastle fans were desperate for something to lift their season and once again they turned to the FA Cup. Moving towards the end of the twentieth century, with Brighton firmly anchored at the foot of the Third Division and facing oblivion, it seems odd to think that just fourteen years ago the mighty Newcastle United actually started as underdogs against them in their third-round cup tie. They were merely a mid-table Second Division side pitted against the high-flying Seagulls. The Geordies earned a draw at the seaside and were widely fancied to win at home. However, Brighton grabbed the lead, and then the referee disallowed not one, but two Newcastle goals, and needed a police escort to get him out of the ground in one piece.

Out of the cup at the first hurdle, already out of the League Cup by Christmas and well out of the promotion race. Chris, himself, was struggling for form, struggling in a way for a sense of direction. For once it seemed that the Keegan magic was not going to work.

chapter 13

As the 1982–83 season progressed, the team gradually took shape. Without ever threatening really to take the division by storm they finished a respectable fifth. Players came and players went as Arthur sought for the elusive piece of the jigsaw puzzle that would finally present a complete picture to the adoring fans. Among the arrivals and departures was Howard Gayle, the first black player to pull on a Newcastle shirt.

Although the Newcastle fans had a reputation for racism at the time, in the north-east it stemmed from a fear of the unknown, rather than a hatred of something different. The black population of the area was small, and most black faces came up white again once the coal-dust was washed away. In his short stay, Gayle actually endeared himself to the terraces, scoring twice. 'He's black, he's brown, he's playing for the toon,' they chanted. But his loan terms didn't allow him to play in the FA Cup, he missed the Brighton matches, and the early exit from that competition meant there was no money to sign him.

Chris himself has never seen any racism among the players, although he has certainly heard it from the terraces. Bobby Barnes of West Ham was on the receiving end of a cascade of bananas thrown on to the pitch and guttural 'native' chants every time he got the ball. 'I put it all down to ignorance and thankfully it's much rarer now. I think that's because there's been such a great contribution to our national game from the likes of John Barnes, Paul Ince and Les Ferdinand.'

A more permanent and, as time would prove, a more relevant signing was John Anderson from Preston. 'Ando' became a fixture in the side over many seasons. Time and time again his position was threatened by more expensive signings, but he either saw them off or resurfaced as a utility player in another role. Chris recalls: 'I liked Ando as a player and a person. He had a dry Irish sense of humour apart from being very quick on the field. The club got ten years out of him on a free transfer which can't be bad business.'

By the end of the season, Chris was able to look back on a year when he'd been ever-present from the end of October after winning back his place. He'd scored only seven goals, but then Keegan and Varadi had netted forty-two times in the league between them and Chris was gradually, imperceptibly, turning towards being a provider, a creator, rather than a scorer. He felt more settled and was looking forward to his wedding in June. The club were not particularly interested in his personal arrangements and he had to depart with them for an end of season tour of the Far East, leaving Lorna behind with the organisation.

'I was rather relieved that Chris was away,' Lorna recalls. 'He would only have got in the way. As it was, my mum and dad made all the arrangements for the wedding, even down to decorating the house. It was while they were doing the painting that my aunt, who was helping them, fell down the stairs and smashed her face in, just a week before the wedding. I'm sure that if we'd put Chris up a ladder he'd have done something even worse.'

They'd never actually got formally engaged. Chris had wanted to buy a house and asked her to move in with him. She'd declined, but without saying that marriage was a pre-condition of their living together. He assumed that to be the case and got on with the business of naming the day. They did eventually buy a house in Springwell Village, but again Chris's footballing commitments meant that he saw it only once before it actually became theirs.

The tour was a nightmare. The players were propositioned by the gay population wherever they went, their athletic figures drawing the locals towards them like moths to a flame. When Kevin Carr, the 6ft 2in, 13½st keeper, became the target for one love-lorn individual, he eventually snapped: 'Look mate, if you don't go away and let us alone, I'm going to kick your balls off.' The local just smiled, taking it as some form of encouragement.

Jet-lag and food poisoning took their toll and travel around Kuala Lumpar was never the height of luxury. One drive across the island saw Chris becoming horribly travel sick, so it was with a feeling of utter relief that he saw the gleaming sea and beach. He raced away to dive into the cool waters and looked back to see everybody waving to him from the shore. He cheerfully waved back before lip-reading 'sharks'. He was never the quickest of swimmers, but he's convinced he would have broken the Olympic record for the distance.

He kept in touch with home by writing letters, for the club's budget did not extend to paying for calls back home. By the end of the tour, the 'them' and 'us' syndrome within the camp was well and truly entrenched. Arthur, somewhat surprisingly, was one of 'us'. When somebody found a photograph of the younger Cox and pinned it on the notice board, Chris anonymously added the name 'McVicar', a reference to the recently convicted killer. There were marked similarities between the most wanted man in Britain and the Newcastle manager, with the close cut hair and the six o'clock shadow. Arthur said nothing, but never forgot, and when he left Newcastle he told Chris he had known it was him all along.

By now a close-knit, if beleagured group, they moved on to Japan. 'This wasn't yet the football-mad country where my friend Gary Lineker was to play, but it was incredibly expensive. For what it cost to play a round of golf, I could have bought my own golf club back home. My lasting memory, though, is the fact that they showed films about Pearl Harbor every night in the bar!'

Newcastle were chosen to compete in an obscure tournament for the Japan Cup, against the Japanese national side, the Japanese league champions, the Syrian national team (who were on war alert to return home) and Botofogo of Brazil. In the first match, Chris grabbed a hat-trick in a 4–0 defeat of the Japanese national side. 'There must have been about a hundred journalists there with television cameras and all,' Arthur Cox says. 'Chris was the man they all wanted to interview, but he just got changed quickly, lay on the back seat of the coach and told me he couldn't face them. That was typical. It was another year before he'd even speak to Metro, the local radio station.'

Newcastle ran out winners of the tournament, with the highlight a goalless draw against the Brazilians, who included internationals Josimar and Nunez in their ranks. The trophy was less than impressive, looking like a big blue flower vase that Chris's mum might have kept on the dresser if she'd not been particularly choosy.

Yet clearly any trophy meant something to the fans on Tyneside. Keegan and Terry McDermott stayed over in London on the return leg, leaving Chris to bring the cup home. To his astonishment, there were hordes of fans waiting to greet their heroes. So starved were they of success that even victory in this nonentity of a tournament was regarded as some kind of triumph. Chris held the vase high in the air, promising himself that some day he'd bring them home something really worthwhile. At the time, although he did not realise it, the silent promise he made to the fans waiting at the airport was less than a year from being fulfilled.

For once in his life, Lorna turned his attention away from football to their wedding. His date with destiny was 25 June 1983. Keith Mullen was to be the best man, being marginally more responsible than Gary Durham, and inevitably it was Gary who caused the stag night to descend into chaos. None of the players attended the night, and indeed it is an interesting comment on the man that throughout his life his hard core of friends have always remained the same.

They started out at the Swan in Howarth, where Keith poured a bottle of Spanish Fly he'd bought at a local sex shop into Ray Waddle's pint of beer. Ray downed it, smacked his lips and expressed a reluctance to move on. However, it was he who went over to sort out an argument in which Gary had become embroiled. A youngster born at Wallsend was claiming he was Geordie and Gary was having none of it. Before Ray could open his mouth, the youngster hit him on the chin and the wedding party had to beat a hasty retreat, with Gary laughing helplessly and Ray worrying about how he was going to look in the wedding photos with a black eye, bruised jaw and broken tooth.

Chris was the only one to remain stone cold sober, despite the efforts of his entourage. That was fortunate, as Keith took his duties seriously and was so worried that he turned up at Chris's home at six in the morning. The cars, in contrast, were late.

There was neither time nor money for a honeymoon. Pre-season training was already beckoning and they had so much to do in the house. 'People think a footballer's life is a doddle, but if you're with a successful team nowadays and are also an international, you can go years without having more than a week off. Yes, the money's there, but it's certainly not paid for old rope. It's only paid for hard work, like in every other job.'

chapter 14

At the start of each season, every club's manager makes the public declaration that his team will win something, even if in his heart of hearts he knows that the only realistic target is mere survival. Arthur Cox, still tinkering with the engine of his team, made the decision to sell Imre Varadi, which was initially regarded as the final nail in his own coffin. Varadi had not only been the previous season's joint top scorer, but had also been very popular with the fans and his fellow-players, despite being somewhat vague. In one conversation with him, Kevin Carr mentioned that his wife worked for an estate agent. 'So you're all right for cheap holidays then,' said Imre.

There was no public indication of the signing of a replacement, and Arthur had merely dipped into the transfer market for the signing of an expensive defender in the shape of Oldham's Under-21 England international, John Ryan.

Although Lady Luck always plays her part in any team's promotion campaign, she is never available for transfer. She goes wherever she pleases. It was vital to get the campaign off to a positive start, so when Newcastle grabbed the lead at Elland Road against Leeds through an isolated John Anderson goal, it looked as if the Lady may have pulled on a black and white shirt. Then Kevin Carr, who had just won the battle for the number one goalkeeper's slot with Martin Thomas, fell awkwardly and clearly could not continue. 'I volunteered to go in goal,' recalls Chris. 'It was me or Kevin, and although he was up for it he looked a bit lost at his size between the sticks. I was so keen to get on with it that I pulled the jersey off Kevin Carr whilst he was still on the ground. He screamed in agony and it was only later that I discovered that he'd actually broken his arm.'

It was never going to be easy. Chris was ambling back towards the goal when he heard his team-mates screaming at him. He looked up to see a Terry McDermott back-pass creeping towards him, with two Leeds players in hot pursuit. He scrambled it away and somehow or other managed to keep a clean sheet for the remaining forty-three minutes of the game. His communication with the team for the rest of the game left a lot to be desired. 'I was having problems with goal-kicks. They were all going out to the left, and when Kevin and David Mills drifted out to the wing to meet the ball, I finally got it right and started banging it down the middle. Eventually Kevin yelled at me to ask where I was going to hit it next.'

Somehow or other, Newcastle and their makeshift goalie held on. Chris was so relieved to hear the final whistle that he raced off the field, with a small child behind him shouting, 'Keeper, keeper, you've left your bag in the net.'

If Arthur Cox was the architect of Newcastle's success, then his next signing was to be the spark that brought his designs to life. October 1983 saw Peter Beardsley join Newcastle United for the first time. Not only was he to bring his mercurial skills to the club, but he was also to be the man to help Chris fulfil his potential.

'You could see Peter was special from the moment he started training with us. I'd heard a lot about him when he'd been with Carlisle, and we'd all thought it a bit odd when he'd vanished from English football to go to play for Vancouver Whitecaps in the North American League. Now I experienced for myself his vision and technique. He has an incredible love of the game, an enthusiasm that seems to have grown as he's got older. We were never that close at Newcastle, but I really got to know him when we were together with England. When I was commentating recently for the BBC on the Metz–Newcastle game in France, I was out on the pitch getting soaking wet in the pouring rain. Peter came running out and gave me his wet-top and then told me to keep it when I tried to return it at the end of the match. Typical of the man.'

Married life had given Chris a sense of stability, as did the feeling that his position in the side was now held on merit, no longer under threat either from within or from some big-name signing.

Arthur Cox never permitted Chris to remain complacent, though. Having scored in early-season matches against Oldham, Palace and Barnsley he scored twice against Portsmouth in a 4–2 demolition – then found himself substituted because the manager thought he was not trying sufficiently hard to get a hat-trick.

'Chris and Peter, at the time, were chalk and cheese,' Cox says. 'Peter was always bright-eyed and bushy-tailed, there with the balls at the start of training, whilst there were moments when Chris seemed as if he couldn't care less. I'd say to him, "I want you to be a footballer more than you do." I couldn't understand him. He seemed quite happy to spend his time on the training ground with players of lesser ability as it meant he didn't have to extend himself.'

An early exit from the Milk Cup to Oxford was a blessing in disguise as the focus centred on the league and promotion. Nobody actually put the thought into words, but certainly for Cox himself, and perhaps also for the club, this was the crossroads. It was now or never, and as a series of victories took them into second place, it looked very much as if it were going to be now.

A place behind them were Manchester City, who visited St James' Park on 29 October. A huge crowd of 33,500 saw an irresistible performance from the home side. It is unlikely that a front three of the likes of Keegan, Waddle and Beardsley will ever grace the lower divisions again and City had no answer to an all-out attack that saw all three score in a 5–0 win, with Beardsley getting a hat-trick.

Yet, had they peaked too early? As United were to discover in the 1995–96 season when they were twelve points clear at the top, it was far easier to be caught when trying to lead all the way from the front. They were unconvincing in a narrow win over lowly Fulham and then proceeded to lose three of their next four games – the most aggravating being when they threw away a two-goal lead against Derby to go down 3–2, and the most embarrassing being another crushing 4–0 defeat by Chelsea. It was clear that with what was becoming an all-star team, a match against Newcastle was every opponent's cup final.

Somehow Arthur got them fired up again and Chris was back in the headlines with a brace of goals against Huddersfield in a 5–2 win. Over the next three games – a win, a draw and a defeat –

Newcastle scored only three goals and Chris got them all, giving him a personal record of scoring in five consecutive matches, a feat he has never repeated.

'I always felt Chris should score goals and I was always on to him to go for goal,' Cox says. ' He was so consistent in that promotion year. If he and I had stayed together, then I'm convinced he would have scored a lot more times in his career. Somehow he liked making them more than putting them into the net himself. A lot of people suggest he was one-footed. I thought he had two great feet. Defenders would find the greatest of difficulty in getting him into the corner because he could pass or cross with both left and right and they just didn't know what he was going to do. He was good in the air, too, but somehow nobody seemed to work on that after I left.'

Chris missed out in a 2–1 New Year's Eve victory at Oldham, but was back on the score-sheet with the only goal of the match in a victory over Barnsley. It was a shot hit with the outside of his left foot from some twenty yards at the Gallogate end, described by Ronnie Glavin of Barnsley as 'sheer magic, world class'.

So it was that Chris and the rest of the team had every reason to look forward with confidence to the third round of the FA Cup and their daunting opposition – Liverpool at Anfield. It was a challenge in more senses than one. Chris knew he needed a national platform upon which to build his international career. Disappointed not to have been invited to join up with the Under-21 side again, despite the recommendations of his manager, he felt he still had something to prove. The cup game, televised live before an audience of millions, would be an opportunity to measure the club's progress against top-class opposition rather than the likes of Fulham, Shrewsbury and Cambridge. And then

6

there was the final ingredient, the ultimate twist of spice in the brew – Kevin Keegan coming up against his old side.

Yet once again the fans were led down the primrose path to the rainbow's end, only to find that the pot of gold belonged to Merseyside. 'This is Anfield,' says the stark notice at the end of the players' tunnel. Indeed it was. 'I was really looking forward to it, although I was very nervous. I didn't find anything particularly special about playing at Anfield, although it was my first time. Since then it's always been a ground I've enjoyed visiting. The fans understand their football and that helps.'

It was as humiliating as it had been at Wembley a decade before. A 4–0 victory for Liverpool told only half the story of the gulf between the two sides. For Chris, there was the added ignominy of missing Newcastle's best chance of the night when he allowed Bruce Grobbelaar in the Liverpool goal to make a relatively easy save.

'I enjoyed the game despite the result. They were a yard faster than us, never giving us time to settle on the ball, and I realised that even if we got promotion, if we were going to play the likes of Liverpool every week then we still had a long way to go.'

If the match taught Chris a lesson, it also gave Kevin Keegan the message that he could no longer compete at the highest level, and he immediately announced that whether or not Newcastle got promotion he was going to retire at the end of the season. For Keegan the perfectionist, if he could not do himself justice then it was time to pack it in.

Keegan's decision was one that was to echo around Chris's own mind in the autumn of 1996. 'I never forgot that. Yet, when all the managerial and coaching offers were coming in, I kept thinking to myself, I can still play. Once I give it up and move over to the other side of the fence I can never return.'

Keegan's decision, dramatic as it was, together with the exit from the cup, once again focused the minds of the team on the only honour now available to them – promotion. It was the league or nothing, and nobody – the fans, Arthur, the players or the board – none of them – would be satisfied with nothing.

chapter 15

A debutant in the Boxing Day side against Blackburn Rovers was Glenn Roeder, who had joined Newcastle from QPR. Roeder was to prove a wonderful servant to the club, captaining the team after the departure of Keegan until he, himself, moved on. He was most unlucky never to receive the international recognition his talents deserved. It was not until 1996 that his first opportunity came to join up with the national squad when, retired and newly dismissed as the Watford manager, he was appointed by Glenn Hoddle to the England scouting staff.

While Chris and Terry McDermott were the only ever-presents throughout the season, Glenn wore the number six shirt in every match after his signing and was able to see the blossoming Waddle talent from close quarters.

'Since I'd last seen Chris, he'd improved immensely,' Glenn recalls. 'He'd filled out and was getting far more involved in the game, although it wasn't until he went to Spurs that he was actually lasting ninety minutes. His main problem, although some would have seen it as an asset, was that he was laid back to the point of being horizontal. He was just so contented in the north-east, happy-go-lucky, really only comfortable with his local mates like Steve Carney. I think he was very fortunate in marrying someone like Lorna who was always prepared to push him on. She was, and is, a huge influence on his life and I'm sure she had a big say in his decision to go to London. That was the making of him. He left Newcastle a shy, Geordie lad and his first year in the south turned him into a fully grown man.'

After the defeat by Liverpool, it was the weather that began to beat Newcastle. Snow and ice reduced them to road running or merely kicking around in the snow. Even when they returned to the playing arena, a trip to Crystal Palace brought only a 3–1 defeat. That disappointment did not stop Chris picking up the *Evening Chronicle* Hennessy Cognac Player of the Month award – his first, but not his last, individual prize of this nature.

It was back to basics with another loss at home to Grimsby that certainly did not represent championship form, and Newcastle slipped to fifth place. But that was as bad as it got. Mid–February saw them beat Manchester City again, this time at Maine Road by two goals to one. The Toon Army took to the road in numbers, some 12,000 of them helping to swell the crowd to nearly 42,000.

'I've played in lots of places since then, at Tottenham, Marseille, Sheffield, not to mention for England at Wembley, but nothing can rival the passionate support that Newcastle take with them,' says Chris. It was as if they were not just following a football team, but a dream that could help them escape from the greyness of their lives, from the closures of pits and factories, from the unemployment queues from which football had also helped Chris to escape.

Suddenly the show was back on the road. From that match at Manchester on 18 February, right the way through to mid-April,

Newcastle went nine matches without defeat. Although the goals were shared around, it was Chris who was catching all the headlines – and catching the eye of all the leading clubs, including Manchester United. Bobby Robson, the England manager, had also watched the young Geordie personally. Tow Law seemed an awfully long way away.

He made an immediate impression on Robson. 'I always felt an empathy with Chris, we shared the same roots,' Robson said from his precarious position as manager of Barcelona. 'I could see, even then, that he had wonderful technique. He could go inside or outside, which was a huge asset, and together with his pace made for a great combination. Cruyff, Best, Maradona and Pele all had it and although, in those early days, I didn't think Chris would ever be that good, I really believe that his career since then has put him alongside those all-time greats.'

Now there was no doubt as to the board's feelings as chairman Stan Seymour publicly warned other clubs to keep their hands off his emerging star. 'There is no way Chris will be allowed to leave this club,' said "Mr Newcastle". 'We have him under contract until the end of next season and we expect him to be a Newcastle player beyond that.' It was all such a different story from just three years ago.

Expectation was one thing, the ability or willingness to deliver another. The Newcastle United of the mid-eighties was not the same club that Sir John Hall recreated in the nineties. There were more important things for Chris than any new contract, for he was still desperate to get his club back into the top flight. Just as suddenly as they had run into form, so they lost it. Despite the impressive string of results, they were still only third, behind Chelsea and Sheffield Wednesday and with

Grimsby and Manchester City breathing down their necks. It was still a case of automatic promotion for the top three, and although they would obviously have liked to have taken the title, the fact was that once promotion was achieved nobody really remembered, or indeed cared, in which order they'd come up.

The game against Sheffield Wednesday on 14 April was a real six-pointer and Newcastle disastrously lost it by the only goal. A draw at Blackburn, an easy win against Carlisle and then all they had to do was go to bottom club Cambridge, who'd played twenty games without a win, get a result, and they were up. Once again they pressed the self-destruct button and went down 1–0. Grimsby had drawn. A supporter who let his feelings get the better of him and barged into the dressing-room summed it all up: 'Blew it again, you stupid bastards.'

There was no way of hiding the team coach as it travelled the endless journey back up the motorway. Coachloads of supporters who had been ready to celebrate could scarcely conceal their disappointment. Horns blared, not in triumph but in anger, and instead of scarves flying with pride out of the windows, there was a succession of two-fingered gestures to the men who had let them down yet again.

There were three games left – against Derby, Huddersfield and Brighton – and there was no room for error.

chapter 16

More than 35,000 fans filled St James' Park on 5 May 1984, ready to celebrate the bank holiday in a big way. Derby County were the visitors, fighting what would prove to be a futile battle against relegation to the Third Division. This time everything went according to the script. Top beat bottom 4–0 and the trinity of Keegan, Beardsley and Waddle all scored.

It was far better than the Japan Cup, although from the club's point of view it did not feel like it. There were the usual celebrations on the pitch, the laps of honour and the champagne in the dressing-room. There were tears as well, certainly in Kevin Keegan's eyes, but being Keegan there was no turning back from his decision to retire – and if he was to go out on a high, where better than the passionate north-east?

Once the players had left the ground it was an anticlimax. The club had organised nothing for the players or the families, although it would not have needed too much optimism to have predicted promotion that afternoon. If there was a moment when Chris began to doubt that his long-term future lay at Newcastle United, at least under its existing regime, then that was it. 'When you win something like that, you think there's going to be a massive party with everybody going crazy; but in a way that sort of success is more for the fans than the players. It's a bit like your own wedding. Everybody enjoys it more than you on the day. As it was, after we'd cracked open the bubbly in the dressing-room, we all just went home in our own cars.'

The fans knew nothing of the politics behind the scenes. They travelled down to Huddersfield to swell the crowd to over 25,000, almost treble most of the home gates the Yorkshire club had been receiving all season. The 2–2 result was irrelevant. It was the only game of the campaign that Keegan missed, but there was no way he was not going to play in the final match at home to Brighton, who'd been relegated the previous year.

There could be only one result. With the pressure lifted, Newcastle played relaxed, cultured football. There were no takers for any bets on the three scorers. A goal each for the striking trio in a 3–1 victory meant that Kevin had scored twenty-seven, Peter twenty and Chris eighteen, an astonishing sixty-five in the league between them.

The rest of the squad, Chris included, did some half a dozen laps of honour before leaving the stage to Special K. They would have other opportunities; he would not. He had not only played his last game for United, but his last competitive match in the English league. The Keegan career as a player was over; his future as United's manager was years away. The ground was filled to capacity both for the match against Brighton and, later in the week, for a friendly against Liverpool. The fans were there for one reason only – to say goodbye and thank you to Keegan. Yet again Kevin knew just what was expected of him. He didn't score, but he was collected from the pitch by helicoptor and taken to the reception that the club had got round to organising – as well they could afford to do, given the gate receipts for what was, after all, a non-competitive match.

That was as far as it went. There was no holiday offered as a gesture of thanks, and the players breathed a sigh of relief that there was to be no post-season tour. The appreciation shown to Arthur Cox was even less impressive: they offered him a one-year contract. Arthur was never one to negotiate in the face of what he perceived to be an insult. If the board doubted his ability to keep the club in the top flight and were looking to hedge their bets, he was having none of it, and promptly resigned.

'I was sad to leave the club and sad to leave behind such a talent as Chris,' he said. 'I was lucky enough to have three players under me of the likes of Beardsley, Chris and Keegan. They all looked as if they'd been born with a ball at their feet, it was so natural for them. I'd had Chris for four years. The difference in the lad I found and the man I left was largely one of confidence. When I first had him into my office, he'd look at the wall, the floor, the ceiling, anywhere rather than at me. By the time I left, he was already prepared to talk football at length. Now he's confident enough to talk to anybody about anything. He's improved his ability and his knowledge, and has to be one of the most respected footballers in the world.'

Outside Newcastle, Cox was certainly one of the most respected of managers, and there was no shortage of takers for such a talent. By the time Chris and the rest of the players returned from holiday, Arthur was the manager of Derby County – charged with the task of rescuing them from the Third Division to which he'd helped consign them.

■ Chris Waddle

Newcastle had not delayed long in making a new appointment, and from Chris's point of view it was not an encouraging one. Arthur Cox might have appeared dour, but he had produced a team with flair and character. While Jack Charlton had carved a niche for himself as a media 'character', the teams he had managed, such as Middlesbrough and Sheffield Wednesday, did not play in a style that appealed to Chris. There was also the small matter of Charlton's 'little black book', which had caused such a sensation a few years before. Chris did not really fancy being managed by a man who, as a player, had actually compiled a 'hit list' of players upon whom he'd sworn revenge. Charlton's criteria as a manager seemed to relate to work-rate and he was not known as a man who liked stars in his team. Although Keegan may have gone, there was now no doubting that Chris and Peter Beardsley did, indeed, have star status. However, Chris was always one to give a man a chance. He'd fulfilled his silent promise to the fans and played his part in giving them promotion. Now he wanted to reap the rewards himself by making his debut in the First Division. There was no way Jack Charlton or anybody else was going to stand in the path of that.

Charlton arrived at Newcastle without bothering to familiarise himself with any names. Later it appeared there was nothing personal in this. He was never that good with names. He just got the players in a circle, pointed to David McCreery and said, 'Introduce yourselves.'

It didn't take long before the more skilful members of the side became disillusioned. Terry McDermott was the first to depart, never to play under Charlton's management. He and Chris were playing in a five-a-side match when Big Jack told them to stop.

'I don't want you playing one-twos on goal. I want you to play one-twos with God.' The players looked at him as if he'd taken leave of his senses, or had some kind of religious experience. He told two of them to stand on benches at the end of the gym and the rest of them were to chip the ball into their hands.

'That's what I mean,' he said. 'You can't get hurt as long as the ball's up in the clouds.' It was anathema to the likes of Chris and Terry, who'd been used to playing the ball along the ground, but Charlton was the boss. Fortunately Willie McFaul was reappointed first-team coach. McFaul had done his time at the club both as a popular goalkeeper and coach and was well liked by the players. As long as he took the coaching sessions and Charlton, with his eccentric ideas, stayed away, then life was tolerable.

When he did turn up at the Benwell training ground, something was always sure to happen. Once, the squad were about to set off on a cross-country run when Charlton suddenly pointed at Steve Carney and designated him as the pace-maker. Steve had many attributes as a player but long-distance running was not one of them, and gradually the rest of the squad, tired of plodding behind him, kicked on for home. Only Chris obeyed instructions and stuck with him, but when the pair finished so far behind the rest, Charlton must have thought they were taking the mickey. 'Right it's a lap of Benwell for you,' he said, promptly grabbing a child's bicycle so he could personally supervise the additional circuit. He cut a comical figure with his coat flapping, his huge frame crouched over the tiny bike, the inevitable cap on his head. It would not take long for Chris to realise that what Jack Charlton was trying to do to Newcastle United was not the slightest bit amusing.

chapter 17

In the top flight, Chris discovered that pace and first touch were everything. Newcastle's baptism, away to Leicester on 25 August 1984, was the fastest game in which Chris had ever played. He scored the winner in a 3–2 victory and for a moment began to have some doubts as to the justification for his internal criticism of Charlton. Three days later, those doubts were intensified when it was the same again against Sheffield Wednesday at St James'. It was still the holiday season, but the crowd of 29,700 was well below capacity and perhaps showed an element of discontent at the departure of Arthur Cox, as well as a suggestion that Charlton and his methods had not yet captured the imagination of the Tyneside footballing public. Still, a 2–1 victory and maximum points spoke for themselves.

'To be fair to Jack, it had been his suggestion that I played up front in the pre-season friendlies, and I certainly felt much happier in that role at the time,' Chris says.

The team generally felt much happier as a whole when Charlton was not around – which was quite a lot of the time. Even before the season had started, the only time they had played real flair football was in a 5–1 destruction of Hibernian, when Willie McFaul had been in charge and they had ignored everything Charlton had told them. It was one of the best team performances Chris can recall from his time with Newcastle. The manager seemed to have many prior commitments, which meant that day-to-day control was with McFaul, who seemed far more in touch with the feelings and strengths of the team he had known for so long. McFaul had made a huge contribution over the years to the club, as well as being instrumental in recommending that one particularly troublesome apprentice be offered full professional terms. His name was Paul Gascoigne.

Gazza did not come into the reckoning for selection for the third match of the season against Aston Villa and Chris nearly missed it as well. The night before the match, he was woken by a call from his brother Ray: 'I didn't want to ring you, because I knew you had a game, but we felt you should know that Dad's had a stroke.'

For some time Joe Waddle had been under pressure, much of it self-inflicted, as he pushed himself to the limit in his social life since retiring. 'He'd go dancing every night. He'd only discovered dancing when he was sixty-five, but he acted like he was a twenty-one-year-old Fred Astaire. He'd drink Carlsberg Special Brew and dance the night away. He knew all the times of the buses to and from the dance-halls and went to the same clubs in strict rotation. Seeing him at the bus stops each week must have been a bit like watching *Groundhog Day*.'

However, he bore the inheritance of his years down the pits and had already suffered a bout of pleurisy which his weakened chest never quite shook off. Now, as Chris rushed to the hospital, he saw not his father but an old man, unable to speak properly or move. His dad had always been a man obsessed with a smart appearance, shaving twice a day, rarely seen without a jacket and tie. Chris was shocked, but it simply did not occur to him even to tell Jack Charlton, giving the manager an excuse not to play him. Instead, in an unchanged side, he rolled up his sleeves and turned in his best performance to date, scoring twice in a 3–1 win and earning himself the Man of the Match accolade.

One reporter wrote: 'Anyone who has any doubts that Waddle is a genuine contender for an England cap should just ask Aston Villa's defenders.'

Jack Charlton also appeared complimentary, although there was some subtly implied criticism in what he had to say: 'Waddle saves his energy and then explodes. When he does, he's terrific.'

Peter Beardsley added: 'No one in the world would have stopped Chris today. Those goals were magnificent.' He was right about nobody in the world stopping him. He'd had his first exposure to serious illness, and somehow felt that he could distance himself by what he did on the field. Both those goals were for his father.

That match against Villa was the high point of United's season. As was so often the case with newly promoted sides, they had taken the First Division by surprise: their tactics were different and there was an unfamiliarity with their players. However, the next five games did not bring a single victory.

The long-ball technique of playing over the midfield for Beardsley and Waddle to chase foundered on the rocks of Arsenal's defence at Highbury. In the dressing-room after a 2–0 defeat that hardly recognised the difference in class in the sides, Charlton blamed the players and not the tactics. Glenn Roeder had tried to slow things down at one stage by putting his foot on the ball before hoofing it upfield. Charlton's response was short and to the point. 'I never want to see you do that again – you could slip.'

What followed at Old Trafford the weekend after was even more embarrassing. A 5–0 defeat before a massive 54,000 crowd left absolutely nothing for the travelling Geordies to sing about. Charlton stubbornly persisted with the same side and the same tactics against Everton at home and the result was also the same – a 2–3 defeat. In a space of less than a fortnight, the side had slipped from top to eleventh in the table.

If Charlton was becoming frustrated, then after the visit to QPR on 22 September he must have been starting to tear out what was left of his hair. At the time, the London club were still playing on their artificial astroturf surface, so Charlton took his players to the Gateshead stadium to acclimatise them. Obviously it worked for the attackers, and Chris in particular, but the defence need not have bothered. United were 4–0 at half-time, then incredibly threw it away in the second half as Rangers clawed their way back to draw 5–5.

Chris had got a hat-trick and felt he could not have done more, but Charlton completely lost it in the dressing-room. He had already kicked the advertising boards around the pitch as he jumped out of the dug-out, but now he was like a man demented, swearing and ranting, apparently close to hitting somebody. He even had the goalkeeper, Kevin Carr, by the throat. Chris took to the showers then, but on the coach and train on the way back, the manager still went up to every player, telling them exactly what he thought of their performance.

Glenn Roeder, had, of course, already had ample experience of playing on QPR's astroturf when a player with them. 'Ignoring the result, Chris's performance that day was the best I ever saw on that surface. Of the five goals, he got three and made two more. He was left up front on his own and we kept hitting long balls up to him. They had to be to his feet, because if you tried to use the channels the ball just shot through to the keeper. Jack Charlton had been the only manager who got results at Loftus Road when I was a player there, and he was obviously disappointed he'd not done it again. But that day was all about Chris Waddle's skills and not Jack Charlton's tactics.'

Charlton had already made a couple of changes for the Rangers match, but everybody within the club and on the terraces knew he had to sign some players to strengthen the side. It wasn't yet the Premier League where money was power, but it was still clear that any promoted side had to buy to compete. Charlton's first foray into the market raised some eyebrows, as few people knew anything about the man he signed – Pat Heard from Sheffield Wednesday. As Charlton was to prove throughout his managerial career, he tended to go for players with whom he was familiar and he had, of course, been in charge at Hillsborough before taking over at United.

Heard was little more than a journeyman, but he did bring some stability to the under-used midfield, and through to mid-November the team went undefeated for eight matches, although six of them were drawn, which meant they still hovered only just above mid-table.

Chris's reputation continued to grow. With goals against Ipswich and Chelsea (where they laid to rest their bogey with a 2–1 win) and a goal against Bradford City in the Milk Cup second round in October, he brought his tally to nine and again there was pressure in the media for his selection for the England Under-21s, if not the full side itself. Jack Charlton had his views on the subject. 'I don't want him to play for England just yet,' he said, without offering any reason.

Charlton may, in due course, have had some influence on the Irish national team, but the England selectors made up their own minds, and just four years after leaving non-league Tow Law, Chris Waddle was called up as the over-age player for the England Under-21 side against Finland. He read and re-read the letter of invitation as if it might disappear from sight if he did not remember every word. Today that letter, creased as it is, still has a treasured place in the Waddle scrapbook.

chapter 18

England selection was a far cry from Valley Parade, just as Chris's England career seemed a long way in the past when he finally joined the Yorkshire club. Being a real part of the Under-21 squad for the first time, under Dave Sexton, with a real chance of selection was a new experience.

He and Gary Shelton of Sheffield Wednesday were the over-age players and within fifty-five seconds Chris had got his name on the score-sheet. Trevor Steven put in a cross from the wing, Paul Rideout headed it into the path of Waddle, who had made an instinctive run, and he lifted it over the keeper into the net. The result was encouraging. England won 2–0 at Southampton with a side containing many stars of the future, such as Barry Venison, Trevor Steven, Tony Cottee and – indubitably the most famous of them all – David Seaman.

Chris noted: 'It was very different, even at that level, from playing in the English league. The European-style football meant tighter marking. There was far less flow in the game, much less of the end-to-end stuff I was experiencing every week.' Just as he was to do after every new experience, he thought about it for weeks afterwards, analysing what he had learned.

Chris's goal and all-round performance were enough to attract Bobby Robson to St James' Park to watch him in a 1–1 draw with Nottingham Forest. 'I knew the England manager was watching me and I was aware of it all the time. Every pass I made, the thought ran through my head – got to get it right or else I've no chance.'

Although he did not excel that day, the late, great Jackie Milburn took it upon himself to write an open letter to the England manager in his newspaper column. 'Waddle is your man, Bobby .... Surely his England chance cannot be long delayed.'

He'd learned more than just footballing matters whilst in the England camp. Footballers, when they get together, are never shy about telling each other what they earn. It did not take a mathematical genius to work out that Chris was very much the poor relation, for the Newcastle wage structure as a whole was not generous, and Chris was nowhere near the top of its ladder. Charlton treated the club's purse as if it were his own – and he was never renowned for his generosity. The bonus scheme was also less than generous. It increased by a miserly £20 for every match won up to a maximum of £120, and then if the team strung six wins together, hit the top of the league but then drew a match, say at Liverpool, it went all the way back to the original £20. Some three years later, after Chris had left, it was to lead the players to the brink of a strike until the club reluctantly renegotiated in the face of player power.

After Chris won the Sun Canon Player of the Month award, he gave an interview, which appeared under the headline: 'Pay up or I go.' Substantially misquoted, Chris had once again been let down by a journalist. He found that the more publicity he got, the more embarrassed he felt. He has never courted the media and indeed turns down most interviews, doing absolutely nothing with the press for months at a time. 'Yet, the more you play Greta Garbo, the more they seem to want to speak to you,' he says.

However, his contract *was* up at the end of the season, and although he would not have put it so brutally, he did expect Newcastle to be more generous this time. He had served his time, and indeed they had even haggled with Tow Law when the little club had sought an extra bit of money for the player they had sold at such a knock-down price. It was remarkable really that he kept his feet on the ground, but nobody who knew him from the old days felt he had changed in any way.

Unfortunately for Chris, he was forced to pull out of the Under-21 team due to an injury picked up against Chelsea. So instead he concentrated on the next big test: Anfield on 18 November. Once again Newcastle were given the opportunity to measure how far they had come against the best. In fact, although they would eventually finish runners-up, Liverpool did not look like the best at that particular stage of the season, and were actually below United in the league. But it didn't seem that way as they disposed of the home side with almost arrogant ease.

Once again, Chris had the best chance of the match early on. He was clear through, then slipped on the wet surface and completely fluffed his shot. Liverpool won 2–0, but what was worse from Chris's point of view was that he badly aggravated his injury.

He struggled on with his fitness and on 8 December played in a match that was to change his life, when Newcastle were the visitors to White Hart Lane. Although they lost 3–1, it was

■ Chris Waddle

a Waddle goal that stayed in the memory: a sublime Beardsley chip, Chris brought the ball down in the box, body-swerved Paul Miller almost in the same movement and hammered in a goal that was shown over and over again on television. Perhaps of more importance, it was replayed time and time again in the mind of Tottenham's chairman, Irving Scholar.

Peter Shreeves, Spurs manager at the time, was public in his praise: 'Some of the things he did were world class. He always frightened me when he had the ball.' The refrain would be echoed by opposing managers across the world. There are some players who cause the crowd to draw in their breath when they have the ball, who make them wait for the unexpected while expecting it all the time, who send a frisson of excitement down the spine in that split-second just before they receive the pass – and Chris Waddle is one of them.

chapter 19

One of Chris's lasting regrets in football was that injury forced him to miss the New Year's Day game against a Sunderland side who were to begin their slippery slide to near oblivion with relegation that season. There being no room for compassion in football, Chris had buried all his childhood support for Sunderland. In this local derby, he wanted there to be only one winner, and they were the team in the black and white stripes. He got his wish as United roared home 3–1 with the huge partisan crowd singing 'And man shall live for evermore because of New Year's Day' to the tune of 'Mary's Boy-Child', a song that was to roll around the terraces for many years to come, to the mystification of opposition supporters.

Chris had recovered sufficiently to play against Forest in the third round of the FA Cup, but although they did the hard work getting a draw at the City Ground, they once again failed at home. Chris got the consolation goal in a 1–3 defeat and could see that the season was going to have little in store beyond a struggle for mid-table respectability.

The early exit from the cup did bring one consolation in the shape of a mid-winter break for the players in Benidorm, where

Chris had the chance to see Charlton in a more relaxed mood. They all went to see a local match where one of the sides had Mario Kempas, the Argentinian, on the wing. In the first half, Kempas started off in the sun and apart from taking a couple of free-kicks hardly moved. After the break, he switched wings so that he could continue to improve his sun-tan, and at the end of the match all the spectators threw their cushions on to the pitch. Charlton was less than impressed.

He had a camp-follower who went everywhere with him, calling him 'Mr Jack' and who was inevitably nicknamed 'Mr Jack' himself. He led Charlton, Chris and a couple of the other players, Pat Heard and Gary Megson, off to a local restaurant. The food arrived but their hosts seemed reluctant to start and suddenly Jack realised that a speech was expected from him. He rose to his feet, an incongruous figure. It was about eighty degrees at night, yet he was still wearing his jacket and the flat cap under which he carried all his money.

'When in Rome,' he began, 'do as the Romans do. When in Italy,' there was a pause, 'when in Italy, eat pasta. When in Spain,' there was an even longer pause. 'When in Spain . . .' he desperately sought the right thing to say. 'When in Spain . . . get pissed.'

Chris never actually disliked Jack as person. Indeed, he was the sort of man he'd be happy to sit down with for hours and talk football. It was just his tactics with which he could not agree. It was those tactics that were just not working out either for Newcastle United or for Chris Waddle.

Although relegation wasn't an immediate prospect, he had no desire to play again in the lower divisions. He'd played against the likes of Arsenal, Liverpool and Manchester United and he'd enjoyed it win, lose or draw. The *Mirror*, never one to miss an opportunity to sensationalise, picked on a chance comment and carried the headline, 'If they're down, I'm off.'

Charlton's 'big-money' signings were not particularly helpful to the cause. He pursued the giant striker George Reilly – who was to finish his career at Barnet, which was probably more suited to his enthusiastic, but limited, talents – and then when he failed to get him first time around, he turned his attention to the likeable Tony Cunningham, who'd joined Sheffield Wednesday after Jack's period in charge. The rumour was that Charlton had never actually seen Cunningham play and, when he went to meet him at the station, walked straight past him because he didn't know he was black. When Reilly then became available, Charlton was so keen that he bought him as well, thus ending up with two strikers who were well over six feet tall, and neither of whom was renowned for his speed or ball control. Chris's days up front were at an end, and he was despatched to the left wing with Beardsley playing on the right.

The basic concept was for Chris and Peter to launch a barrage of crosses to the heads of the front two, but in order to do that they first had to get the ball. The service was non-existent and Chris found himself patrolling the touch-line on the periphery of the game while long, hopeful balls were hit down the middle from the back.

The statistics at the end of the season told the whole story. Peter scored seventeen, Chris sixteen, whilst Reilly got three and Cunningham (or TC as he came to be known) only one. Chris, himself, scored only once after the change in position.

The more he was exposed to the world outside the north-east, the more certain he was that he had to get away. He was no longer the gawky naïve kid who had been prepared to do exactly what he was told by whoever happened to be in charge at the time. He now had a team of professional advisers, having appointed an agent in the shape of Alastair Garvie, as well as a lawyer and accountant – the team of Mel Stein and Len Lazarus.

Garvie had first seen Chris play as a raw youngster when he was assistant secretary at Newcastle United. He was an odd character, a tall, chain-smoking, quietly-spoken Scot, seemingly self-effacing, who eventually got out of his depth when trying to cope with the pressures and profile that representation of high-flying stars brought with it. However, he did have a great talent for spotting young emerging talent and was (ill-advisedly as it later proved) to give up his secure job to enter player management on a full-time basis. He was last seen driving a mini-cab in the Durham area, a sad and forgotten figure.

Not only did his agent keep Chris advised as to which clubs were becoming interested in him but he also obtained news by his involvement in the international scene. In January he had been invited to join up with a full England squad get-together, but to his disappointment that had to be abandoned owing to bad weather. Then in February he received a call from a journalist to tell him he had been named in the England party for the match against Northern Ireland. He thought at first it was just another wild rumour, an opportunity for the caller to grab an interview, but when he switched on the radio, he had confirmation.

'It's hard to put into words how I felt. It wasn't so much excitement, but pride, not just for myself, but for my family and the whole of the north-east.'

There was no doubt that all the Newcastle fans had been

willing him into the team. For too long they had been caught in the backwater of international football. Malcolm Macdonald had been their last capped player a decade before, and although they'd had their sprinkling of Scottish, Welsh and Irish internationals it just did not carry the same prestige as pulling on the white shirt of England.

The match against Northern Ireland on 27 February was not just any game. It was a World Cup qualifier in a group from which England would eventually emerge triumphant. The team which would play was a star-studded cast: Peter Shilton, Viv Anderson, Alvin Martin, Terry Butcher, Kenny Sansom, Trevor Steven, Ray Wilkins, Gary Stevens, Tony Woodcock, and Mark Hateley, while on the wing was the man with whom Chris would battle for a position over the next ten years, John Barnes. Also included in the squad were two other men who would play such important roles in Chris's future – Glenn Hoddle and Trevor Francis. There was never any real prospect of Chris actually making the starting line-up, but once again the experience and, as the Irish themselves put it, the 'crack' were invaluable.

Chris's name had already been linked with Spurs and Glenn was quick to tell him how happy he was at the club, suggesting that if there was ever a chance that Chris might join him, he should give him a ring. Ray Wilkins, by then in Italy with AC Milan, was equally enthusiastic about Manchester United.

The training routine was very different from what Chris was used to at Newcastle, far more sophisticated. Once Don Howe, with all his wealth of experience, had dealt with the warm-up, the accent was on set-pieces, comfort on the ball and shooting practice. Chris was a little nervous about flying into the troubled Belfast, but the security was very tight and the only trouble was bottles being tossed on to the pitch at the end of a match that England won by a single Hateley goal. Chris's sole contribution was to jog along the touch-line wearing his number sixteen shirt, just to remind the players on the pitch that there was a fresh pair of legs waiting should their enthusiasm wane. Yet as the team celebrated their victory he felt very much a part of it, and when he returned to the north-east and Jack Charlton, it was with a sense of anticlimax and despondency.

He was also faced with a whole spate of transfer rumours. He might not yet have received his first England cap, but it was only a matter of time. In terms of a move to another club, he was now in a different league and a different price bracket. It was not so much a question of whether he would move, but when, to which club and at what price.

chapter 20

Newcastle's season drifted on with more and more discontent. They sank as low as seventeenth by the beginning of February, and although a brief spring revival saw them climb away from relegation worries and to mid-table it was never going to be enough for the fans. Charlton seemed unable to cope with what was now a meteoric rise to fame for Chris. Against Sheffield Wednesday, for example, at the end of March, Chris was really turning it on, even though the team lost 2–4. With the home fans getting at him, to try to put him off his game, he just cheerfully waved to them. Charlton promptly substituted him, saying he didn't think he was playing up to the mark. Later, as Chris got on the team coach with a huge bottle of whisky, Charlton asked him what he thought he was doing with it. 'I got the Man of the Match award,' Chris replied. Charlton didn't respond.

On 26 March 1985, luck gave Chris the main chance. It was good luck for him and bad luck for John Barnes, who had picked up an injury. Clearly Bobby Robson had come to see Chris as the natural alternative to Barnes, and now he made his England debut on the wing in the friendly against the Republic of Ireland, the same country whose fortunes his then manager was to turn around with such outstanding success some years later.

It was his first experience of Wembley. 'I went out on to the pitch some forty-five minutes before kick-off and the stadium was half-empty, which made it look even bigger. The pitch looked enormous and one part of me thought I could really use that space to show off my ability, whilst the other thought I was going to be knackered before I started.'

That was always going to be part of the problem. He did look exhausted before he even got out of the tunnel, and until the manager and the fans got used to him it could be very off-putting. David Hodgson, a fellow-Geordie from Gateshead, now manager of Darlington, remembers playing against him at schoolboy level for Elgin against Heworth Boys. 'He had a unique style. That's the only way to put it. He looked ungainly, lazy even, and I think that's why he slipped through the net as a schoolboy. Managers just couldn't see past that.'

Bobby Robson could, and after a 2–1 victory with goals from Trevor Steven and Gary Lineker, he told Chris how pleased he'd been with his efforts and that there was every chance there would be a next time. First time for England, first time at Wembley and also the first time he had played alongside Gary Lineker, with whom he now works closely for the BBC.

For the moment on the opposite side of the media fence, Chris made his television debut when he was interviewed by ITV for their *Mid-Week Sports Special* after the match. It was another first.

Back at Newcastle, Jack Charlton told the board that he would deal personally with Chris Waddle's new contract. Whether or not it would have been better handled by the likes of Stan

Seymour, who can say, but the fact of the matter was that his first offer to Chris was nothing short of insulting. The interests of other clubs were now public knowledge, with Chelsea leading the way. Chris could stand it no longer. Ignoring his agent, he went straight to see Seymour, with whom he'd always had a good relationship. It was a Wednesday night, after a reserve match, and Stan was sitting in the manager's chair exuding that paternal charm for which he was famous.

Chris was very upset and came straight to the point. 'I'm leaving,' he said, almost in tears.

Equally perturbed, Stan tried his best to persuade him to stay by making an increased offer. It was too late. The club had tried to get him on the cheap; Chris knew it and disliked them for it. Seymour was totally honest with him, telling him that they had received two formal offers – one from Chelsea and one from Spurs. 'Where do you want to go?' he asked.

At the end of the day, it was not a difficult decision. He had not forgotten what Glenn Hoddle had told him about Tottenham, while his memories of Chelsea were somewhat tainted by the heavy defeats he had suffered at their hands. Mel Stein and Len Lazarus, with Newcastle's knowledge, opened discussions with Irving Scholar at Tottenham. It was the first time they had dealt with him and the club, and they were impressed by his direct and generous attitude.

'I don't want the lad to come down as a poor relation,' said Scholar, as he proudly showed them round the club he had supported as a boy, bought as a man and taken to the stock-market as chairman. As a matter of courtesy, Lazarus had lunch with Ken Bates of Chelsea, who did his best to sell the club to Chris's accountant, but by then it was really a one-horse race.

Jack Charlton still wanted the last word, calling Chris into his office and making him yet another offer. 'You don't want to go to Spurs,' he said, adding some criticism of the club's ownership and supporters. Chris did. He liked the way Tottenham played, even though he'd not yet had the chance to spend any time himself with either Scholar or Peter Shreeves.

He told Seymour in mid-April of his final decision – that he definitely wanted to leave and that he wanted to join Tottenham Hotspur. Seymour seemed resigned to it. 'You'll be a Spurs player by the end of the week. We'll call you out of training and you can go down, meet the people and agree your final terms.'

His advisers spoke to Spurs, who laid on a plane to bring him down after training on the Thursday. Chris trained normally, said his goodbyes and then waited patiently for the car to take him to the airport. And waited and waited. It didn't come. Chris wrote a letter that he delivered by hand to secretary Russell Cushing, making it absolutely clear that he would not be re-signing for the club, just in case they were still under any illusions. The mind games continued. Seymour called Chris into his office and with some embarrassment told him that there had been a turn-about. Newcastle would now keep him to his contract. What he really meant was that the club were reneging on the deal. 'I can't be seen to be the one who let's you go. You'll have to stay with us until the end of the season.'

The problem was that Chris was the first big name to leave arising from Charlton's management. Everybody wanted to come out of the situation looking the cleanest. Chris did not feel he was being greedy, but certainly did not feel the club were offering him what he deserved. The club were now claiming that they had offered the player what he'd requested but omitted to say when that offer was made. Frustrated as he was, there was nothing left for Chris to do but play out the few remaining matches of the campaign in a black and white shirt. London would have to wait.

chapter 21

It was hard being left in limbo. While Newcastle had nothing to play for, Spurs were third in the table – and had they won the rest of their games, they could actually have won the title. But the transfer deadline passed and Chris remained on Tyneside. He was not the most popular of figures. The United public relations machine had seen to that by painting him as both greedy and disloyal. It got worse as the media, short of stories, began to create them.

Injured for the match against Sunderland, yet again, Chris chose to watch Wickham play in the FA Vase, rather than be the centre of attention at Roker Park. A press photographer asked for a shot, Chris declined, but he took one anyway. Newcastle's game ended in an uninspiring goalless draw, and although Chris could not have played anyway, the story carried by *The Journal* implied that he simply had more important things to do than turn out for the club to whom he was still contracted. Normally the most mild-mannered of men, Chris completely lost his temper. The pressure was getting to him, and the sooner he was away the better.

He did his best on the field, but the fans did not appreciate it. He was booed whenever he touched the ball and was greeted with a constant chant of 'Judas'. All too often the roulette wheel that is the fixture list tosses up relegation and promotion battles for the last games of the season. Newcastle's final home game had neither of those elements, but for Chris it was just as dramatic – United were playing Spurs.

He would have loved to have left behind him the memory of a great goal, but it was not to be. The goal of the match came from Glen Hoddle with a stunning free-kick; but Newcastle did at least get a point.

The Spurs players could see the funny side of things, even if Chris could not. After he'd left Tottenham defender Paul Miller for dead on more than one occasion, Paul finally caught up with him to say: 'Let me get near you so I can give you a good kicking before you become one of us!'

In the players' lounge after the game, almost instinctively Chris ended up with the visiting players. It was not unnatural for, after all, he had been made to feel like a visitor himself. Chris had not fallen out with the other members of his team, but no longer felt a part of Newcastle United. Ray Clemence, Paul Miller and Graham Roberts understood and sat with him to keep him company. He had, of course, still not signed and even then Jack Charlton was trying to influence his decision: 'You should go to Chelsea rather than Spurs, they've offered us more money.'

Paul Miller, never short of a word, put Charlton in his place. 'Hello, Jack, nice to see you at a game, I thought you'd be off fishing.' Charlton was not amused. Perhaps the joke was too close to the truth.

All his former team-mates, without exception, attended his

leaving party. George Reilly, fresh from a car crash and with a collar round his neck and a row of broken teeth, looked like something out of *Dracula*, although Chris suggested he might have won the fancy-dress prize even if he had come in his normal state.

There was only one more game – away at Norwich. Just before the final whistle, Chris took a corner in front of the Geordie fans. The more loyal of them gave him a cheer and one of the most fanatical, a kid called John Dodds who'd followed them everywhere and was known by name to all the players, shouted: 'Waddler, give us your shirt.'

As the referee blew for time, he did just that and then went home. It was all over bar the shouting. But there was still to be some of that, for the two clubs had failed to agree a fee and the dispute had been referred to the FA tribunal. There could not even be a clean break in that respect.

The differences between the clubs did not stop Chris and Lorna finally making their way down to London for the grand tour of White Hart Lane. Although St James' Park today stands amongst the finest of grounds in Europe for its facilities, in the late eighties it was positively Stone Age compared to Tottenham's ground. As Chris walked around with Peter Shreeves, Scholar sat down with Stein and Lazarus to thrash out the final terms of his contract. It did not take long. As would be the case with Paul Gascoigne a few years later, Irving wanted the player and was determined to get him at any price.

However, one of the best kept secrets of Chris's career was the fact that he nearly failed his medical at Tottenham. What he had thought was merely a formality revealed in an X-ray what appeared to be a deformity in his back – and his spine in particular. Due to join up at Windsor races with the rest of a syndicate, with whom he shared an interest in a racehorse called Aztec Star, he found himself undergoing further tests that put his transfer on a knife-edge. Eventually, after much deliberation, the specialist asked if he had any pain. When Chris replied that it had never troubled him, the specialist told him that most of the players he examined had something wrong with them. In fact it was just Chris's stooping posture that had caused the 'deformity', and there was no reason why it should interfere with his career. The specialist concerned was John Browett, who was to be responsible for putting together Gascoigne's shattered knee. It was a most unpleasant and tension-filled twenty-four hours, during which Chris could hardly sleep with worry. 'I had visions of going back to Newcastle with my tail between my legs.'

As it was, Chris had left Newcastle with no regrets save the abandonment of their magnificent fans. Gradually, over the years, though, those wounds would heal and he would once again be regarded as one of Tyneside's favourite sons. Although, at the time, he did not leave with their good wishes, he did leave with several awards. He got the North-East Player of the Year trophy, which was presented to him by Bobby Robson, and was selected as the *News of the World* Player of the Year. Amongst his peers he had already been runner-up in the PFA Young Player of the Year and had been in the top five of the PFA Player of the Year main category. Best of all, he had been invited to join the England party for their tour of Mexico and the USA.

Even before that there were two internationals, the first away to Finland, the second against the old enemy – Scotland. In

Helsinki John Barnes was restored to the left wing, but Chris came on as substitute for Trevor Steven on the right.

'I always felt more comfortable on the right flank so I was delighted. But in any event, at that time it wouldn't have occurred to me to argue with the manager of the national side. As long as I was getting a chance I would have played in goal if he'd asked me.'

He wasn't asking, and Chris did get another chance as substitute against Scotland. He was feeling more confident of his ability, more reassured that his selection was not just a dream from which he'd eventually awake and find himself back at Tow Law – or worse still, the sausage factory. He went on a long mazy run in that game, taking on player after player and leaving them trailing in his wake. Instead of shooting, he put in a deep, unselfish cross. Robson was impressed and told him so. He had everything to look forward to in South America.

chapter 22

There have been two players with the nickname 'Psycho' in Chris's footballing life. One, Stuart Pearce, was to miss a penalty in the 1990 World Cup semi-final just before Chris's desperate effort and then to line up alongside him again in a soul-cleansing Pizza Hut advert in 1996. The other, Mark Hateley, was his England room-mate on the American tour. Pearce had earned his reputation by his hardness on the pitch, while Mark's was awarded for his fearlessness.

Although he was rooming with Hateley, the player he had became closest to in the squad was Glenn Hoddle. Their backgrounds could not have been more different – Hoddle the sophisticated southerner, Chris the naïve boy from the north-east. The common bond was music. That and the fact that both had chosen to stick with their old friends, rather than abandon them for the fly-by-nights when fame came wandering by. They spent hours talking about their musical tastes, and in those conversations were sown the seeds of the musical pairing that was to see them flying high in the pop charts, actually appearing on *Top of the Pops* and even gracing the stage of the London Palladium.

The first game of the tour was against Italy. 'It seemed a long way to come to play another European side, but there it was.' England lost 2–1, and although Chris started the match, he was substituted by Barnes in what had become a Tweedledum-Tweedledee situation. It was not just a question of facing the opposition. There was the altitude to contend with as well. The twelve-minute runs Robson and Howe insisted on seemed like marathons to Chris and most of the rest of the squad.

Even at that early stage in the respective careers of Barnes and Waddle, Bobby Robson was thought, by the media, to regard them as alternatives. 'That simply wasn't so,' Robson says. 'They certainly could play together and were very important to Lineker and Beardsley, neither of whom were giants. The sort of low crosses they could supply from the wings were premium and crucial. Whenever they were fit and available, I always considered the pair of them for selection.'

A bit of light relief was a cricket match at the Reform Club in Mexico City. It was like an English country club with everybody there playing in white, drinking tea and eating cucumber sandwiches. Gary Lineker, who could well have carved out an alternative career in the summer game, hit a half-century, while Chris merely fielded and decided that perhaps he wasn't cut out to be a fast bowler.

Against Mexico in a 1–0 defeat, it was turn and turn about again for Chris and John Barnes. Barnes started, Chris replaced him and then kept his place for the match against West Germany on 12 June 1985. It may only have been an invitation tournament, but between those two countries there can never be such a thing as a friendly. The match was highly competitive and England won 3–0 with Chris turning in his most complete performance to date for his country.

'Waddle Wins His Spurs,' wrote Bob Harris in Newcastle's *Evening Chronicle*, the very headline reminding United what they had lost. Bobby Robson was equally complimentary: 'This was easily his best match for England. He looked fitter and stronger than before and played with great tenacity and a lot of confidence. He grew in stature as the match progressed.'

Chris was thriving on being given a right-wing role, where he found to his surprise that he was more effective. It looked as if he had won the battle with Barnes for what would now be described as the playmaker role, yet neither of them could have realised then that both of their careers would be parallel roller-coaster rides of emotional peaks and troughs.

Chris has always got on extremely well with John Barnes and, indeed, they are distantly related by marriage, John's wife, Susie, being Chris's mother's great-niece. Chris certainly has never felt there was any competition between them for one particular spot in the side, nor that either one was better than the other.

'It seemed to the public to start out as the battle of the wingers, as Bobby Robson obviously felt we were both match-winners on our day. Playing on the wing for England has to be the hardest position in the world. Other teams don't play wingers, so you end up playing as a full-back. Suddenly you look up and see the goal is seventy yards away and you're supposed to run for it and make a chance. However, in a 5–3–2 formation I ended up playing in mid-field with John up front until he got injured. In any event, I'm convinced that John is the one of the most skilful players this country has ever produced, even if he didn't always demonstrate that in an England shirt. Whatever the case, we've both had our fair share of stick from the England fans, especially at Wembley.'

The tour ended with a 5–0 victory over the USA in Los Angeles, the sort of result that was not likely to be repeated once the Americans got to grips with the fact that football (or soccer) was a world game – and they simply had to be a successful part of every world sport.

The tour had given Chris a cutting edge to his game, and he could not wait to start the new season with his new club. He left Lorna back home to sell their house while he came south on a permanent basis. He had forgotten how lonely it could be staying in a hotel, but Tottenham did their best to ensure he was left on his own as little as possible. There was one piece of administration yet to be settled – his transfer fee.

At the independent tribunal, Newcastle were represented in force. Stan Seymour, Jack Charlton, Russell Cushing and Gordon McKeag, the club solicitor and fellow-director who would inherit the mantle of chairman from Seymour, all arrived together.

Newcastle put their case forward at length, taking more than three-quarters of an hour to present their arguments. Chris's evidence took about ten minutes. He spoke sincerely and without malice. When asked why he wanted to leave Newcastle, he simply said: 'I want to better my career. I feel I have more chance of European and international honours with Tottenham.' Asked if he wanted to add anything, he told the tribunal that he would like Newcastle to look after Tow Law. He never discovered whether or not they did.

Newcastle had been asking £750,000 – a trifling fee by today's standards. Spurs had been willing to go to £600,000 and, rather oddly (although to Scholar's delight), the tribunal picked on the figure of £590,000. 'I reckon they knocked off the odd £10,000 because they went on so long,' a member of the Tottenham party was heard to comment. The Newcastle contingent had nothing to say. Charlton departed without a word to Chris, and the rest of them merely said a cold goodbye. Nobody wished him luck. As divorces went, it was not a happy one.

chapter 23

The 1985–86 season, which at times had promised so much, started with pain and ended with a mild feeling of disappointment. Before leaving Newcastle, Chris visited the dentist for what should have been a simple extraction. However, the tooth snapped and had to be drilled out, so that for days afterwards every effort to run was sheer agony, sending pain throbbing through his head. As soon as he began to train with Spurs, he realised it wasn't just the couple of days that he had missed with the tooth problem that put him behind the rest of the squad. Their entire expectations were far more demanding than those he had left behind at Newcastle.

Peter Shreeves and John Pratt (the former Spurs player) were far more hands-on than Big Jack when it came to training, but the warm-up was left to the physiotherapist, Mike Varney, who utilised two big speakers to blast out music and instructions to the players to do aerobics. He'd get a handful of players out front every day, and Chris was terrified he might be invited. He even watched Mad Lizzie, the then star of *Breakfast TV*'s keep-fit slot, in order to ensure he didn't make a total fool of himself. He was never called upon to perform, but the embarrassment came when he was allocated a nickname – as essential a part of a player's equipment as his boots. It was Hoddle who blew the whistle on him, telling the rest of the lads that in the England team he'd been known as 'Widdley' and so 'Widdley' he became. The London boys teased him about that, as well as complaining that they couldn't understand a word he said and needed the Sunderland-born Mickey Hazard as an interpreter. It was all in good fun, but Chris was still painfully shy and quiet, responding only when he was spoken to, feeling comfortable only when alone with Glenn.

One of the attractions of joining Spurs had been the chance to play alongside Clive Allen, a proven goalscorer. As it was, although Allen scored twice in the first pre-season friendly, he also picked up an injury that kept him out of the first team until the end of November, perhaps putting more pressure on Chris than he would have liked.

'As I settled in at Spurs, Clive's runs helped me enormously. If I was dribbling and running at pace, I had to whip the ball in to the centre because there was no time to control and place it. Clive would invariably gamble and get ahead of his man. It was a rare talent, and only Gary Lineker of the men I've played alongside could match Clive at it.'

As it turned out, it was Chris, rather than Allen, who pulled on the number nine shirt for the first league match of the season against Watford, with the rest of the attack comprising Mark Falco and Mickey Hazard, supported by Tony Galvin and Ossie Ardiles. On paper it looked a strong side with real championship potential: Ray Clemence in goal, Steve Perryman as captain, Chris Hughton, Paul Miller and his old friend Danny Thomas making up the rest of the defence. With the injured

Glenn Hoddle, Clive Allen and Gary Mabbutt waiting in the wings, there was a strength in depth, thanks to the generosity of Scholar's purse, that the north London club had not had since the halcyon double year.

They certainly looked all-conquering as they arrogantly ran riot against Watford in a 4–0 victory. Chris scored twice and could not have had a better start. Yet, it never really took off from there. One win in the next four games and they had slipped into the bottom half of the table. They seemed to have got back on the rails with a 4–1 win against Chelsea, but Chris wasn't playing well, and he knew it. The crowd knew it too, and the brace of goals in the first match were soon forgotten as they began to wonder whether or not he was worth the big fee.

The big personal test for Chris was going to come on 7 September against Newcastle at White Hart Lane. Tony Galvin had been injured and Chris had been switched to the left flank and the number eleven shirt to replace him. As if he didn't have enough pressure, the media added some more. He'd been asked by Jack Steggles of the *Mirror* what differences he'd found at Tottenham. Chris naïvely told him he thought that although they were both big clubs, Tottenham were fulfilling their potential whilst Newcastle were not. He added that the London club were better at looking after their players, citing the example of fresh kit every day, while at Newcastle they'd had to make do with the same kit all week. Pushed a little further, Chris went on to say that his old club's idea of a meal after a match was fish and chips on the coach, whereas Spurs would provide a three-course meal of the player's choice. It was no great surprise when he ran on to the pitch and waved to the Black and White Army, that in addition to the usual taunt of 'Judas' they also chanted 'fish and chips'.

The Newcastle fans felt that success had gone to Chris Waddle's head, that he was trying to forget where he came from. The key to his popularity on Tyneside, apart from his footballing skills, was that he was a Geordie. He might well have supported Sunderland, but he'd watched them from the terraces and not the comfort of the stands. It was exactly the same with Gazza. Although the fans would respect the expensive imports, they would never regard them with the same passion as a local lad who had made it big. Now they believed, quite wrongly, that this local lad had crossed the border and betrayed his own roots. If he was going to try to deny them, then they would be sure not to let him forget.

It seemed for a few moments as if the travelling fans would have the last laugh and that it was going to be the visitors' day. Alan Davies, the former Manchester United player and Welsh international, who was years later to die by his own hand, a sad and forgotten man, put Newcastle ahead with a stunning goal. But then Falco equalised, John Chiedozie grabbed a couple, Hazard put another nail into their coffin and Hoddle stamped his class on the match with a near-definitive performance and a memorable goal. A few minutes from the end, United put on a slightly overweight teenager who showed some nice touches. He was called Paul Gascoigne. It finished 5–1, and when Kenny Wharton, his former team-mate, begged for a few cans of lager for the Geordies to take back on the coach, Chris knew he had made the right decision to leave.

chapter 24

Living in Broxbourne in Hertfordshire was a far cry from living in the Waddles' native north-east. The locals were used to footballers living in their midst, so Chris and Lorna could go out for a drink in their local or to a restaurant without being badgered by autograph hunters or head-cases just on the look out for trouble. Initially, Lorna in particular found it very hard to settle. She'd been sadder than Chris to leave Newcastle. They had no children, she had no job here and all her family were in the north-east. Some of the first friends they made on their arrival in London were Pat Nelson and his wife, Cheryl.

They met up in the players' lounge at White Hart Lane, where Pat was already a regular visitor. The Nelsons took the Waddles under their wing, showed them around London and introduced them to a social life through their own friends. Pat got Chris so many sponsored cars that at one time they had three on their driveway and were spoilt for choice. It is a friendship that has endured the series of career moves that has taken Chris around the British Isles and into France.

'London was, of course, a much bigger place than Newcastle in every sense of the word. You could get lost there, unlike

Newcastle where you felt you were in a goldfish bowl all the time. There was also this great expectancy at Tottenham that something was about to happen. I'm not saying that one is better than the other. I'm sure that somebody moving from London to Newcastle would find it equally hard to settle.'

Tottenham's season stop-started along its way, the expectancy disappointed at every turn. Although the league title was, by Christmas, a mere pipe-dream for Spurs, the growing feeling amongst both players and fans was that this could well be a year for a cup run in one or both of the competitions. In the Milk Cup they'd already beaten Orient and Wimbledon, and a home tie against Portsmouth in the fourth round suggested an easy passage to Wembley. As it was, Portsmouth twice battled to a goalless draw, before winning by the only goal of the match at Fratton Park on 12 December. To Chris it was beginning to feel like Newcastle all over again, as Tottenham flattered to deceive.

Ninth in the league at the turn of the year, out of one cup and with a tricky tie at Oxford to look forward to in the third round of the FA Cup. The fans and management were getting restless and Peter Shreeves knew that he had to turn the season round if he still wanted to be in a job, come May. He was given the best of all opportunities to prove his intentions on New Year's Day, when Spurs made the short trip across north London for the local derby against Arsenal. It was Chris's first exposure to the internecine warfare of this particular fixture. It ended 0–0, and with Arsenal a couple of places higher in the table that would have seemed to have been a satisfactory result.

'To the Spurs fans it wasn't enough. If we'd thumped Arsenal 5–0 and finished just above the relegation zone, that might have

Chris at 12 in his West Ham away strip demonstrating his lethal left foot (background) © Newcastle Chronicle and Journal

Chris (holding the ball), captain of the 1971 Charity Shield-winning side in his first football strip — the green and yellow of Bill Quay (below)

Lorna and Chris on their wedding day, 25 June 1983 (above) © Bonney Agency

Ebullient celebrations from Gazza and Waddle as the two Geordies score for Tottenham in a 2–1 win over Norwich (below left) © Express Newspapers

The Newcastle team celebrate promotion to the First Division in time-honoured fashion (below right) © Newcastle Journal & Chronicle

Chris gets off the mark
for Tottenham as he
heads the ball past Tony
Coton on his debut in a
4–0 win against Watford
(background)
© Express Newspapers

Glenn Hoddle and Chris
prepare for pop stardom
(left) © Express
Newspapers

Typical Waddle skill — Chris drops his shoulder
against Egypt (left) © Sporting Pictures Ltd

'Tweedledum and Tweedledee' - John Barnes and
Chris Waddle (below) © Express Newspapers

'Let's Have a Disco' — Chris Waddle and Terry Butcher celebrate victory over Belgium in the World Cup, 1990 (background) © Empics

'If ever I saw a man who could be described as absolutely flattened, then it was Chris Waddle that night in Turin' — Bobby Robson. (below) Chris Waddle is consoled by Lothar Matthaus after that infamous penalty miss. © Empics

Marseille v AC Milan European Cup semi-final 1991, Chris is surrounded by photographers after scoring the only goal of the game (centre) © Empics

Chris holds his head in his hands while coach Raymond Goethals (right) gazes mournfully into space after Marseille lose the 1991 European Cup Final to Red Star Belgrade (bottom) © Empics

Chris celebrates his first goal for Falkirk. 'I don't think anybody who saw him play will forget that brief, but glorious time when Chris Waddle played for Falkirk' — Neil Binney, Falkirk chairman (background) © Scottish Daily Record

Chris Waddle and Trevor Francis in happier days as Chris signs for Sheffield Wednesday in 1992 (centre) © Steve Walsh

Graham Taylor makes a point to Chris Waddle. 'I think I knew in my heart of hearts that once Graham Taylor was appointed England manager I wouldn't be around for long' (bottom) © Express Newspapers

Against the old enemy — Chris Waddle playing for Bradford against Sheffield Wednesday in the FA Cup, 1997 (centre) © Empics

Making his debut for Sunderland, Chris Waddle emerges from the tunnel with Nottingham Forest's Pierre van Hooijdonk. Both teams were relegated to the First Division at the end of the season (bottom) © Empics

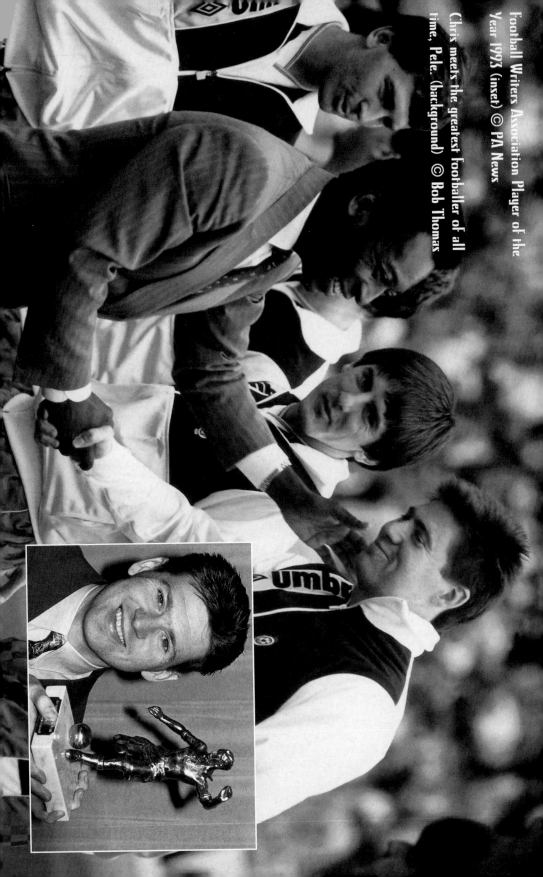

been enough to have saved Shreeves's job. They wanted a team that would excite them, and somehow we just weren't gelling with any consistency.'

It looked as if they were heading for an early exit from the FA Cup as well. They'd beaten Oxford 5–1 in the league, but the little side had a bit of a cup reputation themselves and had already put Newcastle out of the Milk Cup. When they took an early lead against Spurs at the Manor Ground, it looked as if they were about to claim another victim. Then Chiedozie equalised and gave Chris the chance of playing his best match to date in a Spurs shirt in the replay.

He made one and scored another, but the talk was all of the goal that never was. If it had been allowed, it would have been one of the best ever of his career. He got the ball, left three Oxford defenders standing, even seemed to beat a couple of them twice, then hit the ball in from inside the box. To his disbelief, the referee disallowed the effort for off-side against Glenn Hoddle, who could not conceivably have been interfering with play.

The press campaign against Shreeves grew in its volume. Injuries conspired against him as well. He was having to use the likes of youngsters Alistair Dick, David Howells, Mark Bowen, David Leworthy and Richard Cooke and the side lost five of its six league matches after the New Year's Day point at Highbury. David Howells, now the Tottenham captain and the only real Tottenham survivor of those kids, remembers being a little in awe of Chris when he first played alongside him.

'In fact, David started up front, scoring a hat-full of goals alongside Phil Gray, who's now an established Northern Ireland international. He moved on from Spurs, as did all those other promising youngsters. It wasn't that they weren't good enough. They just found it difficult to compete with big-money signings. I'm not surprised that other clubs snap up players from Spurs. The one thing that you always get coming out of White Hart Lane is a well-educated footballer.'

A fourth round FA Cup replay with Notts County saw Spurs safely through by five clear goals, but the final death knell for Peter Shreeves was probably sounded in March, when Everton knocked Spurs out of the cup by a 2–1 score-line. The axe did not finally fall until the end of the season, though. There was a bit of a revival in the league, as the club only lost one of its last twelve matches – including an away draw at St James' Park.

It was strange for Chris going back for the first time as the enemy, and he felt for a moment as if he were in the wrong changing-room. When he was asked to lead the team on to the pitch, the rest of them held back by prior plan so that Chris found himself totally alone on the pitch. Once again he greeted the massed Geordie fans, who responded with the cry of 'fish and chips'. They were not yet prepared to forgive and forget, and when Chris scored the equaliser in a 2–2 draw, they were even less likely to greet him with any enthusiasm. He ran automatically towards the Gallowgate end, where he was greeted him with stony silence. 'Cut it out,' said Glenn Roeder as he ran past him, and Chris could not tell whether or not he was joking.

It was, in fact, the fourth consecutive match in which he'd scored and he was beginning to feel as if he were finally in tune with the Tottenham style of play.

Despite the average season being enjoyed by his new club, Chris was still chosen for the vital World Cup qualifier at

Wembley in October against Turkey. The opposition were by no means as strong as the side that qualified for Euro '96 a decade later, but they had to be beaten, and England did the job with clinical professionalism, strolling home 5–0. There was a growing army of dissenters amongst the press who thought Chris too inconsistent to merit a place in the England side, but he silenced them – at least temporarily – with a goal from an acute angle after a solo run down the left wing. Whatever the media might say publicly, from what Bobby Robson told him privately, he felt a permanent member of the England squad, if not of the team itself.

The other results meant that England would be going to Mexico and Chris just had to maintain his form to be invited to the party. Once he knew they had qualified, Robson lined up a whole stream of friendlies to have a good hard look at all the players with whom he'd not been able to experiment while the serious business of booking their place for the finals had been underway.

The goals had dried up for Chris at Spurs, so that by the time England played Northern Ireland in a match that the Irish had to draw to be sure of joining England in Mexico, he'd scored only three more times since the first game of the season. It was not therefore surprising that he failed to find the score-sheet – nor did any of his team-mates as Pat Jennings was magnificent in the Northern Ireland goal. Inevitably there were suggestions from the other teams in the group that the result had been rigged, but Chris dismissed suggestions of match-fixing and bribery. A decade ago was a less cynical time in football.

'Since then I've heard so much about match-fixing, particularly when I was playing in Europe, that you start to ask yourself

– could it happen here, and the answer has to be why not? There's so much money in the game and money always attracts the wrong kind of people.'

The eighties were also a different era with regard to priority of country over club. Then, because Spurs had a fourth-round FA Cup replay with Notts County, the club insisted that both Chris and Glenn were left out of the England side that travelled to Egypt in January. Nowadays it is always England that comes first, and all too often a club is left bemoaning its fate as one of its star players returns injured from international duty.

The game in Cairo was only a friendly, which meant that Robson could experiment, with opportunities afforded to Peter Beardsley, Gordon Cowans and Danny Wallace. Clearly Robson did not see the wide-berth positions as being a straight contest between Waddle and Barnes. Beardsley, Cowans and Wallace all did well as England won 4–1, and Tottenham's cup victory was small consolation for Chris, who was beginning to worry about his England place. He was always a worrier in those days, although it was mostly football he worried about. The older, more mature Waddle seems to have left even those cares and pressures far behind him.

Despite his worries, he was back for the next international against Israel in Tel Aviv, and it was after the match at St James' Park that he went straight from Newcastle to Luton Airport to fly out with the England team to the USSR. If there was to be a signpost along the way of Chris's England career, pointing the way to success, then there would be little doubt that one single place-name would be carved upon it – Tbilisi.

chapter 25

Life in the Soviet Union was grim, as was the England team's greeting at the airport. They were used to travelling and arriving as VIPs, not being kept waiting in the customs hall for over an hour while all their newspapers were confiscated. Their hotel was supposedly the best available, but if it was, then Chris shuddered to think what the worst might be like. The room he shared with Mark Wright was tiny and the thin towels were in proportion to it, making it virtually impossible to dry oneself after a bath in tepid, bracken coloured water. Unsuccessful darning could not conceal the holes in the thin blankets.

'The worst thing as far as I was concerned,' remembers Chris, 'was that there was only one television station, that was in Russian and the reception was crap.'

Fortunately the England team had taken with them most of their own food supplies, including baked beans which most of the players adored. They did try one of the local delicacies, a thin soup with floating dumplings, but it did not suit the English palate. There was nothing to buy, the shops being virtually empty of stock, and in desperation the squad went to see a circus. Even the animals seemed sad, and there was nothing amusing about the clowns. They was no opportunity to speak to the ordinary Russians, nor even to their opposing players. 'When I returned to England and heard people in my local moaning on about their lives and England generally, I thought to myself, go and live in Russia for a week, you'll soon be back. You just don't realise how good England is.'

The England team got a great reception at the match, where most of the spectators regarded themselves as Georgian rather than Russian and hardly spoke the Russian language. When the break-up of the Soviet Union came a few years later and the new Georgian state emerged, Chris for one was not surprised. Travelling the world had taught him something about politics.

Despite the fact it was a friendly, the entertainment-starved locals turned up in their thousands, virtually filling the 90,000-capacity stadium with its hard concrete seats. Spring came late to the area and it was bitterly cold, but Chris had had enough of hanging around and was determined to warm the crowd.

He teased and tormented the Russian defence throughout the match, then finally played a one-two with Peter Beardsley in his own half. His fellow-Geordie then dragged the ball back while Chris made a run into the box and Gary Lineker drew a defender away to the near post. Peter flicked it back to Chris, who cleanly struck it home. The game was marred for him when towards the end he suffered an ankle injury and was substituted by Trevor Steven, yet all that was forgotten when he arrived back in England to see the headlines. 'Tiger of Tbilisi' was an echo of the famous tribute to Nat Lofthouse as the Lion of Vienna some thirty years before.

Within hours of his return he developed a throbbing pain in his stomach and began to vomit. He said nothing to the manager and managed to struggle through the match against Arsenal, which Spurs duly won by the only goal. He was foolish not to have confided in Robson, for of all the managers under whom Chris has played, there is no doubt that Bobby Robson was the most understanding. 'The great thing about Bobby was that he really cared about his players and took an interest in their personal lives and problems. Like Arthur Cox, he was also never one to bear grudges. If a player stepped out of line or went out and had a drink, as long as he came and apologised then it was all over. With some bosses you can blot your copy-book forever for just one misdeed or one hasty word.'

After his return from the Arsenal game he begged Lorna to get him home. Although he felt dehydrated and sick, a night's sleep convinced him he had recovered enough to play in mid-field against West Ham on the Monday in the absence of the injured Hoddle. Without feeling particularly well, he kept that role against Leicester, but by the time he had played another ninety minutes against David Pleat's Luton, all he wanted was his bed. In fact, rather than going home to bed, he had to go to Coventry for an award ceremony, but felt worse than he had done immediately on his return from Russia. With the tiredness and the nausea came depression. He had wanted so much for the season to bring him and his new club a major honour, but it was not to be. He was playing on auto and it showed. There seemed to be no rest. If it wasn't a club match, then he was on international duty; if it wasn't England, then there was something on for the club; if it wasn't for the club, then he'd committed himself to some worthy cause. And all this without the sort of off-the-pitch commercial activities that most high-profile players undertake as a matter of course nowadays.

He virtually had to drag himself out of bed to join up with
England for yet another friendly, this time against Scotland. He
knew that if he cried off, he could lose his place, and it was getting
too close to the World Cup to take the chance that he might not
be able to grab it back. England duly won 2–1. Trevor Francis
was up front, although he failed to score and his international
career drew to an end.

Chris confided in Glenn about his own insecurity. Hoddle,
statesmanlike even then, told him to keep plugging away, to
believe in himself and his own ability. He had the skill, and
the rest would follow. He was right. What Chris had failed to
realise was just how much the bug he had picked up in Russia
had taken out of him. It was not a country that he was likely to
put at the top of his holiday list.

'I think, looking back, that the change of life-style had a lot to
do with my feeling down. I'd left behind all the friends I'd grown
up with. I think depression affects a lot of players, particularly
those in their twenties who can't break into the first team and
whom nobody wants to buy or take on loan. I felt at the time
that what I'd got wasn't the life I'd anticipated. I wanted to
turn back the clock and go back to my old life-style, despite
all the material benefits I'd achieved. Glenn really helped me
through it. He told me that even though I thought I hadn't
done well at Spurs, everybody who mattered thought I had.
My advice now would be for anybody feeling low to try and
recognise the symptoms. I felt tired and drained all the time,
unable to sleep. They should then try and ring somebody more
experienced than them. I suppose I should have called Arthur,
but I didn't. I bottled it all up inside.'

By the time of the last match of the season against Southampton he was flying again, scoring the first in a 5–3 win. He finished the season with fourteen goals, Spurs finished in eleventh place, and once again without any medals, Chris was left to he worry about whether or not he would make the final squad for Mexico.

chapter 26

By April 1986, Chris knew his fate as far as World Cup selection was concerned. He was in as were Barnes and Hoddle, but there was no room in the squad for his other principal rivals, Danny Wallace and Gordon Cowans. 'I was a bit surprised to be picked. I'd only played a handful of games.'

He needn't have worried. 'He was always in my plans from the first time he pulled on an England shirt,' Robson now confirms.

Chris felt an enormous surge of anticipation as he assembled with the rest of the squad on 6 May and was dying for the preliminaries to be out of the way. The photographs, the usual ghastly record (which inevitably became a hit), an appearance on *Wogan* and finally a formal reception at the House of Commons with the minister of sport would all have wounded Joe Waddle's socialist beliefs to the core.

It was a relief to get on the plane and fly first to Colorado for some exposure to the blistering heat they knew they would have to endure in LA, where the game was being held. In fact, a friendly against Mexico was on the agenda. England won 3–0, Chris started, Barnes finished. They both wondered if that would be the shape of things to come.

The preparation and the training were very thorough, leaving nothing to chance. In the sixteen years since an England team last visited South America for a World Cup tournament, they had learned a lot. A whole medical team tested the players constantly. If the blood tests revealed low haemoglobin levels, then iron tablets were immediately prescribed. An hour-and-a-half walk up a mountain was followed by a fifteen-minute run down again, followed in turn by blood pressure and heart tests. At times it was more like preparing for a moon probe than a football tournament. The strain finally got to the medical team, rather than the players, when the popular Dr Vernon Edwards, the principal team doctor, suffered a minor heart-attack. It did not stop him insisting on joining up with the squad in Mexico, though.

The opening ceremony was due to take place on 31 May, with England's first match in Group F against Portugal scheduled for Monterrey on 3 June. Just a week before, Bobby Robson was still shuffling the pack in the last warm-up game against Canada. Chris Woods, who would in fact play in the new US MLS for Colorado in 1996, was given a chance to play a half in place of Shilton. Goalkeepers seem to last forever, and over ten years on Shilton had played just over 1,000 league games. Glenn Hoddle is the England manager whilst Kenny Sansom ended his career at Croydon and is now running a football school for children. Such are the vagaries of life as a professional footballer.

Peter Reid came on for Ray Wilkins – both players who would move into management with varying degrees of success – while Beardsley replaced Lineker and, of course, Barnes came on for Waddle. The match ended in a 1–0 win for England – and if Bobby Robson was any wiser about the formation which would play in the first competitive match, then, of those watching, he was probably the only one. But as time would tell he was also the only one who counted. What was becoming clear was that some of the players were just there for the ride and would get to play a meaningful part only if some disaster befell their team-mates. Viv Anderson and Kerry Dixon fell into that category, while Bryan Robson's persistent shoulder injury was also becoming an increasing worry.

The opening ceremony momentarily took the players' minds off the task ahead. It was very impressive, the millions of dollars spent upon it contrasting vividly with the poverty that the players could see as they moved from luxury hotel to luxury hotel. It was frustrating being unable to help, but the people seemed cheerful enough, particularly the small street urchins, who followed the England team devotedly wherever they could.

England were favourites to qualify from a group that comprised Portugal, Morocco and their old bogey team Poland, yet the start of the campaign was nothing short of disastrous.

Everything that they had worked on in training seemed forgotten in their first match – against Portugal. They had an enormous amount of possession, but seemed to freeze when they got near goal. It was almost as if they were scared to raise the pace in case the heat and the altitude got to them. After an hour, Chris was replaced by Beardsley, rather than Barnes, but it was to no avail. Portugal seized upon a rare English defensive mistake and grabbed the only goal of the match. It may have been against the run of play, but the record books show Portugal 1 England 0, and nothing Robson could say by way of explanation or apology to the thousands of fans who had spent fortunes travelling to follow the team could change that.

The team had watched the opening match between the other two sides in the group, and although neither Poland nor Morocco could be taken seriously as potential winners of the tournament, Morocco had scrapped hard for a goalless draw and did not look as if they would be the pushover which had been anticipated. They had one or two players who were appearing regularly in the French league, which, as Chris was to discover, was not a league for no-hopers.

The game against Morocco was scheduled for 6 June. It was D-Day in more ways than one. In the face of a barrage of press criticism, Robson kept the same side that had begun against the Portuguese. The result was a sterile, goalless draw, although the result did not tell the whole story. Bryan Robson's shoulder finally gave in and ended his participation in the tournament. Ray Wilkins, somewhat uncharacteristically, lost his temper and was sent off. Chris buckled down to the task in hand, having to work twice as hard to fill the midfield gap left by Wilkins' departure. 'The Boss told me to play down the right, and at times I felt I was running through thick soup. I would almost have welcomed being substituted this time around.'

It wasn't to be. He played the whole ninety minutes and finished the game five pounds lighter than he had started. The burden upon the whole England side was much heavier. Now their destiny was no longer in their own hands. They had to depend upon the results of others. It looked as if it had been a very long way to come for an early trip home.

chapter 27

As it was, the dice finally began to roll in England's favour. Both Poland and Morocco beat Portugal, and as long as England could beat Poland, then they would be through. All those months of qualification and preparation, and it was coming down to a single match to decide whether there might be a chance to make it all worthwhile.

Bobby Robson took Chris aside to break the news. He was out of the side. In the absence of Robson and Wilkins, he was going to dispense with wingers and play 4–4–2. Barnes and Waddle were to be the losers. England, as it transpired, were to be the winners. Robson, kindly as ever, did not put it to Chris as if he had been dropped. It was a tactical decision, based on the need to have a solid mid-field. He chose Steven, Reid and Hodge, with Hoddle as his only real playmaker, Beardsley in front of them switching between a central striking position and the mid-field, and Lineker as the out-and-out front man.

Gary had grabbed a hat-trick before half-time, so that by the time Chris came on to replace the tiring Beardsley, England were as good as through to the next round. When Chris did come on to the pitch, he was asked to take on some bags of water. He grabbed a handful, the manager told him to take a few more, and he ended up with about twenty. As somebody said, all he needed was the goldfish. The scene was straight out of *Monty Python*, and as he tossed a bag to each player it promptly broke. The image clearly made an impression back home, as when he returned to Tottenham he found a bag of water in his locker with a note saying, 'You left this in Mexico and they sent it over!'

Their opponents in the next round were Paraguay, who had had a fairly convincing passage, beating Iraq and drawing with Belgium and Mexico. England left behind them the beauty of Monterrey and flew to the madness that was Mexico City.

There were certainly no opportunities for any high jinks on the flight. 'We had a nightmare flight through an electrical storm, and there were moments when I thought our number was up,' Chris recalls. There were also problems with their hotel, which was on the main road and so noisy at night that the team could hardly sleep. It had been checked out before by the England manager and various Football Association officials – but they had presumably seen it during the day-time, and it had certainly not then been subject to the deliberate attempts to keep the England players awake at night with the blaring of horns and the playing of loud music.

After some political pressure, they were moved to the hotel already occupied by the Italian squad. The power of the lira had already spoken when it came to their choice of accommodation, and Chris was left in no doubt that their budget was virtually without limit. For the first time in his life, Chris was able to see at close quarters how the other half lived. It wasn't just their stylish Diadora kit that impressed him, but their designer clothes and the ease with which they carried the trappings of their obvious wealth. If he had been told that within ten years Italian players would be coming to play in the Premier League for wages that would match or exceed their own back home, he would have dismissed the idea as an absurdity. Mark Hateley, of course, knew many of the Italians from his time in Serie A and was able to speak the language fluently. Although he couldn't understand a word, Chris sat quite happily listening to Hateley chatting away to Paolo Rossi, whom he considered remarkably modest, considering his wealth and fame. It never occurred to him that one day he would be doing the same in French.

At least he had been on the substitutes' bench against Poland, but he did not even get that far against Paraguay in the magnificent and awe-inspiring Azteca Stadium on 18 June. Alvin Martin came in for Terry Fenwick, but apart from that it was the same side that had demolished the Poles. One could hardly blame Robson for not wanting to tamper with a winning formula. It worked again as England cruised into the last eight with another 3–0 victory, including two goals from Lineker. The campaign was beginning to get up a head of steam and as Argentina and Maradona waited in the next round, there was a feeling amongst the squad for the first time that it was actually within their powers to win the Jules Rimet Trophy itself.

The four days they had to wait between the matches were purgatory. Everybody was wanting to know if they would be playing, and whatever diversions were available were endured rather than enjoyed. It was virtually impossible to go outside the hotel. Security was tight; they were driven crazy by fans, of whom the travelling English supporters were the least of their problems; and Mexico City seemed to be a permanent traffic jam. The players organised race nights for themselves, watching videos of horse races, with Kerry Dixon and Peter Shilton acting as bookmakers. The bookies never lose – as Shilton was to discover later in his life when, by his own admission, he lost fortunes to them.

It was not until the night before the match that Chris learned that he was once again only to be substitute. However, it did at least give him a chance to be involved. He had hated just watching the Paraguay match and had feared his career was in irretrievable reverse.

The first half of the match was pure chess, with each side jockeying for position. Goalless after forty-five minutes, it left even the gamblers in the England team finding it impossible to call. The second half is, of course, in the annals of English folk history. Still 0–0 with the English side playing above themselves, actually threatening to take the lead – and then 'The Hand of God'.

Sitting on the bench, Chris was fooled, along with the referee, and thought it had been headed home. So did most of the players on the field. Only John Barnes protested immediately, his fervour gradually spreading to the rest of the side. There was no argument about Maradona's second, and it was time for a last desperate effort to attack and get back in the game and the tournament itself.

Chris was sent on to replace Peter Reid with the orders to get in as many crosses as he could. John Barnes was on the other wing and suddenly England had reverted to the system with which they had started and which had actually got them to Mexico in the first place. A cross from Barnes saw Lineker get one back, but try as the wide men did to get the ball across, the English attack was hardly strong in the aerial power department.

Neither Lineker nor Beardsley had the height or capabilities to score consistently from headers and Hateley had not been called upon. There was one more close call, when a Lineker shot was cleared off the line, but as the final whistle blew the lads knew it was all over.

'It was different in 1990. Then we were nearly all crying, but this time we were too angry for tears. We'd been cheated by Maradona, a player with such skill that he had no need to cheat. For some of the players it would be their last chance to play in a World Cup. Kenny Sansom, Mark Hateley, Kerry Dixon wouldn't be with us in Italy. But as far as I was concerned, the four years started the minute that game ended. I'd been a part of the greatest football circus in the world and I was determined to be a part of it again.'

chapter 28

By the time David Pleat arrived in Monterrey to commentate on the World Cup, he knew that he was the new manager of Tottenham Hotspur. Three of his squad were with the England party – Chris, Glenn and Gary Stevens. When he met up with them, they asked what they should call him. He told them that he didn't mind. When the Spurs team got together for pre-season training, however, and his three internationals chorused a greeting of 'Good morning, David,' he was not amused. He was the boss now, and England players or not, he had the power of selection over them. There is no doubt that the same problem arose when Pleat took over at Sheffield Wednesday to find the, by now, senior citizen Chris Waddle amongst his playing staff. He could never come to terms with the fact that Chris certainly regarded himself as an equal, to be treated with the due respect that he felt he never received.

Despite the apparent public differences between the men, Pleat recalls those early days with Chris with some affection. 'When I first arrived at White Hart Lane, I found Chris still very shy. He wasn't enjoying the position in which he'd been playing so successfully for Peter Shreeves, which was out wide on the left.

I converted him to a wide right wing role, but he wanted to be involved more from a central position. However, that role was already allotted to Glenn Hoddle and Chris would have to wait until Glenn left before he could assume his mantle. I remember after one match against Aston Villa where we'd had a resounding victory and found the net three times, Chris came up to me and said he wasn't happy playing wide on the right. I told him the team was doing well, we were winning and I wasn't changing anything.'

Yet all that was in the future. In the summer of 1986, with the glory and disappointment of the World Cup behind them, Chris and the rest of the Tottenham squad were looking forward to a season that would promise so much and eventually deliver so little. With Pleat came the ebullient Mitchell Thomas from Luton, a likeable character who would shake his dreadlocks and describe even his hair as relaxed. Although Mitchell was never the greatest of players, nobody could ever doubt his whole-hearted efforts. Yet another example of the circularity of the world of professional football saw his career come full circle when he ended up back at Luton Town, trying to help them escape from the Second Division. Pleat also brought with him his own training methods. He had a series of code-words for various moves. 'Sid' meant take over, 'Jack' was let it go, 'Fred' a back-heel. It was fine, except that for the life of him, Chris could not remember which was which. As he stopped to think, he'd find himself dispossessed. It descended into chaos when Spurs played Luton later in the season, for Pleat's former team were still using the same tactics, although the names meant different things. Anybody sitting near enough to the field would have been puzzled to hear the twenty-two players screaming names at each other that seemed to have no connection with anybody on the team-sheet.

The season got off to a flying start, as did Clive Allen with a hat-trick in a 3–0 win against Aston Villa, but a solitary win in the next five matches meant that they slipped to twelfth place by mid-September. Despite Pleat's reputation for bright, attacking football, the team had managed only six goals in six matches and Clive Allen had scored five of them. Chris hadn't found the net once, despite being handed the number nine shirt.

Arthur Cox observed the goal-drought from a distance: 'His scoring seemed to disappear once the two of us had split up. I think other managers weren't on to him all the time as I was, but then they didn't know him like I did.'

Obviously Bobby Robson was not impressed by Chris's form – or lack of it – and he was on the bench in a friendly against Sweden in Stockholm on 10 September, coming on for the last ten minutes. Almost to Chris's relief, England lost 1–0. It seemed throughout his career that whenever he didn't play a substantial amount of the game, or if he didn't play at all, either through injury or simply because he wasn't picked, whoever took his place failed to grasp their chance.

He scored his first goal of the season in the Littlewoods Cup in the first leg away to Barnsley, which Spurs won 3–2. They put five past them in the home leg to move smoothly into the third round, and a week later Chris was once again feeling all was right with the world as he began the European Championship qualifying match against Northern Ireland. He scored in a 3–0 victory, with Gary Lineker getting the other two.

'The longer I've been in football, the more I realise what a roller-coaster ride of a career it is. One goal, one win, one defeat can change an entire season. Winning is as much a matter of habit as is losing. I really felt that we'd win something that season and somehow that confidence came across on the park.'

The league season was beginning to come together as Spurs put together a five-match unbeaten run that had them climbing into fourth place in the table. Clive Allen was having a season to end all seasons and by 18 October had already scored eleven league goals. There was no doubt that he was benefiting from the service provided by Chris and Tony Galvin. But, just when it seemed they had a platform for a championship challenge, the squad suffered a whole stream of injuries. Mark Falco, Galvin and Gary Stevens were the first to miss a string of games, followed, as the season progressed, by Nico Claesen, who had joined the north London club after impressing for Belgium in the World Cup, Ossie Ardiles and, most sickeningly of all, Danny Thomas.

Chris was getting concerned over his own goal drought, until a change of tactics – in part enforced by the injury to Falco – changed all that. Clive Allen was left alone up front, while Chris became one of a five-man mid-field. He scored for the first time in the season as Tottenham progressed in the Littlewoods Cup with a 5–0 thrashing of Birmingham.

He was really enjoying playing with Allen. He has still not seen a more effective player at the near post, likening Teddy Sheringham from today's Tottenham team to Allen in that respect. Time and time again, Chris would whip the ball in for Clive to score with a little controlled flick. It is an art form to be able to beat defenders at the near post, and Allen hit the back of the net an incredible forty-nine times in all competitions that year. Had he not missed one match, he would almost certainly have reached the magic half-century. Although there was a lot of media pressure for him to be given an England chance, it never came. Perhaps he was a little unlucky to be playing in the same generation as Lineker, another arch-predator in front of goal.

Chris kept his place in the England side for another European qualifier against Yugoslavia, although he was substituted by Trevor Steven ten minutes from the end. England had a comfortable 2–0 victory and were looking good to top the table. Meanwhile, the Spurs bandwagon was still *en route* for Wembley. Chris scored twice against Oxford and found the net again four days later in a 3–1 win at Cambridge in the Littlewoods Cup. Although Spurs slipped to sixth just after Christmas, the results were still good, and their lack of progress up the league was due more to the consistency of the teams above them than to their own shortcomings.

As 1986 moved into 1987, Chris seemed to have everything to look forward to: Spurs in a position to challenge for the title, still in the Littlewoods Cup, a third-round FA Cup tie against Scunthorpe that offered an easy path to the fourth round, and a whole series of qualifiers for the European Championships. Perhaps most important of all, he was being given a chance at club level to express himself without being confined to one particular role. He just hoped that Bobby Robson would take note.

chapter 29

It wasn't all serious football at Tottenham. The board made sure there was always enough money for them to relax and feel important, and in December they were taken on a busman's holiday – a winter-break trip to Bermuda. Staying at the luxurious Hamilton Princess Hotel, they did not allow a game against the Bermudian national team to interfere with the serious business of playing golf. Although Chris has never been as obsessed with the sport as some of his contemporaries, he can still play a competent round.

The island is renowned for its golf courses, Castle Harbour being the most prestigious. They were not prepared for Mitchell Thomas. Mitchell was no great golfer himself which didn't stop him accompanying Chris and Glenn around the course. It was all very American, with everybody using motorised buggies, rather than walking around the cliff-top course. Glenn made the mistake of asking Mitchell to drive him over to Chris, who watched in horror as Mitchell set off down a hill at top speed. Realising that Mitchell had no idea how to stop the vehicle, Chris leapt out of the way as the buggy approached. Glenn also abandoned ship, jumping out in what seemed like slow motion. Mitchell careered on down the course until a tree loomed up ahead and brought him to a crashing halt. Incredibly, Mitchell climbed out without a scratch, but the buggy was so firmly embedded in the tree that it took the combined strength of all three players to shift it. They finally freed it up and Mitchell drove the battered buggy back up the fairway, oblivious of the loose pieces of metal churning up the beautifully laid grass with all the efficiency of a farm tractor.

The man in charge of the greens looked from his buggy to his beloved grass, almost in tears as he asked what had happened. Mitchell thought quickly: 'I heard someone shout fore, went to avoid the ball and went straight into a tree.' Grateful the footballer hadn't been hurt and wasn't filing a law suit against the golf course, the man let it go at that. Bermuda may appear to be very English, but geographically it's very close to the United States with their enormous awards for damages.

Mitchell went for broke the following day. Having insisted on driving again, he parked his buggy on the cliff-top without ensuring that the handbrake was properly secured. Glenn whirled round as he heard the click, and the three valuable players dashed after the runaway vehicle, catching it in true movie style just before it went over the edge.

It wasn't just on the golf course that Mitchell made his mark on the island, whose roads are so narrow and winding that even long-term residents are restricted to one car per family. It is not possible to hire a car on Bermuda, so tourists are allowed to rent small motor-bikes, yet even those lead to several fatalities a year. Mitchell Thomas seemed intent on adding to the statistics when he was the only one of the Spurs party brave or foolhardy enough to choose the bike over taxis. Chris and a couple of other players were heading back for their hotel with Mitchell in hot pursuit behind them.

'Make a right,' Chris said, without any idea of where he was going. Another couple of turns were directed and the players watched poor Mitchell desperately trying to manoeuvre his bike to keep up with them.

On his return to England, Chris lost another friend from the club. Graham Roberts, with whom he'd roomed, was moving on to Rangers in Scotland. Graham had become a folk-hero at White Hart Lane for putting Charlie Nicholas over one of the advertising hoardings in a north London derby and earned himself his own special chant of: 'Who put Charlie in the box? Robbo did, Robbo did.'

Now manager of Yeovil Town, Graham has maintained a close friendship with Chris over the years. 'I remember on a flight that Chris lost his wallet. He was convinced that a couple of teenagers in the seat in front had stolen it, because they kept averting their eyes whenever he looked at them. As we got off the plane, he had me follow them into the toilets while he went off to look for someone in authority. The kids were terrified, but there was no sight of the wallet. It was only when they had to let them go that somebody told Chris they'd found his wallet down the back of the seat. He never found them to apologise, which was perhaps just as well.'

Graham Roberts may have moved on, but the rest of the Spurs team he left behind still had to play Arsenal in a live televised match on 4 January. It had a special edge because Arsenal were top of the league and looking good to stay there, while Spurs were fifth and desperate to close the gap. They failed as Arsenal won 2–1. It was always bad to lose this derby, but even worse to lose at home in front of 37,000 fans, their biggest gate of the season. There was a feeling after the match that if Spurs were going to put some silverware in their showcase, it would have to come from one of the cup competitions.

Arsenal seemed to have the hex on Spurs that year. After beating West Ham 5–1 in a replay in the Littlewoods Cup, Spurs were two games away from Wembley. The only problem was that both those matches were against Arsenal. On 8 February, Spurs went to Highbury and did the difficult part by winning 1–0. Clive Allen got the goal, but Chris's contribution was the most telling, as he gave Gus Caesar the Arsenal defender such a torrid time that it marked the start of the decline in his Arsenal career.

'At most clubs where you play, there's always one performance you remember more than most. You always know that, if you're playing to the best of your ability and seeing a lot of the ball, you'll give the defending full-back a difficult time. On that day I had a good game and Gus had a bad one. I never set out to make an opponent look foolish, but I do try to entertain. The crowd love it when you send a player this way and that, with the odd nutmeg thrown in for good measure, and it sticks in their minds. I can't say I felt sorry for Gus at the time. If he'd have marked me out of the game he'd have been doing his job and I was just doing mine.'

Chris had a brief respite from the English winter when he travelled with the England team to Madrid for a friendly against Spain. He was so focused on the league and the cups that it was almost a distraction, but England won 4–2 and although he was substituted again by Trevor Steven, he felt that was just to give Bobby Robson the chance to have a look at Trevor, rather than any reflection on his own performance.

He was in a hurry to return to England and the second leg of the Littlewoods Cup semi-final. However, it was a different story at White Hart Lane on 1 March. Gus Caesar was gone and the Arsenal defence now consisted of Tony Adams, David O'Leary, Kenny Sansom and Viv Anderson. Clive Allen got his inevitable goal, but Arsenal got two, and the matter was still unresolved after extra-time. So it was a replay at White Hart Lane on 4 March, when again Clive Allen scored, but again Arsenal got two. It was cruel. Chris had longed for a Wembley appearance. With no way of knowing that he was to get another chance come May, all he could think of was that he had let the fans down and that at work-places across London the Spurs fans were having a torrid time from their north London neighbour's supporters.

Meanwhile, in five league matches between 24 January and 22 March, Tottenham gave their supporters fresh hope, winning them all and scoring twelve times without conceding a goal. The match against QPR on 7 March ended in a 1–0 victory for Spurs, but the result was made virtually irrelevant by the terrible career-ending injury suffered by Danny Thomas, following a tackle by Gavin Maguire of Rangers. The incident ended with legal proceedings for damages and a negotiated out-of-court settlement. Although Danny eventually carved a new career for himself as a physiotherapist, his loss to the club, both as a player and a sunny personality, was incalculable.

Chris didn't score until the last game in the winning sequence, but when he did find the net, it was memorable for being the only goal of the game against Liverpool, who by then had replaced

Arsenal at the top of the table. A mis-hit shot that skidded and bounced over the always unpredictable Bruce Grobbelaar, it was by no means a great goal, but was no less than he deserved. The *Mirror* said:

'Chris Waddle's brilliance and Bruce Grobelaar's blunder have set up an exciting climax to the Championship. Waddle is the winger England fans love to hate. He's frequently booed at Wembley – but now he is silencing the critics and his will be one of the first names that Bobby Robson will write into his England team for the game against Northern Ireland next month.'

Spurs moved into fourth place, still fourteen points behind but with five games in hand. Having made progress in the FA Cup, too, they had brief visions of the magnificent double year repeating itself. They'd beaten Scunthorpe 3–2 in the third round as expected, then put four past Crystal Palace without reply. For Chris, judgement day was 21 February when in the fifth round Spurs were drawn at home to Newcastle United. The prospect of his old club getting to Wembley at his expense did not bear consideration. Both teams fancied themselves as cup sides, although Spurs had much more impressive credentials. United hadn't actually made it to Wembley since 1974 and hadn't won since 1955, while Tottenham had put their name on the trophy in both 1981 and 1982. It wasn't a pretty game. There was too much needle, too much at stake and Spurs squeezed home a little luckily by a solitary goal.

'It's always hard playing against your old club, particularly in the cup. The fans were chanting abuse, trying to wind me up, but I'm not the sort of player to react to that. It was all very close and Albert Craig missed a sitter at the end for Newcastle. But we were through.'

Wimbledon were their next victims, on 14 March, with Chris scoring the first of Spurs' two goals and Glenn getting the other.

'I went wide and everybody thought I was going to cross, including the keeper. That left a gap and I squeezed it through and into the net. Glenn's effort was a magnificent thirty-yard free-kick. He vanished under a huge heap of our players and I got to the celebrations a bit late. I went to leap on top of them, they all moved and I fell flat on my face.'

Vinny Jones had been man-to-man marking Hoddle, who eventually rolled the ball to his opponent and said, 'See if you can do anything with it.' It was that kind of day. Spurs were celebrating getting to the semi-final and the Tottenham faithful did not believe that their team could lose twice at the penultimate hurdle.

chapter 30

It might have been April Fool's Day, but there was no joke about England's convincing 2–1 win over Northern Ireland in the European Championship qualifier. Chris got the second just before half-time and played the full ninety minutes.

'At that time I was a lot happier playing for my country away from Wembley. A fair number of the England fans were getting on my back, and there were too many of them just to be regarded as Arsenal supporters booing a Spurs player. Eventually I had to work really hard at blocking out the noise from the crowd and just concentrate on what was going on about me on the pitch.'

There was no question of the crowd not getting behind him on 11 April when Spurs faced Watford in the semi-final of the FA Cup at Villa Park. Watford were playing a different style of football than in the days of Graham Taylor, but considering the shoestring budget afforded to his successor, Dave Bassett, they were doing miraculously well in holding a position in the top half of the table and getting this far in the cup. On this occasion, though, they were beaten virtually before they got on to the pitch. Tony Coton and Steve Sherwood, their two first-choice goalies, were unavailable and into their place stepped the young debutant,

Gary Plumley, son of the Watford chief executive, Eddie.

As David Pleat had said during the preceeding week, he was always going to be a hero or villain, and after he'd conceded three goals in the first twenty minutes, it wasn't hard to figure out the category into which he'd fall. Spurs took their foot off the pedal, but it finished 4–1 and Chris had achieved the ambition of a lifetime. He was going to play in an FA Cup final.

He was in tears at the end of the match, although he still found time to ruffle the hair of young Plumley and give him a few words of comfort. The adrenalin was running high and all the way back down the motorway the team coach had an escort of euphoric supporters tooting their horns and waving their scarves out of the window. It was a far cry from the abuse he'd received as part of the Newcastle party making their way back from Cambridge. Ossie was on his way to Wembley and not just his knees, but those of all the squad had gone all trembly.

Ardiles' name was not the only one to make the pop charts. Back in 1986, with Chris still feeling the after-effects of his trip to Russia, he and Glenn had gone out for a meal and a few drinks in Coventry. They had been summoned up on to the stage to sing a version of 'Hey Jude', which had gone down well enough for the fellow diners to request an encore in the shape of 'Can't Buy Me Love'. His friend, Pat Nelson, who had some contacts in the music business had suggested they might like to try to make a record.

They'd laughed it off, but a few more glasses of wine later he got the go-ahead to try and set things up. A meeting with the record producer and song-writer, Bob Puzey, was followed by a session at a recording studio and a single called 'Diamond Lights'. Puzey hawked it around the studios without success.

Nobody wanted to know about a couple of footballers singing a non-football song. It was not until they met up with Jeff Weston, a Spurs fanatic who at the time had his own record company, that the project saw the light of day. Weston, who now works as an agent with Jerome Anderson, recalls the circumstances with a smile on his face. 'I had a season-ticket at Spurs and Glenn's mother always sat in front of me. She knew I had something to do with the music business and told me that her son and Chris had made a record and could I help to get it released? I liked it so much I put it out on my own record label and even published the song as well.'

Suddenly the record had a release date and within weeks was in the charts, making its first entry on 18 April. They appeared on *Top of the Pops* and at the London Palladium, where Chris got himself into the *Sunday Times* quotes of the year by saying that he thought that being in the dressing-rooms at the theatre was very much like playing Hartlepool away. As the record soared to number twelve in the Top Twenty, both Chris and Glenn found there was a down side to pop music fame. Their fan base changed to teenage girls as their pictures began to appear regularly in the teen magazines, while the football fans delighted in taunting them on the pitch with such chants as 'Stick to making records'.

'There's an enormous similarity between the worlds of football and pop music,' Chris believes. 'Three-quarters of musicians are frustrated footballers and the reverse is also true. Most of the people in both professions come from working-class backgrounds. You don't need money to make it, you just need to be good enough and have a little bit of luck.'

With that success and luck in both fields, he should have been feeling on top of the world as the build-up to the Cup final began and Spurs launched their final assault on the elusive double. But disaster struck. In March Lorna had told him that she was expecting their first baby. Now she was being rushed to hospital, where she suffered a miscarriage.

Chris wasn't told until after it was all over. It was 29 April 1987. He was on the plane travelling back from Turkey after a goalless draw in a European Championship qualifier, when Bobby Robson sat him down and broke the news to him gently. 'Don't worry. There'll be another time,' he said, and although he was proved right, the flight back seemed like an eternity.

Glenn Hoddle drove Chris to Holly House Hospital in Buckhurst Hill, Essex, and as he saw Lorna lying there, Chris would have exchanged everything that football had to offer to get back his baby. Yet, the news was not all negative. The specialist, Mr Gattack, told them that Lorna had suffered no permanent damage and there was no reason why she should not be able to have another chance. It seemed little enough comfort at the time.

Other problems appeared less serious, but were problems for all that. Wembley proved to be a distraction rather than an incentive, and of the last nine league games only three were won, while Chris actually missed three of those matches to spoil his ever-present record for the season. By the last home game of the season, it had also become common knowledge that Glenn Hoddle was on his way to Monaco. At the time, Chris was a little disappointed that Glenn had not confided in him, but then Robbo had not told him he was off to Rangers either. As he progressed in the game, he realised that a transfer is a very personal matter. The player concerned becomes so entwined in its labyrinthine plot that the last thing he thinks of is confiding in his team-mates. It is simply one of the unwritten rules of the game.

As the title challenge disintegrated, he just wanted the final to come and the season to be over. The last game against Everton was totally meaningless. The Toffeemen had already won the title and Spurs were destined to finish third. They took the opportunity to field a side of youngsters, resting virtually all their potential Cup final team, including Chris. They lost 1–0, the FA were not amused and the club was fined. Scholar and the rest of the board felt hard done-by, and goodness knows what might have happened had there been someone as aggressive as Alan Sugar at the helm. As it was, the club just paid the fine and looked forward to 16 May and the match against Coventry.

The build-up to the final was remarkably short of drama. The team virtually picked itself and there were no real injury worries. Although Coventry had enjoyed a season unusually free of their usual relegation worries, they had no cup pedigree and the bookmakers had made Spurs hot favourites.

For Chris, on the night before the final, there was the experience of staying at the Pondesbourne Hotel where he had spent his first few lonely nights when he first arrived at Tottenham. That all seemed light years away. Waddle was now almost a senior member of the Tottenham side. People listened to what he had to say and nobody took his silence for stupidity, merely thoughtfulness.

Outside Wembley it felt like a home match. All Chris could see were Spurs fans who had clearly had the greater access to tickets, but in fact the Sky Blue supporters were already in the ground, having arrived early to make a day of it. That was a miscalculation and there were more of them to come.

Probably the two biggest mistakes of the day were the fact that most of the players had forgotten that Coventry had already beaten Spurs 4–3 earlier in the season, and the arrogant action of the Tottenham directors in walking a pre-match lap of honour in their designer suits, waving to the fans as if they had actually had something to do with their team getting to Wembley. It was not a mistake that was likely to be repeated. 'I really think that the directors' place is in the Directors Box [or the Royal Box on this occasion]. They just made fools of themselves and I think they realised it afterwards,' Chris recalls.

As he walked out on to the pitch, the noise was deafening. He shielded his eyes, trying to pick out Lorna in the crowd and noticing that most of the rest of the team were also trying to find their wives and families. He found Lorna and waved, feeling better for that brief moment of communication. The formalities seemed endless. He really did not want to be bothered to be introduced to royalty; he was just there to play football, and there was a momentary feeling of annoyance that this day, which belonged to football, had to be shared with so many people who were just there for the social occasion.

He was only too pleased to take off his track suit. Then somebody noticed that not all the shirts were alike – only a few of the players had the sponsor's name, Holsten, printed on their shirts, whilst the rest of them were plain. Footballers are notoriously superstitious. They had already seen a mirror fall off a dressing-room wall when Jim Rosenthal was interviewing Glenn Hoddle during the week, and now this.

As if sensing some kind of confusion in the Tottenham ranks, the outnumbered Coventry fans suddenly raised the tempo of their singing and broke into a rousing version of 'Sky Blues Forever' to the tune of 'The Eton Boating Song'. The sky may have been a clear blue, but for Tottenham there already seemed to be a couple of clouds on the horizon.

chapter 31

The start for Tottenham was perfect, too perfect. Chris cruised past Greg Downs, the Coventry defender, on the right and, in accordance with their training plans, Clive Allen got to the near post, Chris crossed and Clive found the back of the net. As if in a dream, Chris ran back to the halfway line and Spurs began to play relaxed, cultured football that both delighted and encouraged their fans. In stark contrast, Coventry were relying on long balls punted hopefully upfield to their big striker, Keith Houchen.

Spurs had missed several chances to increase their lead when, against the run of play, Dave Bennett equalised for the midlands side. It seemed a temporary blip in Tottenham's smooth run to victory, particularly when they took the lead again before half-time through a Kilcline own goal. Yet the second half saw a remarkable turnaround. Whatever John Sillet had said to his team was clearly more effective than David Pleat's advice, and it was no great surprise when Coventry equalised again through Keith Houchen.

Extra-time made the season just thirty minutes too long for the Spurs side. Chris was convinced that whoever scored first would win the day, and he was right. The goal, when it came, was tragic for Spurs in more than one sense of the word. An own goal to lose a cup final would leave a scar on most players, but it did not seem fair that this particular cross would have to be borne by the magnificent Gary Mabbutt. As he diverted the ball past Ray Clemence, every Tottenham player felt for him. To be fair to Coventry and their fans, they were generous in victory. It was the only time they had been in front in the match, and it was the only time that counted.

The Tottenham players just wanted to disappear. Chris was numb. He couldn't believe he had come this far only to lose, couldn't see beyond defeat to the rest of his career that stretched before him with other and greater opportunities. If his crystal ball could have shown him the other defeats he would experience at Wembley, he might have retired there and then.

There was no immediate escape for the squad, for win, lose or draw, rightly or wrongly, a reception had been arranged back at White Hart Lane. It took a long time for the likes of Chas and Dave and Chris and Glenn to raise the atmosphere with a song. In addition, a public row between Richard Gough and manager David Pleat, which ended with the defender storming out, did not auger well for the season that was to follow.

'Richard had already said on the pitch, whilst tears were streaming down his face, that he thought we were too cavalier to win anything, that we needed to be more defensive. I think Pleaty must have heard him say, "We'll win nothing," and gone over the top. I know a lot of managers who explode at the end of a match. Terry Venables had the right approach. He'd say that he'd speak to us on Monday when we'd had a bad performance on the Saturday. It gave him time to cool down and us time to think about it.'

As it transpired, Gough would be off back to Scotland by September, and Pleat would be out of a job a month later in the most sordid circumstances. Chris thinks Gough and Pleat now speak to each other regularly on the phone and the whole incident was just between two men who cared perhaps a little too passionately about the game.

Chris was desperate for a rest and a holiday. Lorna needed to be taken away after her traumatic experience with the loss of the baby, but he could not leave just yet. The FA, in their wisdom, had decided to drag out the agony of the season even further, with a meaningless tournament between England, Scotland and Brazil for the short-lived Rous Cup, another trophy which is today gathering dust in some anonymous cabinet.

England drew 1–1 with a young, but nevertheless exciting, Brazilian side for whom Mirandinha, who was later to pull on the number nine shirt at Newcastle with mixed success, scored their goal. It got worse with a drab goalless draw against Scotland, and hardly anybody seemed to notice Brazil beat Scotland to win the tournament.

Still there was no respite. Spurs, in a misguided gesture of generosity, took the players on a ten-day tour of Miami. But their largesse did not extend to an invitation to wives and girlfriends, and the last thing Chris wanted at that stage was a few days away with the lads, many of whom just wanted to let their hair down with a few drinks.

The squad seemed strange without Glenn, and Chris found himself spending more time with his other England colleague, Steve Hodge, and his close friend, Mitchell Thomas. They made an odd threesome. Steve went out with Chris on their first day there to buy some deep-tan sun lotion, claiming that he never burned anyway. Chris lasted about an hour in the remorseless sun, but Steve persisted all day, turning a lobster red rather than the handsome sexy brown he'd anticipated. Turning to Mitchell he asked innocently, 'Does the shower hurt *you* when you get into it?'

Eventually Lorna did fly out, and they joined up with Graham Roberts and his wife and daughter for a holiday which included some coaching sessions by the two Englishmen. Professional football would linger in the disorganised doldrums in the States until 1996, when the MLS was born, but Chris found no shortage of enthusiasm amongst the kids. He was certain, even then, that grass-roots pressure would eventually give the game some kind of profile. The only problem was that almost all the players they coached wanted to be goalkeepers, a fact perhaps reflected a generation later when Jurgen Sommer, Kasey Keller, Ian Feuer and Brad Friedel, all US international keepers, were the most successful American exports to Europe, with the sole exception of John Harkes.

The holiday was too short, but yet again the relentless siren of football was beckoning him away from his wife. The Football League had organised a match against the Rest of the World at Wembley on 8 August, and the first match of the league campaign was due to be played on 15 August. Chris had groaned when he saw who were to be the opponents – Coventry City. Only three short months after the ignominy of defeat at Wembley, they were already coming back to haunt him. For manager David Pleat, they would prove to be a continuing nightmare in a year that would bring one fateful skeleton out of his cabinet of ghosts.

chapter 32

Things began brightly enough for Chris at the start of the 1987–88 season. He played the whole of the game against the Rest of the World, gaining some small compensation for his last losing appearance at Wembley when the League side ran out 3–0 winners. It was particularly satisfying when the opposition contained the likes of Maradona, Platini, Josimar and Berthold.

Coventry then picked up where they'd left off, beating Spurs 2–1 in the opening match of the season. Pleat had made a couple of forays into the transfer market with the money available from the cup run and the sale of Hoddle, but players such as Johnny Metgod and Chris Fairclough, who had both come from Forest, did not kindle any great sparks of inspiration either with their fellow professionals or the fans. The whole season had a trace of 'after the Lord Mayor's Show'.

Yet the players buckled down to their task and played seven games without defeat in a month, which took them to second place in the table. Within a few matches, however, Chris realised there was something physically wrong: he had some twinges across his stomach every time he stretched for the ball. They did not stop him playing, and he particularly enjoyed a 3–1 victory over a much changed Newcastle team in which Gazza was by now well established. He was relieved to be greeted with cheers rather than jeers by the visiting fans and felt that his establishment as an England international had a fair amount to do with that.

He was off with England again for a friendly against West Germany on 9 September, still saying nothing about the pains in his stomach. For his reward, he jarred his heel in an early tackle, being replaced by Hateley at half-time. He was slaughtered by the papers for his performance, but none of the journalists bothered to enquire as to the severity of the injury. By the time he returned to England he could not bear to put his swollen foot on the ground. The medical team looked at it and prescribed an ice pack, but that had no effect and for the next two or three weeks the injury refused to respond to treatment. It was the longest period of inaction he'd experienced in his career and he did not like it.

'He was a nightmare to have at home,' Lorna recalls. 'I was pregnant again, and he seemed to be forever under my feet when he wasn't watching television or moaning.'

It was decided to seek a second opinion. The news was not good. He was prescribed complete rest when an inflammation actually inside the heel was diagnosed. It was while Chris was recuperating that the newspapers really got their teeth into poor David Pleat. The story about his alleged kerb-crawling activities whilst at Luton had already circulated in a fairly low key way back in the summer. That particular fire seemed to have been put out at the smoke stage, but now the headlines were blazing all over again in the *Sun*. It turned Pleat into a bag of nerves, affecting him badly, and all the players as well. They were shocked by the news and upset for their manager, particularly when Arsenal fans cruelly began to wear T-shirts printed up with the *Sun* headline. Neither Pleat nor Tottenham could withstand the bad publicity and he resigned. He left the club without saying any goodbyes. Whether it was out of a sense of embarrassment or a feeling that the board had been less than supportive, who could say?

'Quite frankly, at the time I was so depressed about my own injury that who was actually in charge of the team wasn't really high on my list of priorities,' Chris says.

It wasn't only Spurs' matches he was missing, but also the tail-end of England's campaign to qualify for the European Championships. In October they demolished Turkey 8–0, and although he was delighted that qualification looked certain, it was not comforting to Chris that the national side could get that sort of success without him. In November they again won convincingly against Yugoslavia 4–1, and Chris really began to wonder whether or not he would come into contention for the tournament itself in Germany in the summer.

Irving Scholar took a personal interest in Chris's situation. He had always regarded the player as his signing, rather than that of the manager. Now with Chris sidelined and facing surgery if the injury didn't heal, he sent him off to Monaco to stay with Glenn. Irving himself had lived as a tax exile in the principality for several years and had great faith in its curative powers. He was absolutely right. Chris paddled every day in the warm waters of the Mediterranean and made such a speedy recovery that within a couple of days of his return to England he was able to resume some light training.

At White Hart Lane, rumours were already abounding that

Terry Venables was Scholar's target as the next Tottenham manager, but he was relaxing in the States after his Barcelona stint and had made it clear he was in no hurry to return to an English winter. Trevor Hartley was in charge of the first team for a few games, before being replaced by Doug Livermore with managers-to-be Ossie Ardiles and Ray Clemence assisting with their experience.

The results were not encouraging. It was very frustrating, and without a permanent appointment there was no point in entering the transfer market. The season was threatening to end before it had begun. They tumbled at the second hurdle in the Littlewoods Cup to Aston Villa, and by the time Chris returned in mid-October for one game against Arsenal they were drifting down out of the top six in the table. They lost that one 2–1 and Chris promptly found the injury recurring, so it was back to the treatment table until the match against Liverpool on 28 November.

The Liverpool game was, in fact, Venables' first match in charge. Chris was excited by his arrival, but was at the same time nervous, wondering if he would fit into the new man's plans. Glenn Roeder had always maintained Venables was the best coach in England. Euro '96 may eventually have supported that view, but whether or not the best coach is also the best manager is another question. Richard Gough had departed and Terry was concerned, in his few days in charge before the game, to concentrate on the back four. He always felt that a successful side was built from the defence forward. With the best keeper in the country in Ray Clemence he just had to find a suitable replacement for Gough in front of him. The defensive frailties were demonstrated against an eager Liverpool side, who consolidated their position at the top of the league with a 2–0 win against a Spurs side reduced to ten men after the dismissal of Steve Hodge.

Terry Venables was never one to make changes for the sake of change, but obviously the side needed some kind of pick-me-up. Morale was low. The FA Cup defeat, the loss of Pleat and Gough, the early exit from the Littlewoods Cup, Waddle's injury and, in his absence, Clive Allen's loss of goal-scoring form all combined to ensure that in the early winter of 1987, White Hart Lane was not the happiest place to be.

It was not until 28 December that Chris scored his second goal of the season in a 2–1 win against West Ham, but by then Spurs had fallen as low as thirteenth in the league and could only hope for an FA Cup run to bring some life into their season. Their third position in the league the previous season would normally have brought them a UEFA Cup place, but the ban on English clubs still applied and they were confined to the limits of the domestic scene.

They began their cup campaign brightly enough, with a 4–2 win against Oldham – and with Clive Allen scoring twice and Chris also getting a goal, it was quite like old times. They strung a few results together in the league as well, going four games without defeat. Venables had brought in Terry Fenwick from QPR to bolster the defence, as well as a youngster from Millwall called Neil Ruddock, and despite a 2–0 defeat at Newcastle, they had every reason to face Port Vale in the fourth round of the FA Cup with confidence. The Newcastle defeat was particularly significant. Gascoigne got the goals and both Scholar and Venables decided there and then that he would be their number one target in their efforts to rebuild the side.

'I remember Gazza after the game asking me what it was like

at Spurs,' says Chris, 'and I got the impression even then, despite United winning, that he would soon be on the move.'

With Newcastle, Chris had been used to cup upsets and Port Vale were not without a giant-killing reputation themselves. Yet neither Chris nor his team-mates expected to find themselves 2–0 down before half-time. Although Ruddock pulled one back, Spurs' season was effectively over, unless they found themselves sucked into a relegation battle. A fortnight later, when they drew 0–0 with Oxford in just about the worst match which Chris has ever taken part in, it looked as if that might well be their fate. What was obvious was that nobody, certainly not the new manager, could possibly have realised the size of the task that lay ahead to make Tottenham great again.

chapter 33

In mid-February Chris was relieved to find himself back in the England reckoning for a friendly in Israel, although it was more due to past reputation than current form. However, he was almost the senior member of a weakened squad and was a little disappointed to see the captaincy awarded to Peter Beardsley, rather than being given the chance himself. That was probably the nearest he ever came to leading the national side – another missed opportunity in an international career that had so many disappointments and interruptions.

He played the full ninety minutes in a game which ended goalless – a particularly unimpressive result against a side that had yet to emerge as a serious contestant in world football. Clive Allen also failed to impress, having been given his chance probably a season too late, while Mick Harford was another to win his first cap. Twelve goals scored without Chris in the two previous matches and none with him. It was little wonder that he returned somewhat depressed, although he had enjoyed the sightseeing opportunities in the country. He was filled with a sense of history and wonder as he and the rest of the team stood before the Western Wall of the Temple in Jerusalem, with their heads covered as a mark of respect.

Chris's despondency was not just due to his lack of form on the pitch. In his heart of hearts he knew there was something physically wrong, and having seen the England doctor in Israel, he also saw John Sheridan, the Spurs physio. John, who was to be so influential in the recuperation of Gazza in 1991 and 1992, immediately confirmed Chris's worst fears. He had that bane of a footballer's life, a hernia. He was sent to see a specialist who asked him to undress and then, exploring the area, asked him to cough. When Chris screamed in pain, the doctor told him it was a double hernia that needed an immediate operation. On the following Saturday, Spurs were due to play Manchester United. Stuck in mid-table as they were, it meant little enough to Tottenham in terms of points. For Chris, however, in the knowledge that it would be some time before he would play again, the game took on all the importance of the quest for the Holy Grail. Used to the insanity of his footballing patients, the doctor agreed to let Chris play.

Nobody watching him on 23 February would have realised the pain barrier through which he forced himself. The fans and the media tended to regard him as a soft touch, a player who was comfortable on the ball but was not prepared to go out and battle to get it. Again they were wrong. With Chris it has never been a case of what you see is what you get. He has always been deceptive to watch. Off the ball, he stands around, slouched and looking tired and disinterested. On the ball, he can seem slow and clumsy until he drops his shoulder and suddenly takes on a pace of his own that is made to look deceptive by his sheer awkwardness.

Venables had bought again. This time it was Paul Walsh, who had been out of favour at Liverpool, and he looked very sharp in a creditable 1–1 draw. Chris breathed a sigh of relief when the match was over, and by the following day was in the Princess Grace Hospital in London's West End.

Part of the post-operative treatment for a hernia operation is to get the patient up and about as soon as possible. Having survived the night on pain-killers, Chris was astonished to be woken at eight the following morning and told to get up because the nurses needed to make his bed. He befriended another player, Martin Hinkard from non-league Altrincham, and the pair of them sneaked out for an unauthorised visit to nearby Madame Tussauds. Under normal circumstances they could have got there in a minute or so. As it was, they crawled, half doubled up, for some ten minutes before they arrived. Then, faced with an effigy of Benny Hill, they were suddenly struck by an uncontrollable giggling fit which resulted in them both screaming with pain, to the astonishment of a group of foreign tourists.

After Spurs had beaten Sheffield Wednesday in a league game, Chris and Martin took off in carpet slippers for the local pub. They began a drinking session that had Martin in such fits of laughter that he had to return to the hospital for pain-killers. Chris stayed on to finish his drink, only to hear a voice in his ear saying, 'I thought I'd find you in here.'

He whirled round to see Venables standing there with a broad grin on his face. Although he may have come under fire for the drinking antics of his team, and indeed his ownership of a watering hole in West London, Venables has always been far more in tune with the needs and minds of professional footballers than those on the outside looking in. Instead of blowing his top, he simply ordered a drink himself and sat down with Chris for a friendly chat about his progress. It was not until the beginning of April that he was ready for first-team duty, and he duly came on as a substitute against QPR. The team were already 2–0 down and Chris hardly got a touch before the final whistle blew. But at least he was playing again.

'Chris is quite impossible when he's not fit. I think that's why he's played on so long, when many people thought he'd be in management by his mid-thirties,' Lorna comments.

Incredibly enough, with two games to go before the end of the season, Spurs were still not mathematically certain to avoid being involved in the relegation play-offs. However, they managed a 1–1 draw with Charlton and could relax for the final match against Luton, which they won 2–1.

It had not been the greatest of years, either for the club or for Chris personally. They finished thirteenth, and he finished with just two goals and a degree of uncertainty over his international future. Something drastic was needed to bring new life into the club for the following year – and it came in the shape of a Tottenham bid for Paul Gascoigne.

Some two years before Gazzamania was to sweep the country, he was already regarded as one of the brightest emerging talents in the country. The chief rivals for his signature were Manchester United and Liverpool, but the Merseysiders did not have the ready cash and it therefore became a two-horse race. For a while, it seemed as if United had the edge, but Scholar's friendship with Stan Seymour had not been affected by the sour taste left in the aftermath of the Waddle transfer, and Stan kept his word giving Spurs almost a first option on the player. The option was, of course, meaningless, unless the player himself wanted to sign, and at the time Paul was obsessed with Liverpool. He was almost prepared to wait a year for them to come in for him.

However, Scholar played his master-card in the shape of Chris. Up in the north-east for a weekend, Chris took Gazza out for a drink, the normal motley crew of Gazza acolytes in tow, and did his best to sell Tottenham as a club. Gazza recalls that conversation: 'There was no doubt that my decision to come to Spurs was largely influenced by the fact that Chris was there. I liked Irving and I was impressed by Venners, but I also knew that Chris would make sure I wasn't lonely.'

He was certainly right in that respect, for there were times when he virtually moved in with the Waddles, taking over their home, their freezer (for his freshly caught fish) and their phone. Lorna tried to pack his bags to give him a hint and eventually let Chris know that he had to choose between Paul and her. Then, as now, Paul Gascoigne was not an easy person with whom to share a home.

However, when it came to buying his own place, he created a virtual carbon copy of the Waddle household. He adored them and wanted desperately to live in their image. 'It was odd going to visit Paul. For a long time I felt I'd come into the wrong house, it was so much like my own,' Chris recalls.

Gazza was not yet a serious contender for the full England side, but Chris was relieved to be selected for the second playing of the Rous Cup, this time with Colombia replacing Brazil as the South American contestant.

Bobby Robson clearly wanted to have a better look at him after he had come on as a substitute against Scotland in a 1–0 win, and put him in the starting line-up for the match against the Colombians. He set up England's goal for Gary Lineker and felt generally pleased with his performance, until his lack of match fitness got the better of him and he was replaced by Glenn Hoddle.

There was one more friendly against Switzerland before Robson would name his squad for the European Championships. After the Swiss game, Chris felt unsure of his place. He'd come on at half-time and had done very little. The Swiss had played a sweeper system, which had broken the rhythm of the English side. He found it hard to attack the full-back then, and it was that defensive tactic against which England were to founder in the tournament itself.

There was a strengthening campaign in the media, suggesting that Waddle at his best was a luxury and that he was not at his best. They felt Robson had done better without wingers, and if one wide man should be taken, then it should be Barnes rather than Chris. Robson obviously thought differently, that the real Chris Waddle was not too far away, and both he and Barnes were in the squad.

All the injuries and disruptions, the upheavals and lack of success that had plagued him and his club for the past nine months were put behind him. Something else had been happening in the same period. Something good. Something far more important to him than anything that might occur on the football field. Towards the end of May, just before he departed with the squad for Germany, his first child, Brooke, was born. Chris kissed Lorna and his beautiful baby daughter, promising them that when he returned it would be with a medal. It was a promise he was not destined to keep.

chapter 34

As the squad assembled at High Wycombe, it was almost enough just to be with the England team again. He felt a moment of undisguised national pride as he was given his England blazer before going off to a reception to celebrate the 125th anniversary of the Football Association.

He was familiar with most of the players by now, for Robson had relied on experience for the party. Once again the players quickly felt as if they were part of a family, with Bobby Robson as an avuncular patriarch.

Robson had arranged a few friendlies, just to keep them sharp, and they had a leisurely 7–0 win against Aylesbury. However, nobody had told the local side that it was a friendly and Chris, Trevor Steven, Mark Hateley and Gary Lineker all picked up injuries of varying degrees of severity. As Chris limped off after a knock on the top of his thigh, all he could think was, 'Oh no, not again.'

Fortunately, it was something he was able to shrug off in a matter of hours and, together with the rest of the party, he arrived more or less in one piece at their headquarters hotel in Germany. Robson arranged one last friendly against a local

German non-league side. Once more it turned out to be not particularly friendly, with both Lineker and Steven injured again, together with Mark Wright and Gary Stevens. In fact, Trevor Steven was so badly hurt that he could not start the first match. If there had been any doubt in Robson's mind as to whether or not he should start with Chris or the more combative Steven, then he was rescued from making any such decision.

For Chris, the first game of the tournament was particularly significant, as their opponents, the Republic of Ireland, were managed by an old friend – or adversary, depending upon how you looked at it – Jack Charlton. Clearly Charlton bore no grudges, specifically picking out Chris before the match to wish him luck and shake his hand. It was virtually the first time they had spoken since they had met at the tribunal and obviously Charlton had a selective memory as far as the past was concerned. The friendly encounter added strength to Chris's theory that Jack did not go out deliberately to upset people. He probably didn't even realise he was doing it. It was just his way, and he was oblivious to its effect on other more sensitive souls.

There was no doubting that Charlton's appointment as the Irish team manager had been an enormous success, and with hindsight it was apparent that he was better suited to managing a national team than a league team. He had the flexibility, as far as time was concerned, and he did not have to work within the constraints of a wage structure or the transfer market. Perhaps his time in charge of a club side was best summed up by an episode at Newcastle. A car roared into the training ground one day, with the driver yelling from the window, 'Trout in the Tweed.' Charlton just had time to shout at Willie McFaul to take over the training and he'd see him in a couple of days – and he was off.

Perhaps he brought that same relaxed style to the Irish camp, because against England they looked the better side and deservedly won by the single goal. As they had looked the easiest opposition in a group that contained Holland and Russia, it was clearly going to be an uphill struggle to get to the next round.

Despite the defeat, morale was high in the England camp. They moved on to the palatial Guthohne Hotel near Düsseldorf, where anyone seeing them relax by the pool would have thought they had not a care in the world. Maybe they were too relaxed, maybe Robson's ability to motivate when it really mattered had not fully matured, or maybe they were all just very good actors. Kenny Sansom, who had apparently missed his vocation on the stage, kept the lads in fits of laughter with his impressions of Prince Charles, Norman Wisdom, Ronald Reagan, Harold Steptoe and, more surprisingly, Cary Grant.

When it came to the announcement of the side to face Holland in the next match, however, Chris found it very hard to smile. Robson had decided on a different formation, with Hoddle replacing Neil Webb and Trevor Steven, now restored to fitness, taking over from Chris. There was nothing Chris could do but swallow his disappointment, try to remind himself that this was a team game, and hope England would do well enough for him to have a chance to make an impact on the tournament in its later stages.

The then Minister for Sport, the unpopular Colin Moynihan, who had virtually talked Europe into a continuing ban on English fans, still had nothing good to say about the travelling support when he returned from a whirlwind trip to the tournament. There was no doubt that he knew little or nothing about our national sport, and probably set back the cause of English clubs' readmission to European competition by a year or so.

As it was some 10,000 travelling fans gave their team magnificent support in the stadium at Düsseldorf. They were outnumbered some three to one by the Dutch supporters, who seemed intent on stirring up trouble with their English counterparts, but even when England unluckily fell behind to a Marco Van Basten goal just before half-time, their voices did not flag, and when Bryan Robson deservedly equalised nine minutes into the second half, it really looked as if England were going to pull it off. With twenty minutes to go, Trevor Steven picked up a knee injury and Chris got his chance. 'It took about three minutes from my coming on for the world to go pear-shaped. We were going all out for a win, so I suppose there was always going to be a chance that we'd be caught on the break and we were.'

The Dutch suddenly turned their game up a notch or two, and once Van Basten had scored twice to complete his hat-trick, all that was left was for the manager to reach for his calculator to see what were the mathematical options. There weren't many. Ireland would have to beat Russia, as would England, and then the Irish would have to hold the Dutch to a draw.

For a brief moment, to the team watching the Ireland–Russia match over dinner in their hotel, the impossible seemed possible when Whelan put the Irish ahead. But they tired and the Russians grabbed an equaliser. Whatever result the English achieved against the Soviets, they would be coming home. Football itself would not be coming home for another eight years until, with Chris in the commentary box rather than on the field, England would do their home supporters proud.

The academic third match in the group was supposed to

have been played for pride at the time, but not so you would notice. Chris was not even named as substitute and in an out-of-character piece of poor man-management, Bobby Robson did not bother to explain his decision. Now, he says:

'I thought Chris would have appreciated the fact that he wasn't one hundred per cent fit. He'd had a hernia operation and even he would admit that he'd lost a yard of pace because of that. Yet as early as 1988, assuming I was still to be the England manager, I had him in my plans for the World Cup.'

As it was, this last game was a good one to miss. The USSR won 3–1 and went on to the final, where they were beaten by the Dutch. The fact that the final was contested by two teams who had beaten England was small consolation – certainly as far as the media were concerned – but perhaps Bobby Robson saw a small hint of light at the end of the tunnel that kept him in his job, rather than surrendering to the newspaper demands for his resignation.

Chris was just pleased to be going home. His contribution to the tournament had been only 110 minutes of actual playing time, very few of which had been inspirational. Still, at least he'd done better than Viv Anderson and Peter Reid, who'd gone all that way without getting a kick. He'd hardly been able to spend any time with his new daughter and he wanted a complete break from football. It was already past the middle of June and Spurs wanted him to report for pre-season training the following month. He had an awful feeling that his England career had come to a premature end, but he was almost too tired to care.

chapter 35

Probably one the greatest misjudgements of Chris Waddle's career was to appoint Dennis Roach as his agent before the start of the 1988–89 season. It was a relationship that was to last less than a year, ending in tears, recriminations and acrimony. Yet, when the appointment was made, it seemed the right thing to do. Roach had successfully represented Glenn Hoddle for many years, had master-minded his move to Monaco and was generally regarded throughout the footballing world as a man who made deals happen, not just on a domestic basis but on the international scene as well.

Alastair Garvie reluctantly accepted the financial compensation offered by Roach and his company, PRO. He didn't know then that he would also shortly lose his other star, Paul Gascoigne, after he had joined Tottenham and put the distance between London and Newcastle between him and Garvie. The arrangement was meant to be that Roach would deal with promotional matters, with Stein and Lazarus continuing as Chris's professional advisers, working hand in hand with the agent. That was not how it transpired, however, as Roach virtually ignored the old guard, seeking to control all Chris's affairs himself – both on and off the pitch.

Chris still had two years to go on his contract at Spurs, but Irving Scholar was determined at the time that he should see out the rest of his playing career in that particular corner of north London. Almost as soon as the season began, he opened negotiations for a new extended seven-year contract. It was almost unheard of for there to be a contract of such a lengthy period and the sort of figures being discussed were commensurate with Chris giving such a commitment. That is not to suggest that the club were also not taking a risk, for Chris's advisers ensured at the same time that if anything should happen to Chris, then the club would have to honour the contract. Nobody back in 1988 could have known that Chris would still be playing in 1997, when Scholar was to re-emerge in his life.

In fact, the negotiations dragged on over the whole season, with Roach insisting on his own involvement in the latter stages, which did not particularly please Scholar at the time. However, there is no footballing contract in the world that does not have its price to be terminated, whatever any club, manager or chairman might say to the contrary.

All the ingredients were present for a major upheaval in Chris's life. To say the Tottenham season started moderately would have been an understatement. After five matches they had won but once, against Middlesbrough, and drawn three times. The local wits were asking what was the difference between Spurs and the Star of David – the answer being none as they both had six points. A point against Charlton on 8 October stopped that particular wise-crack, but by 5 November, after ten games, there were still no fireworks as they lost to Derby and slipped to twentieth place in the league.

'If we get relegated, I'm off,' Gazza tried to say to Chris – only it came out as, 'If I stay here more than a season, I'm off.' He was only half-joking, and never tired of reminding Chris that he was only at White Hart Lane because Chris had told him what a great club it was.

The real short straw that Chris drew was having to room with Gazza. On the first occasion, they were staying at a hotel in Mill Hill. Before retiring to bed, Gascoigne turned on every light in the room and the adjoining bathroom, as well as putting on the television. Chris's protests fell on deaf ears and eventually, somehow or other, he got to sleep. Chris must have been groaning in his sleep, but Gazza clearly wasn't convinced the noise was coming from his room-mate. 'Are you awake?' he asked Chris and, receiving no reply, assumed he wasn't. There was more groaning and again Paul thought the source was other than Waddle. Chris was woken by a draught of cold air. There was Paul standing at an open window, stark naked, looking down two floors and asking timidly in a frightened voice, 'Is anybody there?' Chris struggled back to sleep, only to wake three hours later to see Paul lying on his bed, sucking his thumb and sleeping the deep sleep of an infant.

The two Geordies buckled down to their task. Having been with a club in the doldrums before, they knew that just one or two results would see them out of it. They weren't a bad side on paper, with the likes of Terry Fenwick, Gary Mabbutt, Paul Walsh, Paul Allen and Vinny Samways. In addition, Venables had bought the aggressive Paul Stewart from Manchester City, but his goalscoring record with them of 26 goals in 51 appearances seemed as poor a joke as his million-pound price tag when he failed to score in his first five appearances for Spurs. Looking back at the start of that season and the affection with which

■ Chris Waddle

Tottenham fans came to regard Chris and the two new Pauls, Gascoigne and Stewart, it is hard to believe the abuse that those two most recent imports were receiving – not just from the terraces but also the cigar-smoke filled stands. The clatter of seats twenty minutes from the end of yet another home defeat told its own story.

During this unfortunate run, Chris was actually the club's top scorer (with four goals) after Clive Allen's departure to Bordeaux, and although it wasn't immediately obvious to the fans, he knew that he was benefiting from the mid-field service being provided by Gascoigne.

'I loved playing with Waddler,' Gazza recalls. 'Sometimes, I didn't know what I was going to do next, but somehow or other he always managed to read my game.'

Chris's worst fears concerning his England future seemed justified when he was omitted from the team to play Denmark on 14 September. The first qualifier against Sweden for the 1990 World Cup was little over a month away, and he was desperate to be a part of it. A narrow Littlewoods Cup victory for Spurs against lowly Notts County was little enough compensation, although it was with some relief that he found himself back in favour for the Swedish match.

Bobby Robson persevered with his European failures, but they failed to rise to the occasion and both Chris and John Barnes were the subject of the Wembley boo-boys in a goalless draw. England were favourites to top a group that contained Poland and Albania in addition to their first opponents, and neither the result, nor the method with which it was obtained, augured well for the rest of their campaign.

Meanwhile, Tottenham's domestic season was beginning to

turn around. They went through the rest of November without defeat and progressed further in the Littlewoods Cup against Blackburn. In the middle of that run, Chris went with the England party to Saudi Arabia for what, with hindsight, was virtually the nadir of Robson's managerial career. It was, admittedly, a weakened England team: the inexperienced Dave Seaman in goal, Mel Sterland, Brian Marwood, David Rocastle, even the young Gazza coming on as a substitute for Chris himself after eighty minutes.

'It felt a bit odd coming on for my mate, but it was the Boss's decision and obviously I was happy to be getting another cap. The press made a lot of it, my career beginning at the expense of Chris, but it didn't seem that way to me at the time,' Gazza says.

There could be no excuses for the result, a 1–1 draw, although the pitch was poor and the heat was taxing. Nobody was looking forward to the media reception back home, as the travelling press corps, without their usual injections of alcohol, had been scathing enough on the spot. The headlines were fairly predictable. 'For the sake of Allah, go now,' was one of the kindest. Once again, Robson had shown some loyalty to Chris; once again he had been unimpressive; once again the international jobs of both were on the line.

chapter 36

As 1988 came to an end, Chris was having second thoughts about a long-term commitment to Tottenham. He had felt after the Littlewoods Cup semi-final defeat against Arsenal back in 1987 that perhaps he was hurting more than most of the other players. Perhaps it was because he came from the north-east, a deprived area in footballing terms as well as in the economic sense. Everything up there was a battle. There was a feeling deep within Chris that in the south it all came too easy, that nobody, apart from himself, cared quite enough.

There seemed to be a lack of steel in the Tottenham side as they bowed out to Southampton in the fourth round of the Littlewoods Cup and then, more embarrassingly, lost 1–0 in the third round of the FA Cup to Bradford City, then of the old Second Division. By mid-January the season seemed to have little more to offer. Scholar was already juggling with the finances to do his best to keep the fans' interest alive. He bought Erik Thorstvedt – Erik the Viking, as he came to be known – from Gothenburg to replace the unhappy and confidence-shattered Bobby Mimms, and added the exciting Nayim from Barcelona on a loan basis, with an option to make the transfer permanent. But to no avail. Crowds often dipped below the twenty thousand mark, which added to the financial problems that were bubbling under the surface. Towards the end of February, results were still inconsistent. If another club had come in with a serious offer for Chris Waddle in the cold winter of 1988, they would not have had to work too hard to secure his signature.

Then suddenly things started to turn around. It is hard to put a finger on the exact moment, although stunning performances with a goal each from Chris and Gazza in a 2–1 win over Norwich on 21 February may well have been a watershed. Spurs strung together a seven-match unbeaten run in which eleven goals were scored – five by Chris and two by Gascoigne.

Almost imperceptibly, Spurs had moved into the top half of the table, so that a home match against Liverpool at the end of March took on new significance. Once again the Merseysiders ran out winners, although Spurs went on to lose just once more in their next seven matches to finish a surprising and encouraging sixth. Chris ended up as top scorer for his club for the first (and what would in fact be the only) time in his career and, despite the interruptions and claims of international duty, he was also ever-present throughout all competitions.

On the international front, although he had been omitted from a friendly match against Greece, with Robson preferring Rocastle and Barnes, Chris was soon back in favour in his yo-yo England career. He travelled to Albania for a World Cup qualifier and actually started the match, although with the game won at 2–0 he was taken off for Beardsley. 'Albania is just about the worst place I have ever visited in my life. It almost made my previous trips to Eastern Europe seem luxurious. I was wearing my hair long in those days and I was advised to get it cut short just to be allowed into the country.'

When Albania visited Wembley on 26 April, just before the end of the season, England finally turned in a performance to please the fans, winning 5–0. Chris was a constant thorn in the side of the Albanian defence, enjoying the freer role he had been given which led to him scoring the fourth goal of the night. Things were looking a lot brighter for England's chances of qualification.

May brought the Rous Cup, yet again, with Chile added to the domestic ranks of England and Scotland. 'I was feeling that I was beginning to be on top of my game in an England shirt. The crowd were on my side, not against me.'

It was strange that so many flair players experienced a constant battle with the hard-core England supporters in the seventies and eighties. Waddle, Hoddle and Barnes were all men who could ignite a game with one incisive pass, one mesmeric run, one brilliant goal, yet all were put under pressure by their own fans, until at times they began to despair of themselves.

Chris and England played well in a 0–0 draw with Chile and then he was outstanding yet again in a 2–0 victory against Scotland. He scored the first goal and had the Scottish fans holding their breath every time he got the ball. Winning the Rous Cup was not winning the World Cup, but it was promising.

With both England and Tottenham, Chris had every reason to look forward to the next campaign with some expectation of success. Irving Scholar had confided in him that he was trying to bring Gary Lineker to White Hart Lane. The thought of Lineker, Waddle and Gascoigne in the white shirts of Tottenham, as well as the white shirts of England, was a mouth-watering prospect.

What Scholar didn't tell Chris, however, was that there was a serious financial crisis brewing at Spurs, as well as a personality rift between himself and fellow-director Paul Bobroff. As it was to prove in the long run, the purchase of Lineker, the imminent sale of Waddle and the lack of money were to mean that not only Chris would depart from Tottenham but that Irving Scholar would not be too far behind.

Lineker himself had seen playing in the same team as Chris as an absolute plus in his decision to join the London side. 'It was some two to three weeks after I'd signed that the rumours began about Chris's imminent departure. I was more than disappointed. I knew him to be a great crosser of the ball as well as having the ability to read my runs. When I heard he was not going to be there for me, all I could think was, what a choker. There goes fifteen goals a season.'

There was every reason to be optimistic about the future as Chris took off for his holidays in Cyprus with Lorna and Brooke, in blissful ignorance of these commercial issues. Yet while he was away, a man named Bernard Tapie was to enter his life and change it forever.

chapter 37

By July 1989, Chris Waddle had become the most expensive British footballer in the history of the game and was preparing to pull on the blue and white shirt of Olympique de Marseille for the first time. When it happened, it happened with surprising speed and took the whole of the footballing world by surprise.

It was just before the press conference to announce the signing of Gary Lineker that Irving Scholar received a telephone call from a French agent called Barin. Scholar had dealt with the man before, when Clive Allen had moved to Bordeaux. Now Barin told the Tottenham chairman that he represented a foreign club who wanted to buy one of Scholar's players. The player in question was Chris Waddle. Scholar's immediate reaction was to say that he simply wasn't for sale. Barin was persistent, telling Scholar that his client would pay two and a half million pounds. Again the answer was no, but Barin must have thought Scholar was taking up a negotiating position and upped the ante to three million. There was a sharp intake of breath, but still Scholar refused, although Barin was encouraged enough to tell him he was representing Olympique de Marseille in France.

The chairman felt obliged to tell the manager who, to his

surprise, did not dismiss the idea out of hand. According to Scholar in his own book, *Behind Closed Doors*, Venables said, 'You know, he's getting on, isn't he? He's not a spring chicken any longer.'

Chris was twenty-eight at the time, but perhaps the amount of the offer, and the fresh players Venables thought he could bring to the club, affected his judgement. Certainly by then, if it had been put to the vote amongst the Spurs fans, they would have insisted on his retention, whatever the offer. If the best were to be got from Gascoigne, then Waddle would have to be around for a while. Scholar certainly subscribed to that view, but was persuaded by Venables at least to meet with the representatives of the French club.

Bernard Tapie was then – and although a little battered, is still – a larger-than-life figure. He had set himself two aims in life: one to be responsible single-handedly for the rebuilding of Marseille both as a city and a football club, and the other to be President of France. It could be argued that he succeeded in the former, but the latter, after criminal convictions and further accusations, would seem to be beyond his grasp. However, in France nothing is impossible.

At a meeting at the Carlton Tower Hotel, Venables and Scholar decided to go for broke. Every player has his price. Ruud Gullit had just broken the world record transfer figure with a move to AC Milan for £5.5 million. The two Tottenham representatives would ask £5 million for Chris alone and also see if Tapie would buy Paul Walsh, whom Venables was anxious to unload.

At first Tapie offered £5 million for both the players. Scholar could not believe it. But then somebody appeared to have dissuaded the Frenchman away from Walsh and he countered with an offer of £4 million for Waddle alone. Considering Spurs had paid less than £600,000 for him, it represented an astonishing profit. Scholar, however, was not finished yet.

On the Sunday afternoon following the meeting with Tapie, somebody finally got round to finding out what the player thought about it all. Chris was not due to return from Cyprus until the following day, but Scholar invited Mel Stein up to his flat in Regents Park. He briefly outlined the situation to Stein and seemed, quite fairly, to say that the offer was so huge that he simply could not refrain from giving the player the choice. Adding that he hoped Chris would say no, he did not disclose that the manager, at least, seemed to regard the situation as a done deal with money in the bank.

There was one other condition attached. Scholar said that the French people concerned would not deal with Dennis Roach, and that if the deal were to proceed, it would have to be negotiated as far as the player was concerned by his professional advisers. As it transpired that was not correct, but Stein was not to know that.

Lazarus and Stein made arrangements to have Chris call them as soon as he landed at the airport. He took the news extraordinarily calmly and said he would have to discuss it with Lorna. The following day he let Stein know that if the offer really was on the table, and an appropriate package could be obtained, then they had decided to go for it. Stein told Scholar, who expressed some surprise and a little disappointment before advising Stein that the deal was by no means finalised and there could be no direct meeting between Chris and his potential new employers until he had concluded his bargaining with Tapie.

There was then a deathly silence for some two weeks, by which time Chris and his advisers all assumed the deal was off. In fact, Scholar had utilised the time to push the price up once again, this time to £4.25 million.

The way now seemed clear for Chris to make his move abroad.

However, Roach had also returned from holiday and, discovering what was afoot, was most unhappy to learn that the Tottenham chairman had told Stein he was not to be involved. Dennis Roach was not a man to take defeat lightly and immediately contacted Stein, asking bluntly what was going on with Chris Waddle. Stein told him what he knew and also told him that his information was that Roach's involvement could prejudice the deal. Roach was not impressed. He appointed his own lawyer and accountant to advise on the move and insisted on full control.

Not really understanding what was happening, Chris went happily off to Wimbledon to watch the tennis, taking a mobile phone with him. Roach called him to say the deal was back on and that it would be best if he got out of the limelight for a while. Roach secreted Chris in one of his houses in Bournemouth, away from the media as well as his long-serving advisers. If Chris Waddle were to move to France, then Dennis Roach seemed intent on ensuring that it would be in accordance with his plans.

There was one exception to the media blackout. Whilst half of Fleet Street's finest were hunting Waddle, the *Sun* scooped them all with an exclusive interview and pictures – organised by Roach's associate, Dave Shapland, who happened to be a former sports editor of that very paper.

Chris Waddle is very much his own man and has a loyal streak that would put many of the younger players coming into the game today to shame. Although he was prepared to be manipulated up to a point, he eventually told Roach that he was not prepared to sign anything unless and until Stein and Lazarus had approved the transaction. He didn't know what to think about what was going on. 'I was very confused. Dennis had negotiated the moves for both Glenn Hoddle and Mark Hateley to Europe and I trusted him, not only because of his experience, but because Glenn trusted him as well.'

So it was that, on the night of 13 July 1989, Stein was rudely awakened at midnight by a call from France. To his astonishment, it was Roach's associate, John Barr, on the line telling him of terms he had 'agreed' with Marseille, while Chris had been whisked away to Guernsey in the Channel Islands with Roach's lawyer.

Barr agreed to fax the terms to Stein in the morning, but added that Roach and he had got Marseille to push out the boat as far as they would and there was no question of further negotiation. Stein and Lazarus duly discussed the deal and spoke to Chris, who asked them to take the advice of a French tax lawyer on certain aspects. They immediately flew to Paris to try to resolve matters.

Meanwhile Paul Bobroff, who was later to fall out with Scholar in a sensational and public manner, was in charge at Spurs whilst Scholar was on holiday. He could not understand why there was any delay and, without any of the personal feelings that Scholar might have shown in respect to the move, simply wanted the money and wanted it as quickly as possible. It is hard to fathom how he achieved that end, but there is no doubt that Spurs were paid while Chris was still in Guernsey and before he had actually signed on the dotted line for Marseille.

In Paris, certain contractual problems had arisen. Roach's associates were told that Chris could not leave Guernsey for France until they had been resolved. Tapie, meanwhile, on his yacht on the Mediterranean, had spent £4.5 million and still had no player. The message he gave to Chris's advisers was short and to the point: he was not interested in further negotiation; the deal he had struck with Roach and Barr was very generous. Unless Waddle was in Marseille for training the following day he, Tapie, would call a press conference and would tell the people of Marseille, the people of France, and whoever else might be interested in listening, that Waddle's absence was entirely due to the fault of an English solicitor and accountant. It was Stein and Lazarus's first exposure to the unusual business methods of Bernard Tapie, but it would certainly not be their last.

Without matters being totally resolved to the satisfaction of his advisers, Chris duly arrived in France, with Lorna due to follow on after returning to London to pack up the house. If Tottenham had seemed like a different country from Newcastle, then this new world appeared totally alien. He spoke not a word of the language and, although he'd been promised lessons, they were for the future – and right now he had to become a part of the team.

The stadium in which they trained, empty of fans, seemed run down and even somewhat tacky compared to White Hart Lane. The treatment room was straight out of the ark consisting of a bed and a sink, and Chris felt a stomach-tumbling sensation that perhaps this had all been a terrible mistake.

Yet, Olympique de Marseille, or OM as they were called by

their fans, were a big club, despite their ramshackle surroundings. They had been brought back from near bankruptcy by Tapie and had just won the French title. Instead of Littlewoods Cup games against the likes of Notts County, Chris could now look forward to the European Cup and the challenge of facing the best that Europe had to offer. But it was all so different, and in those few early days without Lorna and Brooke, it was once again so lonely.

Jean-Pierre Papin, who spoke the best English in the side, was delegated to look after Chris. Papin, notable for treating the roads along the sea-front as if they were Le Mans, appeared unable to drive anywhere at less than 100 mph. He had a little pet poodle which he took everywhere, and on at least one occasion the poor dog was so terrified by his master's driving that he messed himself. Unfortunately he was sitting on Chris's lap at the time.

The first training session was odd. There was no question of road running or fitness training; everything was done with the ball. The coach, Gerard Gili, made no allowances for Chris. 'The thing that hit me on that first day was the heat. I'd never experienced anything like it, even in the Middle East or the States.'

He was thrown into the team for a league match at Lyons. With Marseille 2–0 up at half-time Chris was brought on for the second half and OM ran out 4–1 winners. Chris played up front with Papin, who limped off ten minutes from the end with a pulled hamstring. As he left the field, he tied the captain's arm-band on to Chris's sleeve. Chris thought he'd done well, even though he had no idea what his team-mates were saying to him. At the end of the match he trotted off to the changing-room, showered and was ready to leave. Papin told him he was expected to be back on the pitch to warm down – as opposed to warming up. Chris laughed, thinking it was a joke, all part of the initiation of the new boy, and left to get on the coach. The following day he received a dressing-down, again which he only half understood, but the bits that got through to him clearly demonstrated that warming down was a vital part of the game as far as Gili was concerned.

The coach seemed generally concerned about Chris's level of fitness. English clubs tend to train for a couple of hours in the morning, four days a week, and that's it. On the Continent, it's mornings and afternoons, every day of the week, with the side being assembled to stay in a hotel the night before a match whether it's home or away. It's a far more dedicated, far more professional approach.

Gili had Chris running in the sun on the pitch, and with the sweat streaming down the player's face, Gili looked at him and said two words in English: 'Not fit.' He got him running again until Chris was close to collapse. 'I can't run in the sun like this,' Chris begged. But there was no mercy.

There was, in fact, little or no time to adjust. When Lorna arrived, they spent a few days with the Papins, and then moved into a squalid hotel called the Amadeus. It was an enormous change from the palatial Papin residence with its swimming pool. That pool and the Papin pet dogs had made Lorna nervous for the safety of Brooke, but now that they were living in one room and without a car, Lorna felt a virtual prisoner. The hotel had only a small restaurant at the side which did not even serve breakfast, and its total absence of laundry facilities was a nightmare for a mother with a small child, as were the incessant hordes of mosquitoes.

Fortunately Lorna found a friend in the shape of the receptionist, Valerie, who helped her through the worst of things by smuggling her into the hotel's own laundry room whenever she was on night duty. Valerie also explained that the hotel had a 'certain reputation', which explained the number of men and women booking in for an hour or two in the afternoons, and together they were able to laugh off a situation that was otherwise depressing. Lorna, herself, was propositioned on several occasions, which led to Chris pressurising the club into helping to find them their promised accommodation. Valerie also taught Lorna French in exchange for English lessons. The club provided tuition on a more formal basis. In his first lesson, Chris listened and nodded, even managing to remember a word or two, but the second was far more intense. As Chris himself put it, '*Quelle catastrophe!*'

The second lesson was also his last. If he was to learn the language, which indeed he was, then he would learn it the hard way, by necessity. If he went into a shop wanting to buy something, he was simply going to have to make himself understood. In fact, by the time he left, he was able to undertake a radio commentary in colloquial French. He had no idea of grammar or how to spell, but as long as he could make himself understood, it didn't matter.

chapter 38

One of the factors that had made him hesitate a little before agreeing to a move abroad was whether or not it might affect his England place. He had not had a large part to play in a World Cup qualifier against Poland in early June which England had won 3–0 and it seemed to him that no sooner did he feel settled in the side either tactics or injury undermined his position. He was therefore delighted to be picked to play against Sweden in Stockholm on 6 September, and with the first round of the European Cup a week later, it looked like being a busy and exciting month.

A goalless draw for England in Stockholm provided little entertainment for the fans, but was a satisfactory result, as was a 3–0 win against Brondby in the home leg of the first round of the European Cup. Chris was astonished when Bernard Tapie came into the dressing-room before the match and gave a team talk. It was totally in French, and every so often he would look at Chris, who was virtually nodding off, and give a big smile. Tapie was, Chris discovered later, holding him up as an example the rest of the team should follow. When you were in favour with Tapie, you could do no wrong. Once you had blotted your copybook, you would be shown the door so fast that your feet would not touch the ground.

There was no denying the man's charisma. Although he was very much a ladies' man (and, indeed, was voted the man most French women would like to sleep with), he could also win over men with equal ease.

What did become apparent early on was that Gerard Gili was a mere puppet. The man really in charge of the team was Tapie. Previously a popular goalkeeper at the club, Gili had been promoted from youth team coach when Tapie took over. However, he seemed to be in permanent fear for his job, a fear that was justified when, after a few unconvincing performances early in the season, he was sacked. Gili was to have the last laugh when, after Tapie's fall from grace and Marseille's demotion for alleged match-rigging, he was restored to his position and guided the club back from obscurity to the First Division.

The stadium filled with Marseille's fans was an awe-inspiring sight. They would stamp their feet until the whole stand threatened to collapse, and the guttural chant of 'Allez OM' was almost worth a goal start. Indeed, when the tragedy occurred at Bastia in a European Cup match a couple of years later, it was the noise and enthusiasm of the OM fans that contributed to the collapse of the temporary stand, with all the resulting casualties. That is not to suggest that there was anything violent about the supporters. They were every bit as fanatical and devoted as the Geordies, and could be every bit as fickle as the Spurs devotees.

Their vocal support, when they were roused by a goal or a piece of Waddle trickery, was something else, matching anything Chris has heard anywhere in the world. 'La Marseillaise' was the stirring song that had begun life in the eighteenth century and been brought to the area by guards from Montpellier. Once there, it became the revolutionary anthem and would reverberate around the terraces as if the people were rising once again.

Tapie's appointed replacement for Gili was the Belgian, Raymond Goethals, who went on to manage the national side. He was a little more of his own man than Gili, but still had to endure Tapie sitting alongside him on the bench at matches, telling him who should be substituted. Anybody who has ever sat with Tapie soon learns not to sit at his side, as his favoured method of communication is a jab in the ribs with his elbow. It was Chris who first noticed that, with his black swept-back hair, Goethals had more than a passing resemblance to a certain rock star. 'You know, if Elvis were alive today, then he'd look just like the Boss,' he said one day – and from then on the manager was referred to by the players as Elvis.

His appointment in no way kept Tapie out of the dressing-room. He would come in before a match and, apart from his lengthy tactical talks, he would also offer all sorts of financial bonuses if the team got a result – particularly when it came to European matches, local derbies against the likes of Nice, or vital championship matches against their principal rivals, Bordeaux.

That first season with Marseille brought many bonuses as the team progressed in Europe. For a while, though, it seemed that Chris's stay there might be dramatically brief. The club kept changing his car, so that he found himself driving a different vehicle every week, sometimes being left without transport for days on end. They should have been able to move into their new house in Aix-en-Provence by the beginning of September, but delays with the infamous French builders meant the property was not ready until the end of October. The hotel was becoming so intolerable that Chris even rang Mel Stein to see if Spurs might be prepared to buy him back for a million pounds less than they'd received for him. Just before the house was finally ready, they both went home to Newcastle and when it was time to return, Lorna didn't want to go. Chris had all the distractions of being involved with the team, but she felt totally isolated. Although Chris told her to stay behind, she was sensible enough to realise that it could mean the end of their marriage, so she plucked up courage and got on the plane, determined to try and make a go of it.

The turning point was moving into their own home, a beautiful villa overlooking the sea, sufficiently secluded to keep the fans and the media at bay. On the day they moved in, the couple decided that this was where it all started and that they would erase the nightmare of the previous four months from their minds. The villa had its own swimming pool and Chris and Lorna liked nothing better than to sit there, having a quiet drink, watching the sunset and musing silently on how far they had come from Gateshead. It seemed too perfect to last.

Just as he had done at Newcastle and Tottenham, Chris tended to pick his friends from outside rather than inside football. The Papins were having marital problems, which made it difficult to socialise with them as a couple, and language was still a problem with the rest of the team.

There was a constant stream of visitors from England, and down the hill in the town there was a bar, the Café de Paris, run by two young Armenian brothers, David and Marcel. The boys essentially worked for their parents, who owned the place and of whom they stood in awe and fear. As Chris walked past one day when the café was being refurbished, the boys shyly asked the Englishman if he'd attend the opening as a star guest. The relationship developed from there, and Chris found that he could sit there in the evening, enjoying a drink without being disturbed by journalists or fans. Lorna certainly feels that the French journalists were less intrusive than their English counterparts, although that was probably due in no small measure to the much stricter laws of privacy that exist in France. The fans were worse. Chris would find himself followed around a supermarket by people wanting to see what he was buying.

It was not surprising that the brothers became fiercely protective of their tame Englishman and, long after they returned to England, Chris and Lorna continued to be regarded as family by the Armenians.

Bobby Robson had not forgotten Chris, even though he was away from the English legaue. On 11 October 1989, England visited Poland for the last match of their World Cup qualifiers, drew 0–0, and could look forward to a whole sequence of friendlies before the real business began in Italy the following June. Again Chris played the whole ninety minutes without imposing himself on the game, and once again the doubts crept into his mind as to whether or not he would figure in Robson's final plans.

It was while he was on England duty in Poland that events arose, leading to a sudden and dramatic parting of the ways with Roach and his company. Purely by chance, it was discovered that Roach had failed to disclose a fairly vital financial element of the transaction he had negotiated, and the relationship was immediately terminated. It was the last time Chris had anything to do with agents. From then on, he would rely on his lawyer and his accountant.

By November, it began to come together for both player and team. There was a goalless draw with Italy at Wembley, a match that Bobby Robson selects as Chris's best England performance. 'It's a hard choice, because he played so well in so many games, but that one sticks out simply because he turned a player of Maldini's talent and experience inside out until he didn't know whether he was coming or going. It was no surprise when he was made Man of the Match.'

There followed in December a 2–1 victory over Yugoslavia and then in March, probably the most pleasing of all, a 1–0 defeat of Brazil. That made five consecutive matches without defeat, and Chris appearing for ninety minutes in all of them.

There was similar progress at club level in the European Cup, with Marseille beating the likes of AEK Athens and then CSKA Sofia in the quarter-finals. In the second leg at home, Chris and Papin combined brilliantly, both scoring in a 3–1 victory, and the crowd were really beginning to take him to their hearts. The game after the move into his new home had been another bench-mark in his career; there had been a fair amount of criticism of his performances in the French press, but in that match he scored a magnificent individual goal in a 2–1 victory. He beat the off-side trap, brought the ball down, flicked it on and then back-heeled into the net with cool arrogance. T-shirts and banners began to proliferate around the ground, Union Jacks were waved, thousands of kids were seen on the street with a Chris Waddle hair-style; and out of the Waddlemania that swept through the city of Marseille came a new name for Chris, *Le Magicien* – The Magician.

chapter 39

If his domestic life seemed perfect, then getting to the semi-finals of the European Cup at his first attempt had a dream-like quality. It was only fitting that the opponents should be Benfica, with the second leg to be played in their magnificent Stadium of Light. Marseille took a narrow 2–1 lead into the match, having scored twice in the first half after Benfica had taken a surprise tenth-minute lead. However, Chris felt they should have won by half a dozen, and that game probably signalled the end of Francescoli's time with the club as he missed a hat-trick of sitters.

It was the away goal snatched by the Portuguese side that was always going to be important, and although the scores finished level, with Marseille losing the second leg by the only goal, they went out of the tournament on the away goals rule. The Benfica goal, scored just six minutes from time, was controversial to say the least. Everybody in the ground, except the referee and linesman, saw it punched into the net in Maradona fashion. Tapie went crazy, raging against the referee, suggesting there was some European conspiracy aimed only at his club. It was all the harder to swallow because he would have come up against arch-rival media tycoon Berlusconi's AC Milan in the final, which the Italians duly won 1–0.

Chris took the defeat more quietly, although it seemed to him in that numbing moment that in cup competitions he was destined always to be the bridesmaid and never the bride. It was probably too much to expect to win Europe's major trophy in his first season at the club, but by the time of their elimination he felt so much a part of the set-up, so fired up with ambition by Tapie, that he was really disappointed.

He'd already had one run-in with the club's owner and had come out of the confrontation with a growing confidence in his own ability, both on and off the pitch. Chris, together with the Uruguyan Francescoli and the other forward Vercruysse, had asked the coach why he would not pick the three of them together. The coach told Tapie, who called the three of them in to see him.

'The coach picks the team,' he said, 'You play and do what you are told.'

'You're wrong,' Chris said. It wasn't the wisest reply to a man of Tapie's nature.

'If you want a war, then there can only be one winner,' he said.

On the team bus, as Chris sat on his own, wondering if he'd gone too far, Tapie came to sit beside him, his manner once again all charm.

'Listen, Chris, I didn't mean what I said. I'm the president. If the other players see you beating me in an argument, then they will think that maybe they, too, can get away with it. I'm sorry.' It was a rare apology from the man and Chris respected him more than ever for it.

After the semi-final defeat, he had other footballing matters on which to focus. The World Cup preparation was really hotting up. Gazza starred with a goal in a 4–2 win over the Czechs and with that performance guaranteed his inclusion in the squad for Italy. Chris had missed that particular match, because of a club commitment, but was back for a narrow 1–0 win over Denmark. Although he was substituted by David Rocastle, he felt that was down to Robson wanting to give everybody a fair chance before he named his final twenty-two.

There was a general feeling that if the unbeaten run of seventeen matches had to come to an end, it would be preferable if it occurred before they got to Italy. They got their wish when they went down 2–1 to Uruguay at Wembley, although neither the team nor Chris played particularly badly.

When the squad was announced for Italy, Chris was not surprised to be included. He had the experience of 1986 in Mexico and the '88 European Championships – and he knew he had been playing well at Marseille. It wasn't conceit, it was realism.

A couple of days after the squad had been selected, there were storm clouds on the England horizon. Rumours had been circulating for days that, whatever the outcome of England's Italian adventure, Bobby Robson would resign as manager and take over in charge at Dutch club PSV Eindhoven. Now, at a press conference, he confirmed that was indeed the case. The tabloids seized on the story like dogs with a bone, particularly as a blonde divorcee was about to sell her story concerning an alleged five-year affair with the married Robson.

Gazza took a little pressure off his manager by getting himself into a fight in a Newcastle car park, and as Chris and the rest of the team took off for a last warm-up friendly in Tunisia at the beginning of June, the *Sun*'s headline of 'World Cup Wallies' was fairly typical. The problems being experienced by the manager and his favourite son succeeded only in cementing the team together, very much in the same way as did the media onslaught prior to Euro '96. 'We all liked the Boss. His personal life was his own and it just didn't seem fair that some woman could set out to try and destroy him just because she'd been offered a few bob from a publisher and a newspaper.'

But then the world was like that, and whatever Chris and the other players thought, the tabloids were convinced that sex in high places sold copies. An uninspiring performance against Tunisia did nothing to boost confidence. The game had been arranged with a view to getting the players acclimatised to the heat of Italy. In fact, the match was played in a torrential downpour more in keeping with Cleethorpes than Cagliari and ended in a 1–1 draw, which told the manager absolutely nothing he did not already know about his squad.

It was a relief to get to Sardinia where the England team was based because it was considered to be easier to police their alleg-edly rowdy fans. It wasn't such a relief when Chris discovered, somewhat predictably, that once again he was destined to room with Gazza. 'I suppose it was inevitable that I was going to be appointed his minder,' Chris concedes. 'It wasn't that he was bad or disruptive. He was just hyperactive. I like my sleep and Paul was up at the crack of dawn, having still insisted on leaving all the lights on the whole night so that he could sleep. It didn't seem to bother him that I couldn't.'

Bobby Robson, with hindsight, is sympathetic. 'How Chris

Waddle managed to play, and play so well, in the World Cup, with Gazza in his room, I'll never know. Yet somehow, the two of them were not just room-mates, they were soul-mates. They had an understanding both on and off the pitch which was quite unique.'

The Ismola Golf Hotel where the squad were staying, not surprisingly considering its name, had a great golf course. Many of the players took the game seriously, so when a tournament was organised nobody wanted Gazza as their partner. 'Again, I volunteered, but because of the numbers we had to go round with a third player. Tony Dorigo was hot favourite to win and he got lumbered with us. It was fine until the TV cameras caught up with us and then Gazza went wild. He started singing and insisted I did a duet with him. That wasn't so bad, but when he began to dance with me and then lay flat on his stomach to try and push the ball into the hole with his nose, I'd had enough. There are times (which are actually most of the times) when a little bit of Gazza goes a long, long way.'

It wasn't just because of Gazza, but Chris couldn't wait for the tournament to get under way. It seemed that the media were looking for scandal in every corner, and when one of the Italian hostesses was summarily dismissed, the press corps put two and two together and with their usual mathematical precision came up with five. Even when the explanation was offered that her English simply wasn't good enough, they weren't satisfied.

The only way they would be silenced was for England to perform on the field of play, and after eight minutes of their first match against Jack Charlton's Republic of Ireland team it looked as if they were going to do exactly that. Chris played a beautiful pass through to Lineker, who made no mistake as he

struck it past the keeper. But Charlton's men were always going
to play out of their skins. Their value on paper could not compare
to the multi-million-pound ranks of England, but they made up
for that with blood and sweat – leaving the tears to the English
when they grabbed an equaliser in the second half to leave the
scores level at ninety minutes.

Holland were next on the agenda and, as one of the favourites,
were likely to prove a sterner test. Chris retained his place,
although he was replaced by Bull on the hour, and England
battled to an honourable goalless draw, in fact looking as if
they could actually win it for much of the match. Now all
they needed was to beat Egypt in the final match of the group.
The Egyptians, who had been a surprise package, drawing with
both the Republic of Ireland and Holland, were fairly cynical in
their physical approach to the game, and England were fortunate
to escape serious injury. However, they got the only goal of
the game and were through to the knockout stages. Bologna
beckoned. As they arrived at the Novotel in Castenaso, it
was left to Paul Gascoigne to say to Chris what a lot of the
players had been privately thinking: 'You know, Waddler, we
can win this.'

chapter 40

Before the tournament had begun, back at the end of May, Gascoigne had celebrated his 23rd birthday. Somebody in Bologna must have got the dates wrong, though, because they presented Paul with a huge birthday cake by the side of the pool. Chris saw his chance for revenge. He was tired of being woken at the crack of dawn because Paul wanted to swim, tired of being dragged off to the table-tennis table because nobody else would play with Paul, tired of the endless jokes that Paul thought were hilarious, and most of all tired because he wasn't able to sleep at night. He grabbed the cake and in slapstick style slammed it into Paul's face. Gazza took it calmly, just sat there with icing dripping down his chin, licked it away and said, 'Lovely, chocolate.'

It was that sort of atmosphere. The longer they were together, the more the belief in themselves grew. Asked what it felt like to be away from his family for such a long time, Chris replied: 'What's six weeks away? People were away for five years in the war.'

The players would have gone through fire for each other, and particularly for the manager. They knew it would be his last tournament, but what they couldn't have known was that their own future chances would be destroyed by their failure to qualify for the USA in 1994. Indeed, of that whole squad only David Seaman and Gazza can reasonably anticipate another World Cup experience in France in 1998.

'I reckoned we had the best squad ever in my time in the game,' Chris says. 'Everybody got on well and we did most things together as a group. Terry Butcher was probably the character of the lads, even if Gazza might disagree with that. Terry was told off by Bobby Robson almost every day and we took to noting down every roasting he got. We stopped at a dozen. Terry had developed as a kid under Robson at Ipswich and there was a special relationship between the two of them. I remember that Terry wouldn't shave until England were knocked out. Bobby asked him what he'd got on his face and there was Terry, with all his size, looking like a naughty schoolboy, trying to explain. "You're vice-captain, clean yourself up," Robson growled, adding, "By God, you're ugly," for good measure. Gazza and I would follow Terry, just to see what trouble he'd find for himself, and then we'd crease up whilst Robson let fly.'

On another occasion, Chris, Terry and Gary Stevens all went down to dinner wearing blazers, white shirts and ties. Bobby Robson expressed his approval. 'Very nice, you all look very smart,' as if wishing the rest of the squad would follow suit. The three players finished their meal and, as they rose to leave the room, revealed that all they had on the lower parts of their body were jock-straps. Butcher then touched his toes, which as Chris says, must have put everybody in the dining-room off their meals.

There was no joking as the day of the next game wore on. Everybody could feel the tension before the match against Belgium in Bologna. Tanks lined the streets as rumours spread of the invasion of the British thugs, an invasion that never came. Indeed, it was the Belgian fans who disgraced themselves by their racial jeering at John Barnes every time he got the ball. It was not Barnes's night. That belonged to Chris Waddle. Once again the media knives had been out both for him and for Bobby Robson for persevering with him, but if ever he justified his selection it was on that warm summer evening in Italy. Pete Davies summed it up in his book, *All Played Out*: 'At last *this* was Chris Waddle, fast, tricky, making it look easy with that shambling, shuffly run.'

Yet after ninety minutes, even Chris had been unable to conjure up a goal. A minute of extra-time to go and the dread of a penalty shoot-out beckoned. Then Gazza earned a free-kick. Chris thought he might take it, but his fellow-Geordie was having none of it. He whipped the ball in, Platt swivelled and England were through.

Exhausted as they were, they suddenly found some strength to celebrate. Chris went over to console his former Tottenham team-mate, Nico Claesen, and exchanged shirts with him. So it was that, clad in the opposition colours, he and Terry Butcher moved to the centre circle to conduct the joyous English hordes in a rousing chorus of what was fast becoming the theme-song, 'Let's Have a Disco'.

The difference for Chris was that at last the manager had given him the free role he had so long desired. He was not confined to the touch-line, not told that the manager wanted to see the white paint on the soles of his boots at the end of the match, which was the instruction given to him later, under the stewardship of Graham Taylor. He could go wherever he wanted – and wherever he went he caused a threat.

With Cameroon to play in the quarter-final, a semi-final place now looked a formality. Yet Cameroon were not mugs. They'd already beaten Argentina in the first match of the tournament, but their disciplinary record had been poor and they were now weakened by suspensions. Before the match, Chris had said in an interview that he thought Cameroon would try to defend, but if England got an early goal then they'd have to come at them and that would play into their hands. He got it partially right. Cameroon didn't play as if they were under-strength, didn't seem to have heard of defensive tactics, and although England went a goal up, it was 2–2 at the end of ninety minutes. Another marathon was on the cards for England. It was Lineker who saved their blushes this time, with the only goal of extra-time. Now there was just one last hurdle between them and the final. 'I'd said before the match against the Africans that the best side didn't always win in the cup, and I have to say we were lucky to get through. But I reckon you make your own luck in football, and whatever help we got that night deserted us in spades in the next match.'

That next match, that hurdle they had to get over before Rome and the final, was against West Germany. The Germans had looked stronger and stronger as the competition progressed. Twenty-four years and six World Cups might have passed since 1966, but it was a date and an event that the reporters simply would not let alone.

The dream final that the organisers, and indeed the English, wanted was Italy against England. But Argentina put an end to that with a half-convincing victory against the hosts. England could live with that, if the Italians couldn't. Maradona was still there and they were quite sure there would be no Hand of God coming to his rescue this time. At the end of the day, though, all the England boys wanted was to get to the final.

The drama of those 120 minutes and the penalties that followed has been written and rewritten to the point of boredom. Yet perhaps too much has been written about Chris's penalty miss and not enough about his actual performance in open play.

From the very start, it was clear it was going to be one of his more effective days. Who could fail to be inspired by the occasion and the magnificent support of the loyal, tired and broke England fans, many of whom had been in Italy as long as the players? It was the 4–4–2 formation again, with traditional wingers – for so long a part of Robson's plans – abandoned again and Chris given his *libero* role to play.

A through ball set Paul Parker on his way, a pass from Beardsley and a cross to Lineker, who was never at his strongest with his head and could not quite connect. Then came what would surely have been the goal of Chris's career. He spotted Illgner, the German keeper, off his line, and with stupendous nerve tried a powerful chip from thirty-five yards. Illgner desperately back-pedalled and pushed the ball against the bar, although the linesman was flagging for off-side against an Englishman who could not possibly have been interfering with play. It was 0–0 at half-time, but with England looking the better side. More of the same followed in the second half, Chris and Gazza combining time and time again as if magically on the same wavelength. But it was always dangerous to underestimate the Germans, and they scored a fortunate goal with a vicious deflection off Parker. 'Even then it didn't occur to us for a moment that we wouldn't get back into it. We'd come too far to go out now.'

Chris was right – for the moment: 1–1 and the players had to summon up some strength from somewhere. Matches lasting 120 minutes were becoming the norm rather than the exception. Gazza's booking, Gazza's tears – they belong to Gascoigne's story, and Gazzamania was the last thing on Chris's mind as he raised his tired limbs for one last effort that hit the post. It was going to be penalties.

After his miss Bobby Robson came across. 'I didn't say much, there wasn't much to say. I knew I couldn't console him. We'd been together for seven weeks and I'd come to respect him as an intelligent player and a man who was extremely knowledgeable about football. I just patted him on the back. Stuart Pearce was crying, but Chris was low, very low. If ever I saw a man who could be described as absolutely flattened, the spirit squeezed right out of him, then it was Chris Waddle, that night in Turin.'

chapter 41

England did, of course, play Italy, but not in the final. They met instead in the meaningless (and now abandoned) third-place play-off, which England duly lost and headed for home, leaving behind them a drab and ill-tempered final that the Germans won 1–0. Yet anybody witnessing the scenes when they landed at Luton could be forgiven for believing that England had brought home the World Cup, rather than a gallant and unlucky semi-final defeat.

Stuart Pearce and Chris looked at each other, hearts sinking. They really believed they would be slaughtered by the fans for their penalty misses and sat down on the bus, while the rest of the team took the accolades from the fans. But then people were shouting for the pair of them – and it wasn't abuse. People were telling them not to worry, they weren't to be blamed, and eventually they stood up alongside everybody else.

Lorna was waiting for Chris in the hotel, where the two of them, along with Gazza, sneaked into the back of a mobile home belonging to John Gascoigne, Paul's father. He drew down the blinds, enabling them to pass through the throng in blissful anonymity.

There was no time to dwell on memories. Back on Tyneside, there was only a brief respite before Chris had to return to France for pre-season training. He decided to keep a low profile. The French season began earlier than England's, they had not taken part as a nation in the World Cup and were unlikely to have any sympathy for a man who had.

Another Geordie also returned to his roots seeking sanctuary and advice. Paul Gascoigne had been overwhelmed by the reaction to his tears. The brief honeymoon with fame was already passing, and it was a somewhat confused young man who sat down with Chris and their common advisers on 12 July.

'Enjoy it while it lasts,' Chris said at the time. 'Only I didn't realise then exactly what was going to happen, although I'm not sure what Paul could have done to stop it. I don't think I could have coped the way he did, and I've never been surprised when things have become too much for him.'

Right then, it was just a case of four friends sitting down in the dining room of the Gosforth Park Hotel, seeing off the autograph hunters and musing on what might have been and what might yet be. For Paul Gascoigne, an England career stretched ahead, with all the switchbacks of a roller-coaster. Chris, who could not possibly have guessed it at the time, would play only one more full game for the national side.

He knew hardly anything about Graham Taylor, the new England manager. He'd done wonders at Watford, although his style of play had dismayed the purists and set the tone for Wimbledon to follow with success. He'd done reasonably well at Aston Villa, but had never played the game at the highest level himself, and amongst the players themselves was not regarded as a footballer's football manager. However, Chris was never one to pre-judge people. He was sad that his mentor Bobby Robson had gone, but could understand his desire to move on. There is only so much pressure a man can take, and Robson had spent quite enough time under the spotlight, receiving more than his fair share of abuse. Chris was delighted that he had been able to leave as a hero rather than a villain. Although he had an open mind about Graham Taylor, the question was whether the new England manager had an open mind about him. John Barnes had been his protégé at Watford and everybody knew they comprised a mutual admiration society. Would there be room for two wide players in any team selected by Taylor? Or would he be sufficiently flexible at international level to permit Chris the midfield role he had so enjoyed in the latter days of Robson's reign?

It didn't start particularly promisingly from Chris's point of view. He was included in the squad for a friendly against Hungary at Wembley in September 1990 – but then so was everybody else who had played in Italy, apart from Shilton, who had announced his retirement from international football. The match itself was by way of being a 'welcome home' for the lads, and Taylor could hardly be seen to be tinkering with the engine when he'd not yet had time to lift the bonnet. However, when it came to the starting eleven, Barnes was in and Chris was not. He was brought on with seventeen minutes left and England 1–0 up, hardly got a touch and returned to France already slightly disillusioned.

The French season had got off to a strange start . He'd returned to Marseille to find none other than Franz Beckenbauer in charge at the club – the same Beckenbauer who'd coached Germany to their World Cup triumph.

'Ah, Chris Waddle, my favourite player,' was how Franz

greeted him, with a broad smile. 'Don't worry,' Chris replied, 'I'll not be taking any more penalties.'

Marseille had also recalled the exciting forward, Eric Cantona, from a loan spell at Montpellier. Chris found him to be a pleasant, quiet, thoughtful man, who did not mix particularly easily. He'd arrive in the morning on a Harley Davidson bike, shake hands, train professionally, then shoot off again on the powerful machine. He was certainly not one to joke around in the dressing-room and was almost reclusive in the way he kept himself to himself. Although a big man, in every sense of the word, he played with surprising grace.

He did arrive with a certain reputation. Marseille had farmed him out once when he had ripped off his shirt and tossed it at an official. After he had left and joined Nimes for £1 million, there was another violent incident when he hit an opponent in the tunnel and then threw the ball at the referee. There was always the feeling amongst the French players who knew him better than Chris that you were walking on eggshells in his presence.

Chris remembers one particular incident. 'We were in Sofia for a European Cup match. We always took with us our own chef and food. Eric and Papin were sitting opposite me and Papin was doing his best to squeeze a sachet of vinaigrette dressing so that it sprayed all over me. Unfortunately, instead of the top coming off, the side gave way and it machine-gunned all over Eric. As he sat there with the stuff in his hair, running down his chin and all over his clothes, there was a sharp intake of breath from everybody in the room. I suppose it was like that moment in old cowboy movies where the new boy in town insults the local gunfighter. I thought he was going to flip, but instead, Eric got to his feet, turned to Papin and said, "Are you stupid?" and then walked out, wiping the dressing from his face, leaving the rest of the team in relieved hysterics.'

Another addition to the team was Basil Boli, the black defender, who'd come from Auxerre. Chris soon realised he was an excellent defender, very quick and with an English mentality for the game. He also liked a beer and a laugh, and enjoyed an audience. The two became good friends. Having experienced a few racial problems in France, Boli found things easier with Marseille, who also had Abide Pele, from Ghana, and Angloma, who was later to join Inter-Milan. Marseille is an odd city, divided between the Algerian/Moroccan community and the native French. A proponent of liberal Socialist doctrines, Tapie was seen as the natural rival to the right-wing extremist Le Pen. If he signed black players, then they were always going to be targets for Le Pen's madmen, but to Tapie's credit, he never gave his men less than one hundred per cent support.

Marseille, who had just pipped Bordeaux for the title by two points, had an early opportunity to make up for the disappointment of the previous year in the European Cup. A week after England's Hungary game, Marseille destroyed Dinamo Tirana 5–1 in the home leg of their first-round match, Papin carrying on where he had left off with a hat-trick. He had found the net thirty times in 1989–90 and seemed determined to beat that target this time around. Cantona got his first European goal and Chris could see that he was playing in a team that could take on and beat anybody in the world.

He could not, with all honesty, say the same about England. When he returned home for a European Championship qualifier against Poland on 17 October, it was the same again, with Barnes on the field and Chris on the bench. He couldn't understand what he was doing wrong. He was enjoying some of the best football of his career with Marseille, yet Taylor did not seem comfortable with his more individual skill. He could see he was not impressing in training where the accent was more on set pieces, including spending fifteen minutes or so on the kick-offs. Chris heard later from Andy Gray, of Palace and Tottenham fame, about one incident when Taylor told him to kick the ball out of play from the kick-off, as far up the field as he could manage, almost rugby-style. Gray had looked at him in disbelief. There was a host of critics saying he had no right to be in the team – and the manager wanted him to put the ball into touch with his first kick in international football.

As it was, in the game itself, England were 1–0 up at half-time and then began to struggle. Chris replaced Steve Bull after fifty-six minutes and immediately, with both Barnes and Waddle switching wide, there was more shape, there were more alternatives. Beardsley got a second and eventually England won with some comfort.

'It's always seemed to me that a substitute needs at least half an hour if he's to make any impact on a game. You've sat on the bench, you've not been able to get into the pace and rhythm and then you're supposed to turn a game around in a matter of minutes. You're on a hiding to nothing. If you score or make a goal, then it was an inspired substitution. If you do nothing, then it justifies the manager's decision to leave you out in the first place.'

Chris felt he was not being given a fair chance, but was determined not to sulk. All he could do was try to prove Graham Taylor wrong where it mattered most – on the pitch. 'I don't think I ever fitted into Graham's plans. He didn't seem to fancy me as a player. I remember beating Villa 2–0 when I was at Spurs, and although I thought I'd played well he was unenthusiastic. I think I knew in my heart of hearts that once he was appointed manager I wouldn't be around for long. It was a shame. I felt I was about to be playing at the peak of my form. We'd finished the World Cup playing 5–3–2, which suited me, and now we were reverting to 4–4–2 and the early, long ball.'

He was almost relieved to get back to France where, once again, Marseille were setting the pace in the league, although this time Monaco rather than Bordeaux were their nearest challengers. They were ploughing on in the European Cup as well. Although they lost away 3–2 to Lech Poznan, Chris scored in that match, and a 6–1 victory at home was both predictable and deserved. Chris was still Tapie's blue-eyed boy, and the Marseille owner was incensed that the man he considered his best player was not considered good enough for his national team. Chris would not have put it past Tapie to phone Graham Taylor and tell him at some length exactly what he thought he was doing wrong!

If there was a crossroads in the relationship between Graham Taylor and Chris Waddle, then it came in Dublin when England were due to play the Republic of Ireland yet again, this time in a European Championship qualifier. There was one surprise inclusion in the squad – Gordon Cowans of Aston Villa. Chris certainly knew and liked Gordon. Their paths had crossed often in the past, and they would play together again as veterans at Bradford City. Cowans was yet another example of a player familiar to Taylor at club level and familiar himself with the manager's methods, but he had not played for England for almost five years.

On the morning of the match, Chris woke with a swollen ankle and told Taylor he didn't think he could play. It was too close to the game for him to have a pain-killing injection, so that was that. With Gascoigne also excluded, the newspapers had a field day with innuendo and suggestions as to why the two flair players were not figuring in Taylor's plans. Nobody seemed to believe that Chris was genuinely injured, and it may well be that Taylor thought that he was fit enough to play but had ruled himself out in a fit of pique. What was worse was that Chris went on to play for Marseille the following weekend. However, this time he did have the pain-killing injection to get him on the pitch and succeeded only in aggravating the injury to the ankle ligament.

The Gascoigne omission was more mysterious, appearing to be a reaction by Taylor to the Gazzamania that was still sweeping the nation some five months after the public show of emotion that set the gravy train rolling. Later Taylor admitted that there had been death threats against Paul and he felt it unfair to expose him to that sort of danger. At the time, though, it looked as if there was no room for talented individuals in any team managed by Graham Taylor.

chapter 42

The actual performance against the Irish was awful. Although England got a 1–1 draw and looked on course to qualify, there was little to satisfy in the game except the result. Although Cowans was and is a consummate professional, his was the first of a series of odd selections for England under Taylor's stewardship that eventually led to his resignation. As a disgruntled England fan said on the plane back to London:

'It wouldn't surprise me if he picked Ross Jenkins for the next match,' referring to the lanky Watford striker who had scored so many goals for Taylor when he'd been manager of the Hertfordshire club.

'He's more likely to pick Luther Blissett,' another passenger replied.

As the season progressed, it seemed that Chris did not figure in Taylor's plans for the moment. In February he was not invited to play in a friendly against Cameroon, nor did he appear when in March England drew at home with the Republic of Ireland in the return fixture. The thought was now firmly fixed in the minds of the public that Graham Taylor did not fancy Chris Waddle.

Yet that was not strictly true. In March, before the return

Irish fixture, Taylor and Lawrie McMenemy, his number two, travelled to Marseille to watch Chris play in the second leg of the European Cup quarter-final against mighty AC Milan. Marseille had already achieved an encouraging result in Milan, drawing 1–1 on a rain-soaked night in the San Siro Stadium, with Papin scoring for the French and Ruud Gullit for the Italians.

In their mountain top hotel, the rest of the squad had decided to turn their playful attentions to *Le Rosbif*, as Chris was now called. Returning to his room, he found everything either upright against the walls (including the bed) or neatly stored on the balcony. He was truly beginning to feel at home amongst them.

Chris had pressures before the second leg as well as during it. Gazza was recuperating from a hernia operation and had elected to stay with Chris to accelerate his recovery. As the stay coincided with the start of the interest of Lazio in the player, Chris found himself caught up in the drama of the transfer as the Lazio delegates had their first meeting with Paul in the lounge of his villa.

Gazza never travelled alone, so his father and another friend were also Waddle house-guests. The telephone became Paul's personal property, and when Brooke was trained to say that she intended to marry Paul when she grew up, a mutual shudder ran down the spines of her parents.

The England contingent watching with Gazza from a private box could not have helped but be impressed by Waddle's performance on the night against the Italians. He mesmerised the Milanese defence all night, deservedly scoring a magnificent goal sixteen minutes from time. It brought the crowd to their feet, waving so many Union Jacks that Graham Taylor must have wished he had that sort of support at Wembley.

The opposition must have believed they'd still have a chance if Chris was out of the way, as one of their number promptly felled him with a rabbit-punch to the back of the head. He was brought round, rising unsteadily, but was fouled again. By now only half knowing what he was doing, he unwisely rose for a header and collapsed for a third time. Shrugging away the French coach, who wanted him to come off, he set off on a typical long, mazy run, twisting and turning away from defenders. He seemed certain to score the goal of his career when he was fouled yet again and hobbled back to his own half.

There was yet more drama. With the Italians pressing forward for an equaliser that would have taken the match into extra-time, the floodlights suddenly failed. There was a substantial delay before they were partially restored, but although the referee thought the light good enough to continue, the Milan coach did not and called his team off the pitch. Obviously he was hoping to get another chance at an appeal hearing if he couldn't get it by his team's endeavours on the pitch. In fact the ruse failed. The referee blew for time, awarded the match to Marseille and Milan received a fine and a ban for their troubles.

In anticipation of a victory, the club had laid on a sumptu-ous twelve-course banquet after the match. Chris's old friend Glenn Hoddle, who had come to watch him, joined the table with Gazza, Mel Stein, Len Lazarus and Lorna. The Marseille players arrived one by one to a hero's welcome until only Chris was absent. Eventually he entered the room to a standing reception and sat down at the table, his face absolutely bereft of colour.

'It's all right,' he reassured his wife and friends. 'I've just got a bit of a headache from that knock.'

He got as far as the first course, then slumped forward, his face virtually in the soup.

Gazza, at least, saw the funny side:

'Typical. You invite us all out to dinner and you can't be bothered even to stay awake.'

Obviously in some distress, Chris was led out into the fresh air after a few moments and sat miserably on the steps of the stadium. The suggestion that the club doctor be summoned was brushed aside by Gazza, whose instant remedy was that Chris just needed a couple of large drinks. As Chris began to vomit, alcohol was clearly the last thing he needed, and eventually an ambulance was called, while Chris was placed on a bed, still on the steps of the ground.

Gazza by now was hugely enjoying what he took to be the cabaret. 'Go on Waddler. Get up on the bed for a few photos, it'll be a laugh.'

To Chris's relief, the ambulance finally arrived, and before the concussion took a firmer grip, he muttered to anybody who would listen, 'Whatever happens, don't let Gazza into the ambulance.'

They didn't. Chris spent the night in hospital under observation, and Taylor and McMenemy returned to England, as did Paul. When the team was selected for the match a week later, Chris was ruled out, not by the manager but by injury. There could be no doubting that on what Taylor had seen, he would have had to pick Waddle. If he had done so and Chris had turned it on . . . if he had taken Chris into Europe . . . if England had done better in the European Championships and qualified for the World Cup in the USA . . ..If . . . If my grandmother were a man, then she'd be my grandfather, as the saying goes. She wasn't, and Chris was not be to be part of the England team again until October 1991. And after that never again.

chapter 43

By April, Chris had recovered sufficiently from his injuries to play in the European Cup semi-final against Spartak Moscow. It looked a harder game on paper than it actually was, for already by 1991 Soviet football was on the decline. After his unhappy experiences in Tblisi, Chris was most careful. Again the club travelled with its own food, the security was good, as was the hotel, the Novotel, so Chris simply stayed there to avoid anything untoward, emerging only to train at Moscow's stadium.

Marseille had discovered a real emerging talent in the shape of Pele, who had named himself after his footballing hero. He scored in both the 3–1 away win and the 2–1 home win, while Papin and the reliable Vercruysse also grabbed goals in the first leg and Basil Boli, who was by now Chris's closest friend at the club, got the second at home. In the away tie, Chris made the goals for Papin and Pele and set up the third with a pass to Papin, who got the ball over to Vercruysse. Chris received the Man of the Match award in the shape of a vase. It was shades of the Japan Cup all over again. In the previous round Pele was awarded the Man of the Match accolade in Italy and had received a watch.

'That's really fair,' Chris said to Tapie. 'He gets a watch in Milan and I get a vase in Moscow!'

A few days later, Tapie called Chris into his office and gave him a small bundle. '*Un cadeau* – a gift,' he said. Unwrapping it, Chris found himself the proud owner of a gold Rolex. If Tapie liked one of his players, he was going to ensure that he was always happy.

If Tapie was spoiling him, then Graham Taylor was certainly bringing him back to reality. England's progress towards the European Championship finals in Sweden in June 1992 continued with a 1–0 victory in Izmir against Turkey, but it was Dennis Wise who scored and Waddle once again was not selected, although Taylor did find a place for the dubious talents of Jeff Thomas. One of the manager's more eccentric choices, Thomas was replaced by Steve Hodge at half-time. The same fate was to be meted out to Andy Gray on his only international appearance in the final qualifier against Poland in November. In just over a year, Taylor had decimated Robson's heroes to such an extent that of the 1990 semi-finalists, only Pearce, Walker, Platt and Lineker survived.

The results, if not the performances, seemed to justify Taylor's methods, so that by the end of the summer of 1991, he had taken the team through twelve matches without defeat. Yet, somehow, they had not captured the imagination of the nation, especially in the absence of Gascoigne, following his suicidal Wembley tackle. The team would always try their best, but never looked likely to extend top-class opposition, and the fact was that the seemingly impressive statistics of those twelve matches did not tell the whole story. Opposition had been of the quality of Australia (where England won through a solitary own goal), New Zealand (twice), Malaysia, and Cameroon in freezing February conditions hardly suited to the cavalier Africans. The team may have qualified for Sweden, but not many journalists or fans were holding their breath.

Chris's consolation was a European Cup final on 29 May against Red Star Belgrade in Bari – the French side's first appearance in the finals of the competition. Tapie gave his usual pre-match encouragement, although on this occasion he did leave the tactical side to Raymond Goethals. Franz Beckenbauer was still at the club as technical director, although Chris felt he was there at the time more as a figurehead to enable Tapie to show the sort of personality he could attract to Marseille if he put his mind and his purse to it.

The first half was a game of chess in which Chris had one half-chance with a volley that he took too early. It seemed, as the game progressed, that Belgrade were content to take the match into extra-time and even to penalties, leaving the French side to chase and harry them.

The thought of another penalty shoot-out drove Chris on desperately, but one header from a distance went over the bar, another was just wide. With no real idea where he would come in the pecking order if all five penalties were converted, he just hoped he wouldn't be needed as the match ended without a goal. He wasn't. Marseille, through Amoros, missed once, Belgrade converted all five, and Chris had yet another runners-up medal. 'I was dreading a sudden death shoot-out. I think I would have let the keeper go ahead of me.'

Tapie was distraught. He simply could not believe that his team had lost. He was not a person to take defeat lightly and it was certain that heads would roll. The dinner after the match was a flat occasion, to say the least, and the following night Tapie hauled them all back to the stadium for a dramatic speech, the atmosphere heightened by making it at the scene of their defeat.

'If anybody wants to leave, then let them come and see me,' he declaimed. Chris and Papin did just that, both telling him they would like to go to Italy. To their surprise, he agreed, although when it came to the crunch, they both found themselves playing in France the following season as Tapie would not countenance their sale in the cold light of day. It is one of Chris's enduring regrets in the game that he did not play in the Italian Serie A. 'I always felt there would be more pressure there than in France, but I just wanted to see if I could have succeeded in what I thought was the strongest league in the world.'

It could hardly have been considered to be a bad season. Marseille had seen Monaco off by four points in the race for the title, although they had lost the French Cup final to the same side by a single goal. What had looked to be a possible treble had resulted in a single trophy. Papin had once again top-scored, although this time with a relatively meagre twenty-three goals. They would be back in the European Cup the following season, although how many of the players and coaching staff would be given the chance to atone for their failure, only time would tell.

Tapie invited Chris to eat on his ten-bedroomed yacht in Marseille's harbour. With Jean Bernes, the general manager of the club, Tapie held a post-mortem with his favourite player as to why they had lost the European Cup final. The meal was splendid and the conclusion, at least as far as Tapie was concerned, was that Raymond Goethals had lost it for them with his tactics. While Chris may have had a clear idea that his England career was virtually over, he had no inkling, once Tapie had decided not to sell him and had taken him into his confidence, that the year to follow would be his last in France.

chapter 44

There were just over 50,000 people at Wembley to witness Chris Waddle's last appearance for England on 16 October 1991. The opposition, Turkey, had lost all four of their previous qualifiers, conceding ten goals without finding the net themselves. Bowing to media pressure, Taylor recalled Chris to the team, insisting that he selected his side on current form and that nobody was excluded. There was an air of an old boys' reunion about a side that contained Bryan Robson (restored to fitness and the captaincy), David Platt (now plying his trade at Bari in the Italian Serie A), Des Walker, Stuart Pearce, Alan Smith and Gary Lineker up front. David Batty added some steel to the mid-field, but there was no room for Barnes or Beardsley.

With only Chris likely to find some imaginative creation, it was always going to be difficult against a team who came to keep the score in check. But the problem was that, although the media were given the impression that Chris had been told to play a free role, in fact his instructions were to hug the by-line (the white on the soles of his boot instruction) and tackle back whenever he could. Waddle under Taylor was not Gazza under Robson and Chris obeyed the instructions to the letter, even when he could see that the plan was not working. Alan Smith came to England's rescue, with the only goal of the match, leaving England needing a point in Poland to be certain of a place in the finals. The same journalists who had screamed for Waddle's inclusion were now equally scathing about his performance.

'I really felt I was the fall guy for that particular result,' he says. 'I didn't play particularly well, but then nor did anybody else. What particularly upset me was that in an eleven-a-side game at Wembley on the Saturday before the match, I was given a free role and played well. Then on the night of the match, Lawrie McMenemy told me to pick a wing and stay wide as he had too many in the middle. I didn't play well, but then I hardly touched the ball.

Chris went public to correct the impression that Taylor had given.

'I said that Graham had set us back five years before the European Championships, and not surprisingly he wasn't too happy. But then I wasn't very happy with his statement that I'd been given a free role, which was simply untrue. We did meet up and talk when I was at Sheffield Wednesday, but although he said that I had the same chance as anybody else in his England plans, I wasn't holding my breath until I got reselected.'

When it came to the crucial match against Poland, the wide berth went to Andy Sinton, and when he was substituted twenty minutes from the end, it was Tony Daley who took his place. Taylor could say with hand on heart that he had given Chris Waddle one last chance and he had failed to take it.

Bobby Robson, for one, certainly felt that Chris had been jettisoned too early: 'He had a lot to offer by way of talent and experience, but some managers feel they have to plan for four years ahead,' he says now.

As it was, in four years' time not only was Chris Waddle absent from the international scene, but Taylor himself had been replaced by Venables. It is a matter of conjecture whether England might have qualified for the World Cup in the States if Graham Taylor had persevered with Chris, yet surely they could not have done any worse in their efforts.

Gary Lineker also believes that Chris was tossed aside before his sell-by date. 'Without Peter Beardsley and Chris, and with John Barnes sidelined for long periods, England were just too workmanlike. There was no flair, no creativity. I know Chris had his views and opinions, but they were always genuinely held or given, and there was no doubting his knowledge of the game. Some managers may be scared of that and confuse it with player power, but from an international striker's point of view, there is no doubt in my mind that we were deprived of his services and talents far too early.'

In Europe with Marseille, the campaign had started convincingly enough. The European Cup had taken on a new format with first- and second-round matches leading to a league system for the semi-finals. Now that English teams were back in the fray, Chris was hoping that Arsenal, who had taken the title in such dramatic fashion the previous year, would meet up with his own club somewhere along the way. It wasn't to be a successful year for either of them.

The French club demolished Union Luxembourg 10–0 on aggregate, but Sparta Prague proved to be sterner opponents in the vital second round. In the first leg at home, Marseille were 3–0 up and cruising with half an hour to go. Chris had started the ball rolling before Papin claimed a brace, and then the referee put his life on the line with two penalty decisions that gave the visitors two vital away goals.

Tapie was furious, talking of conspiracies and the like, but in Prague a couple of weeks later it was still all to play for. A goal for Sparta in the first half brought the scores level, and with the benefit of the away goals, Sparta would win if it stayed that way. When they got another twenty minutes from time, it seemed all over, but Marseille roused themselves for one last frenzied effort. Pele scored with three minutes left – and if they'd got one last goal, it would have been the French team rather than the Czechs who would have made the remunerative league section.

It was that result, more than any other, that probably ensured that Tapie would rebuild the team, although there was still no indication that his phoenix would not be constructed around the likes of Waddle and Papin. The early exit from Europe having thrown his optimistic budget out of alignment, he had to find other ways to keep the club afloat. He used Chris to help him make a last-ditch bid for the injured Gascoigne, offering to buy him for a reduced fee without the need for the stringent medicals that Lazio were demanding. Gascoigne's decision to remain loyal to the Italians who had been loyal to him was another log on the funeral pyre of Chris's long-term career with Marseille, although whether Tapie really had the money to buy him was a matter for conjecture.

Marseille were still the pace-setters in the league, but the heart was knocked out of their season when in the French Cup semi-final against Bastia, a stand collapsed, killing many of their fans and leading to the abandonment of that particular tournament for the season. Chris was injured for that match and did not even travel with the team. He watched on television in horror and then listened to the individual players' stories when they returned. 'The lads had a meeting and decided unanimously that they didn't want the match replayed. We were already sure of winning the league and we simply conceeded the cup to Monaco, and Tapie respected our decision.'

In fact, they finished six points clear of Monaco with the third club, Paris St Germain, eleven points adrift. It was their fourth successive title, but like Rangers in Scotland they could not translate their domestic supremacy into any European silverware. Tapie was always one for making sudden and dramatic decisions. He had said at Christmas that Chris could go if he wanted to at the end of the season, but no more had been said on the subject and Chris had put it down to another passing fancy. Now, however, although Papin may have scored another twenty-seven goals and Waddle may have walked on water as far as the local fans were concerned, it was Bernard Tapie who was the owner of the club, and a government minister, and he had decided that both of his stars could go. It was a wholesale clear-out with Moser, Boscic and Deschamps all being sold.

For Chris and Lorna the news brought mixed emotions. They had both enjoyed their time in France, and had made many friends, but independently of Tapie they had come to the conclusion that it was probably time to go home. Lorna was the sorrier of the two to go. Brooke, by now at the International School, could understand almost everything that was said to her in French, even though she still insisted on replying in English. But they both realised that the club was in turmoil and that although Tapie had his finger in the dyke, it could only be a matter of time before the flood waters came rushing through. With the Premier League setting new challenges for those participating, Chris felt he was still young enough to rise to a new challenge, to cope with the increased standards, the additional fitness that this new super-league seemed to demand. Perhaps, most important of all, the couple were keen to have another child and Lorna certainly felt she would like him or her to be born in England. One way or another, it was time to come home.

chapter 45

It was in May 1992 that Tapie summoned Mel Stein and Len Lazarus to his ministerial headquarters in the heart of Paris to let them know that he would listen to offers for Chris. There were already rumours and allegations concerning Tapie's future, but the man seemed not to have a care in the world, dismissing his visitors' enquiries regarding his problems with an airy Gallic wave of his arms. His huge room contained only an enormous antique desk, an equally ancient carpet which seemed to stretch for miles, and there at the end of the royal approach Tapie himself, chameleon-like as ever, looking perfectly in place.

As it transpired, his protestations of innocence would all be to no avail and the criminal charges that were eventually to be made against him, linked with Olympique de Marseille's fall from grace over match-rigging scandals, would make his resignation inevitable. However, at that moment he was totally in control, outraged at a magazine article that suggested his conduct had been other than exemplary, calling his lawyers on the phone, telling them to sue immediately to protect his reputation. It was no wonder that he would eventually carve out a new career for himself as a movie star. Acting was always his strong point.

He told Chris's advisers that he felt it was in their client's best interests that he should be sold. He would not be difficult over the price, as he felt that he had received good value for his investment over the years. He would seek £900,000, but if it were the right club he might take £750,000, and to help Chris OM would play two matches for his benefit wherever he went. Would the lawyer and the accountant now please find him a club? One condition was that he would not sell him to another French club, as he felt he would be slaughtered by the Marseille supporters. Oh, and by the way, he would like to buy Kevin Campbell from Arsenal and perhaps the London club might be interested in a part-exchange for Waddle. They weren't, and all Stein and Lazarus could do was put the news of Chris's availability out through the Press Association.

Chris was philosophical. He was sorry not to have won a major honour with the club, but did not think there would be any shortage of offers back in England. He was not disappointed. Within days of the news breaking that Chris Waddle could be coming home, Trevor Francis of Sheffield Wednesday was in touch.

When Chris spoke to Francis on the phone, he liked what he heard of his approach to the game and his plans for the future of the club. For all too long, Wednesday had been a yo-yo team, unable to command a regular place in the top flight but too strong for the lower division. Francis was determined to change all that and to bring back stable success. In Chris Woods he had a top class keeper, who at the time looked set to be England's number one for some years to come. Up front he had Mark Bright and David Hirst, both of whom also seemed to have an international future, while the likes of John Sheridan, Carlton Palmer, Roland

Nilsson and John Harkes made up what could be a team with real potential for major honours. When Francis and the club secretary, Graham Mackrell, met with Stein at the end of May, significant progress was made towards agreement for a four-year contract.

However, Chris was not going to jump at the first offer that was made, and told Francis that he needed a week or so to think about it. There had been some enquiries from Italy back in February, and he quite liked the idea of playing elsewhere on the Continent, but when they came to nothing, Lorna certainly was relieved. Domestically, Newcastle and Leeds were the only other two English clubs to show any serious interest.

Howard Wilkinson and Bill Fotherby of Leeds were in contact, as were Sir John Hall, with Kevin Keegan, only recently appointed manager and anxious to bring back the glory days to the north-east club. Although they were both attractive alternatives, Chris felt that if he went to Leeds he'd incense the whole of Geordieland, for they were almost as much the hated rivals of Newcastle as were Sunderland. There was also the fact that Leeds had just won the title and he felt that expectations might be too high. As far as Newcastle themselves were concerned, his gut feeling was that the chairman was keener on his return than the manager. There was no doubting his popularity with the supporters, but they didn't pick the team each week. All the 'fish and chips' chants were long ago forgotten and now there was just a shared pride in his achievements on the world stage. Chris's advisers did travel to Newcastle, where they were exposed to Sir John's infectious enthusiasm, but at the end of the day it was the client who made the decisions and, past thirty, with Newcastle still in the First Division, who could really blame

Chris for not going back? There was always the argument that one should never go back to try to reconstruct success, that it can never be the same second time around, although certainly Peter Beardsley gave the lie to that theory.

Francis was persistent and began to deliver ultimatums. He had the money to spend, and if he wasn't going to spend it on Chris, then he had to spend it on somebody else to make sure his squad was complete before the start of the new season. Eventually Chris made his decision. If Sheffield Wednesday could reach agreement with Tapie, then he would sign.

It took until 24 June before a meeting with Tapie could be arranged. In the meantime, on 19 June, a representative of Monaco telephoned Stein, knowing he would get nowhere with Tapie. The suggestion was that Chris be 'parked' with a non-French club and then sold back to Monaco. Chris thought about it briefly before deciding that, apart from the fact it was simply not worth the risk of enraging Tapie by going down that road, he had given Francis his word on the phone that if it were possible he would join Wednesday. And he was not one to break his word.

Assigned the unenviable task of completing the negotiations with Tapie, Francis flew out to Paris, accompanied by Chris's advisers. It was not to be an easy meeting. Stein and Lazarus had discovered that, notwithstanding the instruction to them to find a club for Chris, Tapie had also instructed Dennis Roach of PRO to test the waters. The inevitable result was confusion about the price – and outrage from the Waddle camp that Roach should be involved. They had already made it clear to Tapie that, given the history of the relationship, they would have nothing to do with any deal brokered by Roach. Tapie denied his involvement, but by the time the meeting took place, Tapie had been afflicted by a mental block concerning the price that he had quoted. All he could remember now was that Chris had cost him £4 million and he wanted to recover as much of that as he could. He said that Leeds had offered £1.3 million, as had Newcastle. Why should he sell to Sheffield for less? That was easy, he was told. It was because Chris had decided not to join either Leeds or Newcastle. Nobody (except Tapie) knew at the time how desperate was the financial plight of the club, and indeed of Tapie's whole business empire. Clearly he now saw an opportunity, with Wednesday committed, to maximise his income, and for the second successive move Chris found himself as a pawn in the game of high finance.

As the day wore on, Francis found himself becoming more and more frustrated. He was out of his depth with so experienced a businessman as Tapie, and it was probably unfair of the club to have given him the sole responsibility of bringing the player home. Endless phone calls were made to the club chairman, David Richards. He was prepared to back his manager's judgement up to a point, but there was also a breaking point. Television money was only just beginning to filter through to Premier League clubs, wages and transfer fees were still within the bounds of reason, and Wednesday were not known as the biggest spenders in the league. There was an air of Yorkshire commonsense, if not parsimony, about the club which still exists today, and the negotiations reached the stage where, if Tapie was not prepared to accept an increased offer of £1 million, then Francis was to come home.

A French lawyer, Olivier Patou, was brought in to try to persuade Tapie that Wednesday had gone as far as they could.

■ **Chris Waddle**

With perfect brinkmanship, having pushed the price up by a quarter of a million from the bottom-line figure he had told Chris's adviser he would accept, Tapie capitulated – if indeed that was ever a term that could be used to describe an action of Bernard Tapie. Now it was all about the bargain that Wednesday were getting, how good and generous the club was to Chris to allow him to leave for such a pittance, and indeed that he didn't really want him to go at all. Yet, his generosity did not extend to the playing of the 'jubilee' matches that he had promised.

Again Chris was philosophical. He had been involved in three French championship triumphs for the club, a French Cup final, a European Cup final and a semi-final. He had given his all and the fans appreciated it, even if Tapie did not. There was one further sting in the tail. The club told him they 'could not afford' to pay him a bonus that was due. It all left a bad taste in the mouth, so that when Chris attended a packed press conference at the Forte Crest Hotel in Sheffield on 16 July, he breathed a sigh of relief. It was good to get back to England and sanity. The true madness of what he had left behind was yet to surface in its entirety.

chapter 46

As Chris waited patiently for the professionals to finalise his arrangements, Graham Taylor and England went off to Sweden without him for the European Championships. If football was to come home in 1996, the only thing coming home four years earlier was the England team and manager with their tails between their legs. In their three matches England managed just one goal in a 2–1 defeat by the Swedes, after achieving goalless draws against Denmark and France. As Basil Boli got off the French team bus before the game against England he smiled at the television cameras and said, 'Allo, Chris Waddle,' as if to make the point that the French, at least, were puzzled, if not relieved, by his absence. Boli went on to head-butt Stuart Pearce, which led the Forest player to query why Chris regarded him as a friend next time they met.

Against Sweden, Taylor substituted Lineker with Alan Smith twenty-six minutes from the end, and could not understand why the public and the media turned against him for that decision. Apart from the sentimental fact that Lineker had announced that he would retire after the tournament and that this was therefore his last international, he had, until then, looked like England's best hope of grabbing a winner with the scores poised at one apiece. 'Turnip' Taylor had to endure the sort of press usually reserved for child molesters and mass murderers. It was unfair, for he was basically an honest man, trying to do his best, but it was possible that his best was never going to be good enough at that level of world football. However, he resisted pressures for his resignation, announced a determination to qualify for the 1994 World Cup in the USA, and Chris felt that if only he could play well in the domestic game, perhaps he could force himself back into the reckoning for selection. 'I thought the whole tournament was disappointing, not just England's performance. The French also fell short of their potential. There were the Danes, called into the competition at the last moment, walking away with the trophy. Everybody else had been training hard, working on their tactics and they'd been called back from sunning themselves on beaches around the world. It made me wonder.'

In many ways it was as if he had never been away from the domestic scene: the banter in the dressing-room was still the same; the same journalists were still around. However, the games in the Premier League had picked up in pace, and Chris soon realised that he could never afford to risk being anything other than one hundred per cent fit. He also realised that the man in charge of coaching, Richie Barker, was not exactly his cup of tea. There was too much shouting, too much of the barrack-room, when he had an experienced bunch of players working with him, and not enough concentration on ball skills. Whereas a few years earlier, Chris would have said nothing and just got on with it, the more mature Waddle was not slow to voice his opinions – and he did not win any brownie points for them.

Lorna was pleased to be back in England. Yorkshire was, of course, far more accessible to Newcastle than London had been, and she enjoyed the social life that revolves around any English club. It was good to be back, mixing with the players' wives, talking in English about their homes, their kids, worrying and at the same time amused as to how the mood would take their husbands after a defeat or a poor personal performance.

On 15 August 1992, Chris pulled on the number seven shirt for his new club in an away fixture at Everton. Although he was soon off the field with a twisted knee ligament, he saw the team collect a point in a creditable 1–1 draw. He couldn't believe his bad luck. He'd gone through his time in France virtually unscathed, and now he had the chance to impress back home, it was off to the treatment table.

When he reappeared against Coventry in early September, there were other casualties in the ranks. David Hirst and Phil King were struggling and, indeed, he cannot recall ever being with a club with such a terrible injury record as that suffered by Wednesday during his time there. They lost to Coventry and then again at home to Manchester City, slipping to seventeenth in the table. As Chris began to doubt whether he had done the right thing, the fans must have been questioning the wisdom of spending a million pounds on a player of Chris's age.

But Chris has never been one to panic, never been a man to give up without a fight. Lorna had found a house in the village of Dore, on the outskirts of Sheffield, arrangements had been made for Brooke to join the local school and Chris was determined to try to make a go of it. He liked the rest of the players and although, inevitably, his social life revolved around his old non-footballing friends, Carlton and Jenny Palmer, John and Cindy Harkes and John and Jeanette Sheridan became particularly close.

Carlton would get particularly worked up with Trevor Francis, with whom he had a running battle before his move to Leeds. One day, collecting Chris on the way to training, he arrived in such a foul mood that he virtually demolished the gates to the Waddles' drive. He didn't do his car any great favours either. 'It's all Trevor's fault,' Carlton declaimed with somewhat faulty logic. 'If he hadn't have got me upset, I'd never have done that.'

John Harkes was an interesting character. Of Scottish parentage, he'd been brought up in the States and looked and sounded like an all-American boy. He was really the first US player to make any kind of impression on the English game, going on to become the first American to score at Wembley. He, too, eventually fell out with Francis and Barker, moving on to Derby, West Ham and then back to the new Major League Soccer in the USA, where his club DC United did the league and cup double in the first year of the league's existence. He also carved out an international career for himself as the captain of the USA team which did so well in the 1994 World Cup. He is the first to admit the debt he owes to Chris in footballing terms.

In mid-October, with Chris restored to fitness and beginning to readjust to English football, Wednesday strung together a run of six unbeaten matches, and although five of them were drawn, the side were proving difficult to beat. That, in itself, was a pointer to what was going to be their main area of success – the cups. In the Coca-Cola Cup second round, their opponents were Hartlepool United. Chris has always had a soft spot for the minnows of north-east football, even toying with the idea of trying to acquire a stake in the club. There was no room for sentiment, however, and Sheffield Wednesday ran out 5–2 winners on aggregate over the two legs. Leicester were destroyed 7–1 in the next round and, although Chris was not scoring, the strikers in the shape of Bright and Hirst, as well as young Gordon Watson, were all benefiting from the ammunition he was supplying.

At the start of December, QPR were dismissed summarily 4–0 in the Coca-Cola Cup, and a narrower 1–0 league win against the same opposition was the signal for the start of a ten-match unbeaten run in the league that stretched from 19 December to 3 March 1993. Wednesday found themselves riding high in fourth place in the Premiership, having by then also progressed to the semi-final of the Coca-Cola Cup, as well as the fifth round of the FA Cup. Rather than their being regarded as relegation candidates, odds were being quoted on them winning the treble. It was an amazing turnaround to the season.

An away draw with Ipswich in the fifth round of the Coca-Cola Cup saw David Hirst carried off with an injury that would keep him out for much of the rest of the season and haunt him intermittently throughout the rest of his career, to the point where his bright England future was totally blighted.

'I always rated David very highly and thought that he was on a par with Shearer,' says Chris. 'He was strong, quick, good in the air and had a sledgehammer of a left foot. He was an old-fashioned centre-forward in the image of Malcolm Macdonald and he had everything going for him except his health.'

The pressure of three tournaments eventually took its toll on a squad that had no real depth. A defeat at Coventry at the beginning of March was followed by only three more victories in the last twelve games of the season and a final position of seventh. Even before the season ended, it was clear that the best chance of success and a swift return to Europe for Chris lay with the cups. Ipswich, having been seen off in the replay, were followed in the semi-final by Blackburn, who were beaten 6–3 on aggregate. A Wembley final against Arsenal on 18 April beckoned and, when an away draw at the Baseball Ground against Derby County in the FA Cup sixth round necessitated a replay, it was difficult to find a date. The treble might be out of reach, but a double helping of cup silverware promised a dream return for Chris.

chapter 47

By the time of the Coca-Cola Cup final, Wednesday's incredible cup runs had continued with victories against Derby in the sixth round of the FA Cup and a dramatic local derby win over their arch-rivals, Sheffield United, in the semi-final. For that internecine battle, what seemed like the whole of Sheffield was transported to Wembley, which was considered the only neutral stadium large enough to contain everybody who wanted to see the match. It was never going to be a classic. There was too much at stake for that. Until then Chris had not found the net in either of the cups. It was an incredible statistic that he'd failed to contribute even one of the thirty-five goals they had scored on their journeys to those stages. But then his contribution had been made in so many other ways.

He may have been impressing the Sheffield fans, his team-mates and the manager, but it made no impression on Graham Taylor. Time and time again Trevor Francis would put Chris's name forward, but he never made the squad. The sportswriters of England were more appreciative, voting him their Player of the Year. As things turned out, it was the only thing he would win during his time at Hillsborough.

Back in November 1992, at Paul Gascoigne's sister's wedding in Newcastle, he'd sat with Lawrie McMenemy, who had been despatched by Taylor to act as Gazza's minder. As the evening wore on and the drink flowed freely, Chris told McMenemy exactly what he thought was wrong with Graham Taylor's tactics as England manager. It probably wasn't the most sensible thing to do, and as Lorna said at the time, 'Well, that's Chris's England career finished for sure.'

It wasn't that Chris thought he knew better. It was just that he loved the game, had thought about it deeply and hard and did not like what was happening to English football under Taylor. What was probably more important than any personal feelings was that he did not think England could find long-term international success with the methods being used. As the failure to qualify for the 1994 World Cup and Taylor's subsequent replacement by Venables was to show, he was right. Once again, the contrast between Robson and Taylor in their relationship and understanding of Chris was underlined.

'I always enjoyed talking football with Chris,' Robson says. 'He was as knowledgeable about the game off the pitch as he was intelligent on it. Once he got started, once he'd overcome his initial shyness, he'd be quite happy to talk all night.'

The knowledge that, if they beat Sheffield United on 3 April, they would be guaranteed three Wembley appearances in the space of six weeks was enough to spur Wednesday on – if any further incentive was really necessary. David Hirst was still not fully fit and the emerging talent of Paul Warhurst, who had been so successfully converted from a defender to a striker, started the game up front with Mark Bright. If Chris needed the platform to perform, then Wembley was it. He might not be invited to play there for England, but he ran the show for his club side. 'I was delighted when I heard the match was going to be played at Wembley. The pitch at Elland Road, the original choice, was in poor condition for our passing game and I knew that perfect Wembley surface was going to favour us.'

He chose that 'Venue of Legends' to score his first goal of the cup run, putting Wednesday ahead with an unstoppable free-kick hit with his left foot from some twenty-five yards. Although Cork equalised for United before half-time, Mark Bright got the winner, and it was the red half of Sheffield which had the blues, while the Blues themselves would be returning to the twin towers on 15 May for the final.

As it was, they were to return with even greater resolve, for in between they lost the Coca-Cola final to Arsenal somewhat unluckily 2–1. Harkes had put them in front, but first Merson and then Steve Morrow scored for the north Londoners. The celebrations that greeted Arsenal's win and Morrow's goal were so enthusiastic that the Arsenal youngster had his arm broken as the other players fell on top of him at the end of the match. Come May, the opposition again was Arsenal. Just nine days before the final, the Owls had beaten them in the league 1–0 through a Mark Bright goal, and with David Hirst pushed back to fitness, 'Tricky Trev's Barmy Army' – as the ever growing horde of fans had dubbed themselves – could look forward to the game with some confidence.

'Somehow we'd convinced ourselves that this was the one to play for. Although the Coca-Cola guaranteed a place in Europe, it didn't carry the same prestige as the FA Cup. I'd seen some of the Spurs players walk away smiling after our Coventry defeat and I tried to explain to my team-mates how much it hurt to lose.'

The match did not live up to the expectation. By now the sides knew too much about each other. Although Arsenal took the lead through Ian Wright and kept that advantage until half-time, David Hirst equalised in the second half and the extra half-hour failed to resolve anything. Five days later, it was back to Wembley again. 'Some players hope to play there once in a lifetime. This was my fourth visit of the season.'

It was a much better contest this time. Again Ian Wright gave Arsenal a first-half lead, but when Chris levelled things with his first goal in a Wembley cup final, Wednesday began to take command. It was still all-square at full-time and, with seconds of extra-time to go, penalties seemed on the cards. Chris could feel his stomach churning. He couldn't bear the thought of another crucial miss, prayed that if it came to it the match would be settled one way or another before it was his turn to step up to the spot-kick. It was Andy Linighan who saved him that agony, but by heading home for Arsenal in the very last second of extra-time, he inflicted another kind of pain. The sharp, but lingering pain of defeat.

As the final whistle blew, signalling Chris's third cup final defeat at Wembley and the fifth of his career, he sank to the ground in disbelief. He could not hold back the tears and did not care who saw them. 'Arsenal must be the worst team in the world to play if you get to a cup final. They never know when they're beaten, and in any event, they were Wednesday's long-time bogey team. Ian Wright is one of the most dangerous opponents I've ever faced. The heartache was that we should have won the replay, but they got their winner with thirty seconds left and the "Lucky Arsenal" tag seemed to fit. All I could think at the end was – why?'

Back in the dressing-room there was a shared pain. To lose once at Wembley was bad enough, but doing so twice in a season to the same opponents beggared description. Once again there was the reception back home at City Hall to be faced, and at that moment he felt for the fans even more than he felt for himself. The great adventure had come to an end with nothing to show for it, not even a consolation place in Europe. He felt they had entertained throughout the season and deserved one of the trophies. Yet in football success does not always go to those who deserve it. The good guys don't always win in the theatre of dreams. He would be thirty-three in December, and in that moment of mind-numbing loss, he felt that a domestic trophy would now always be tantalisingly just out of reach.

chapter 48

Six days after the Wembley disaster Chris was at another cup final. This time it was the European Champions Cup between AC Milan and Olympique de Marseille in Munich. Tapie had insisted he attend as his guest to be with the team as a good luck charm. He was met off the plane by a stretch limo, and was even requested to train with the team on one occasion to show off all his old tricks. On the night of the game, he and Pat Nelson, who'd accompanied him, came into the huge stadium at the wrong end and had to walk through the Milan fans, who had not forgotten his goal in the quarter-final a year before. Just for a moment, he thought things might get out of hand, but eventually they allowed him to pass through, some of them even shaking him by the hand. When he got amongst the French fans he was asked to do a television interview, and up on the gantry he was spotted by the Marseille supporters who went crazy, chanting his name. 'It was an odd feeling to hear myself being cheered like that when I wasn't even playing, and if ever there was a time when I had a pang of regret that I'd left, then that was it.'

Tapie was very nervous before the match, for there was far more at stake than just winning a football match. By then every franc counted in his fight for survival. Chris predicted 2–0 and tried to calm his ex-president down by assuring him Marseille were Milan's bogey team. As it was, they won 1–0 with a goal from Boli, and again Chris was the guest of honour at the lavish post-match party. There were not to be many happy nights ahead for Tapie and that was the last time Chris was to meet the flamboyant character face to face.

June 1993 might have seemed an anticlimax, but there was much to interest Chris Waddle in that month. Graham Taylor now seemed in the twilight of his England managerial career as his team stumbled to an embarrassing 2–0 defeat at the hands of the USA, only a week after they had continued to jeopardise their World Cup qualification with a dire performance against Norway. Meanwhile, Terry Venables was losing his battle with Alan Sugar for reinstatement at Tottenham, a failure that began to clear the way for his ultimate appointment as England coach. And then, right at the end of the month, Marseille were accused of an attempt to bribe the players of CSKA Moscow in the previous season's European Cup – an accusation that would eventually lead to a year's ban, followed by their demotion to the Second Divison and the removal of Bernard Tapie from his autocratic rule of the club.

'I was very disappointed. Tapie had never been anything but straight with me. I couldn't understand why there was any need to bribe anybody; but Tapie was desperate to win all the time. The more he won, the more he was talked about, and that didn't do his political career any harm. Whatever may happen to Tapie in the end, I'm sure he'll be back. He's a survivor, and it's typical of the man that with all his troubles he's still managed to carve out a movie career for himself to add to all his other talents.'

Sheffield Wednesday's double cup runs of the previous year had earned the club a considerable amount of income, even if it had not produced any new trophies for their boardroom. Trevor Francis went out into the transfer market, returning with Andy Sinton from QPR, a player who in his day had been a rival for Chris's left-wing berth in the England team. He also added Andy Pearce, the Coventry defender, and Chris's old England team-mate, Des Walker, whose Italian love affair was well and truly over.

The team started the season as third favourites for the title, and on paper it looked a stronger squad than that which had done so well the year before. But by the end of October, the side were once again flirting with relegation in twentieth spot and living up to their reputation as slow starters. In the close season Trevor Francis had finally lost confidence in John Harkes, selling him to Derby County, and it was only after his departure that he realised what a vital cog he had been in the machine with his ceaseless running and tireless energy and enthusiasm. Chris thought, 'Trevor broke the 92–93 team up too early. Apart from Harkes, who I thought was worth another contract, there was a mass exodus. Danny Wilson and Viv Anderson went to Barnsley, Paul Warhurst to Blackburn, Carlton Palmer to Leeds, Nigel Pearson to Middlesbrough, Nigel Worthington to Leeds. It was the heart and the backbone of the side.'

Chris had started the campaign with a niggling foot injury that led to him missing the first three matches. Just when he was back and playing his brightest football, the injury returned, causing him to miss the entire league season after the Christmas period. From early October until the end of the year, Wednesday had lost only one of thirteen matches, rising into the top half of the table as well as moving smoothly into the fifth round of the Coca-Cola Cup with wins over Bolton, Middlesbrough and QPR.

With Chris sidelined, they eventually bowed out in the semi-final to Manchester United and with a defeat by Chelsea in the fourth round of the FA Cup, the season was virtually over – not only for Chris, but for the team itself. He'd tried to make a comeback in the replay against Chelsea at home after a draw at Stamford Bridge, coming on for Gordon Watson, but it was to no avail as they still went down 1–3 after extra-time. He was hurried back into the starting line-up for the first leg of the Coca-Cola semi-final, but again only aggravated the injury and limped off to be replaced by Bart-Williams. After all the excitement of the previous season, after the promise of the dawning of a new age for the club, it was a bitter pill to swallow.

The real frustration for Chris was hearing from Terry Venables, on his appointment as the England coach in January, that he still figured in his plans for the national team, but having to tell him back that he had little or no chance of playing in the immediate future because of his Achilles injury. 'Terry was very supportive. He said he'd keep an eye on the situation as he was looking to bring more mature players into the squad to ensure that there was a good line of communication between him and them, and them and the younger players, who might be too nervous to talk about their problems to the management. In my absence, Peter Beardsley was the one to benefit from that policy as he was recalled after a long absence under Graham Taylor.'

Chris always got on extremely well with Trevor Francis off the field. They were both intelligent men who could talk football until the wee small hours. But he did not see eye-to-eye with him all the time with regard to team selection and tactics. Chris certainly felt that Trevor did not make full use of his senior players' experience and there were times when Chris felt that Trevor regarded him as a rival.

Certainly at first Chris could not understand how Trevor could have merited the accusations of poor man management that had dogged him at QPR. Yet, as time wore on he sensed a certain inconsistency about Trevor. It seemed that the pressure was getting to the man who was decent at heart, but found it hard to understand some of the abuse and criticism that was levelled at him.

The general feeling among the playing staff was that unless the 1994–95 season produced some success, then it could well prove to be his last with the club. Chris never had a real slanging match with Trevor Francis, but did feel that they were playing a different style from that which had attracted him to the club in the first place.

That issue had reared its head in his very early days with the club. On a tour to South Africa, he'd told Francis and Barker that he felt the team would do better if they could play attractive football. To his surprise, Francis had disagreed, maintaining that it was all about results, while Barker chimed in with the accusation that Chris wasn't playing too well himself. After Chris had pointed out that it was hard to play well if nobody passed to him, things had improved. Now it looked as if they were about to go sour again.

As Chris's *annus horribilis* came to an end, there was only one shining light in the darkness. On 2 December 1993, Lorna had given birth to a son. There was no real dispute over his name. Newcastle's own favourite son, who had worn the black and

white number nine shirt with such distinction, had also been
one of Chris's heroes. He had also been one of the young
player's most eloquent advocates when he'd been struggling
to establish himself in the side. With a famous father and an
illustrious namesake, Jack Waddle had the perfect start in life.
The rest was up to him.

chapter 49

By the time Chris made his seasonal debut in the 1994–95 campaign, storm clouds were already gathering on the horizon. One win in their first eight matches saw Sheffield Wednesday poised just above the relegation spots. Francis had bought the Romanian, Dan Petrescu, to bolster up the defence, but he failed to show his best in the Premier League until he moved down south to Chelsea. Good player that he undoubtedly is, he was not the big-name signing that would give the fans the signal that there was a genuine chance of winning the title. More than 34,000 fans attended the opening match at Hillsborough against Spurs, but by the end of September only 23,227 were there for what should have been a competitive local derby with Leeds.

The pressure eased somewhat against Manchester United on 8 October when Wednesday won 1–0 and a victory at Ipswich gave the club some hope that they could resurrect their season. However, by the time Chris returned as substitute on 3 December, against Palace, they had won only once in a sequence of six matches – and that by the solitary goal against lowly West Ham.

To add to their misery, they had been put out of the Coca-Cola

Cup by Arsenal yet again, losing 2–1 at the end of November at Highbury. There almost seemed no point in playing the matches once their names had been drawn out of the hat together. The only up side for Chris was that the mixture of injury and rejection by the manager allowed his media career to develop apace. A few appearances on BBC's *Football Focus* in the past, as well as some bits and pieces for Tyne-Tees, had given him the taste for it. He had his own column in the well-respected football magazine *Four Four Two*, and with his old club, Newcastle, back in European competition he was regularly called upon by the BBC, both as a radio commentator and a television pundit.

He had begun disastrously on the radio when given his own programme *à la* Gary Lineker, reading pre-prepared scripts with all the woodenness of a totem pole. Yet when he was given the freedom to say what he thought, rather than what the producer might believe he thought, it was a different story. As he was encouraged to speak more slowly and more clearly, his commonsense and humour began to come through. He was more relaxed, clearly enjoying it more himself, and it showed.

'I was told that if I said "to be perfectly honest" one more time, they'd pull out the plug. I began to think a bit more about the whole thing. There's so many times you can use phrases like "if you don't buy a ticket you can't win the lottery", and I started to look and listen to recordings of my performances and work on it from there.'

Even when he was ready to return to the field from the commentary box, Trevor Francis appeared to be in no great hurry to bring him back to the side. It was a frustrating time. Francis had clearly decided that he was better deployed as a tactical weapon, rather than a ninety-minute player, and, indeed, stated publicly that he thought Chris was finding it difficult to take an active participation in the whole of a game. It wasn't true as far as Chris was concerned. He had always promised himself that as soon as he perceived he was not delivering the goods at the top level then he would call it a day, but at the moment he felt as fit as ever.

There were others who felt he could make a significant contribution. Sunderland, with Peter Reid in charge, were forever knocking on the door. However, Wednesday effectively scared them off by insisting that they would not sell the player for less than £1.2 million, only a small discount on the price they had paid themselves some three years earlier. But Chris had been three years younger then, and for that sort of money he did not appear at the time to be a long-term investment. Bryan Robson, newly instated at Middlesbrough, did actually offer a million, but was knocked back as it clearly was not politically expedient to get rid of Chris at the time.

Newcastle also showed an interest. Then Chris suddenly found himself restored to the team as if nothing had happened. His return was soon followed by a successful run that took the club up into the top half of the table and even suggested a place in Europe might not be beyond their capabilities. There were a couple of set-backs with defeats by Spurs and QPR, but then the team set off on a ten-match unbeaten sequence in the league and cup. When they settled an old score with Arsenal with a 3–1 victory on 4 February, they had not only progressed to eighth place, but were also anticipating some progress in the FA Cup.

Wolves, now under Graham Taylor, had held them to a goalless draw at Hillsborough, but they'd had enough chances then to visit Molyneux with some confidence. Yet, at full-time and after an extra half an hour, it was one apiece – and there was only one way to settle the issue. The days of endless replays had gone, pushed aside by fixture congestion, police restrictions and the demands of the great television viewing public for an immediate and dramatic conclusion. As the final whistle blew, it was going to be penalties.

It was almost inevitable that if Chris was ever going to be involved in a penalty shoot-out again, it would be in a match shown live on television – and sure enough Sky's cameras were there to record it all for posterity. It started promisingly enough. Wolves missed their first three, while Wednesday found the back of the net each time. Three–nil seemed an unassailable lead, until first Andy Pearce and then Chris Bart-Williams missed, Wolves converted their next two and it was down to Chris. It never occurred to Chris to decline his turn for the spot-kick, but as he ran in, he could not clear his mind of the nightmare of that traumatic summer's night some six years before in Turin.

'I decided that whatever I did I had to hit the target, so I tried to place it by making the keeper go the wrong way. As it was, he guessed correctly and saved it. He claimed afterwards that he'd seen what I'd done in 1990, but I'm not sure how that would have actually helped him.

'Everybody said I shouldn't have been involved, but if that was the case, then I had no right to be on the pitch. If the same thing happened again I still wouldn't bottle out.'

Don Goodman calmly scored with Wolves' next penalty and Wednesday were out by 4–3.

At that stage, the league season could still have gone either way. There were enough matches left for them to get amongst the leaders if they strung together a series of victories, and there was also the possibility of being sucked towards the dead men if defeats piled up. As it was, neither occurred. They finished the season in mid-table obscurity. It was an interesting statistic that in the second half of the season, Chris either started or ended the game on the bench no less than nine times.

It was all so disillusioning. At thirty-four, he still felt he had something to offer. He'd scored four times in the league between December and March and made countless other chances for his team-mates. But Francis seemed burned out and the club's ambitions were limited. In an attempt to add some fire power, they bought Guy Whittingham, the former Portsmouth prolific scorer. But he'd already failed at Aston Villa in between and, good club man that he doubtless was, he was another at Wednesday who he was just off the highest level.

It was not a great surprise when on 20 May 1995, the board's patience with Trevor Francis was finally exhausted and he was dismissed. It was a little over two years since he had taken the club to Wembley no less than four times in a season – but nobody remembers the losers, and without silverware in the trophy cabinet to remind them, the memories of directors are notoriously short.

Amongst the fans and several local newspapers, there was a strong feeling that Chris should get the job. A poll in a local newspaper put him as clear favourite. The board, however, had other ideas and felt they needed a man with experience. Chris had been outspoken enough about his feelings regarding Francis's increasingly odd managerial decisions for them to perceive Chris as too much of his own man for their tastes. In the event, the man they did appoint was no stranger to Chris Waddle. David Pleat had been his manager at Spurs, and since then had been rehabilitated at Luton after his traumas in north London.

Chris was not too disappointed, although he did feel mildly peeved that, given the public demand for his appointment, the board did not see fit to confide in him regarding the choice of Pleat. He learned about it along with all the other players. Despite that disappointment, he still felt Pleat would be an improvement on Francis. He'd always liked the way he got his teams playing football, both at Luton and Spurs, and also felt that Pleat liked his style of play. With his injuries behind him and a new manager at the helm, Chris entered the final year of his four-year contract at Wednesday with all the enthusiasm of a teenager.

chapter 50

It was clear from the start that Pleat was going to run things his way. It was also clear that he regarded Chris Waddle as a threat rather than an asset. Yet he professed to like the Continental style of play and during his first year in charge purchased Mark Degryse, Kovacevic, Stefanovic and Reggie Blinker from the Continent. However, he did still encourage some of the home grown talent in the shape of Mark Platts and Ritchie Humphreys. He also spoke to Chris about his greater involvement in the coaching side, although the offer extended only to the juniors and not to the senior team. There, once again, he brought in his own men, leaving Chris with the impression that he did not figure in Pleat's long-term plans nor, indeed, those of the club.

Fairly early in the season there was some talk about a new contract, but the club seemed reluctant to discuss the matter with Chris's advisers, restricting themselves to odd comments made directly to the player. Although he would be thirty-five in December, he felt he genuinely had another four or five years in the top flight in him. The club, on the other hand, did not wish to offer anything more than a one-year extension to his contract. They wanted to have their cake and eat it, there was no great enthusiasm about selling him and certainly for some time they resisted any idea of the free transfer to which Chris felt his loyalty entitled him. It was not until February 1996 that they finally committed any kind of offer to writing – and that was essentially only a one-year deal, extending his contract through to June 1997 on virtually the same financial terms that had been negotiated four years earlier, when football had been a much poorer business.

Sunderland had persisted in their enquiries, but there was still a prohibitive asking price. Only when Celtic actually bid £750,000 did they indicate they would accept the offer. Tommy Burns, the Celtic manager, impressed Chris when he spoke to him, but he wanted his players to live in the vicinity and was not prepared to accept Chris's offer to commute. After discussing the proposal at length, the Waddles agreed they were reluctant to move north of the border and, indeed, reluctant to move anywhere that meant they'd have to sell the house in Dore. The only thing that could have enticed them was a return to the north-east and home, but Wednesday's refusal when Sunderland came back with an offer of £400,000 meant that the dream move to the club he had supported as a child could never happen.

The writing was on the wall when, in the very first match of the season, he was substituted by David Hirst in a 1–0 defeat at Anfield. Four days later he was taken off again after scoring the first goal in a 2–1 win over Blackburn, although on that occasion it was an injury that justified the substitution. He didn't return to the fray until mid-September and a 3–1 home defeat by Spurs; and then, yet again, it was only as substitute. He did have a good run after that, playing in the next twenty matches, but was removed from the field before the end in five of these.

The results with or without him were, to say the least, moderate. After the beginning of September, the side never moved into the top half of the table. Wins against lower-division opposition in the shapes of Crewe and Millwall in the Coca-Cola Cup led, almost inevitably, to a fourth-round tie against Arsenal. Equally inevitably, there could only be one result. Although Arsenal won 2–1, Chris was at the heart of everything positive produced by the visitors. The home defence were bewildered as he started the match as an out-and-out striker, then moved into mid-field and finally drifted out to the flanks.

Yet his efforts were not particularly appreciated. He was still awaiting an offer of an extended contract from the club, having received no more than vague promises to discuss the matter after Christmas. Chris was certain that he wanted still to be playing the following season, but he also wanted to know for whom he would be playing. Yet again Newcastle showed an interest, claiming to have made a bid, although Pleat told Chris and his advisers that it was just an enquiry without any firm offer of money. Once more Chris was left with the distinct feeling that, as long as his popularity with the Sheffield public continued and there was a chance that his departure would cause the manager some flak, Pleat would not allow him to leave.

One of Pleat's great talents was an ability to judge the mood of the fans and to manipulate the press accordingly. He was able to say that every encouragement had been given to keep Chris at the club, bearing in mind that if he'd gone to Celtic (a move that Wednesday encouraged) at least he would not have come back to Hillsborough with any other Premier League club. From the moment Pleat had joined, there had been pressure on Chris to move on to the coaching staff, but it simply wasn't what he wanted to do at that stage in his career. What was clear was that Pleat, like his predecessor Francis, was beginning to perceive him as a threat – the crown prince waiting in the wings for the king to make a mistake that would cost him his throne.

As it was, yet another approach came in – this time from an unexpected quarter. John Harkes had returned to the States to play in the newly formed Major League Soccer competition. Kevin Payne, the owner of his club, DC United (based in Washington), was a great anglophile when it came to the sport, and a big fan of Waddle in particular. The system out there was quite different from the domestic picture here. It was not the individual clubs which bought the players of their choice but the MLS itself. They would distribute the players amongst the clubs on a kind of handicapping basis, with the intention that whoever won the title in one season would have last choice in selecting college draft players to their squads the following year.

Sunil Galaty, chief executive of the MLS, was a much tougher proposition than Payne. Because of Chris's age he was prepared to offer only a two-year contract, without any guaranteed extension either as a player or a coach. While Chris was not prepared to uproot his family for anything less than a three-year term, a further and greater problem was that Sheffield Wednesday were still looking for a fee for him, even for a move to the States. Although they were prepared to accept a 'concessionary' figure, the amount quoted of £250,000 still meant that the fledgling MLS simply could not afford to give Chris the extension he desired. Mel Stein wrote to Graham Mackrell, the Sheffield Wednesday secretary, on 4 March saying, 'I think it should formally be placed on record that Chris is somewhat disappointed that yet another potential door in respect of his future career has been closed by the Club's insistence on a substantial fee.'

Martigues of the French First Division also made an effort to get Chris back to France. Struggling at the foot of the table, they were prepared to offer massive incentives if Chris helped them to retain their position in the top flight. They had already made one effort to get Chris to return to the other side of the Channel as early as December 1992. It had seemed a retrograde step then and it seemed so now, apart from the fact that Tapie and his cronies were still engulfed by all sorts of court proceedings, both civil and criminal, and seemed only too willing to implicate anybody who had crossed their paths, however innocent they might be. Chris had certainly done nothing wrong during his time at Marseille, but decided that discretion was the better part of valour and declined the offer to partake in a relegation battle. As it transpired, it was probably the right move as Martigues finished rock bottom of the league, some five points from safety, and were duly relegated, to be replaced by the revamped Olympique de Marseille. He needn't have worried about the French authorities either, as in their efforts to entrap Tapie they had given all the players an amnesty.

As the season wore on at home, it looked increasingly unlikely that his future lay at Wednesday and an early exit from the FA Cup in the third round at Charlton meant there was to be no story-book ending to his time at Hillsborough. On 10 February, against Wimbledon, he found himself replaced by the sixteen-year-old prodigy Mark Platts, who was making his debut. Chris had made his bow before the boy was even born. The message Pleat was sending him was clear. This was a young man's sport and all his experience counted for nothing as far as the manager was concerned.

A fortnight later he sat on the bench at White Hart Lane alongside Mark Platts. Both sets of supporters could not believe he would not have added something to a side that was singularly bereft of ideas. As it was, Wednesday lost 1–0 and the travelling fans showed their displeasure. By now the relationship with Pleat had totally disintegrated. He would not come out and say publicly that he wanted Waddle to leave, but absolutely no effort was made to keep him either.

On 6 March 1996, although nobody could know it at the time, Chris Waddle figured in a Sheffield Wednesday starting line-up for the last time. The match was at Villa Park. Although the visitors led 1–0 at half-time, they ended up on the wrong end of a 3–2 score-sheet. Chris did play the whole game and the turn-around in fortunes allowed Pleat to say with some credibility that he did not believe Waddle was up to ninety minutes of a match any longer. As if to prove his point, Chris figured amongst the substitutes for the rest of the season, only being brought on as a peripheral figure, painted by Pleat as being in the twilight of his years.

Pleat still defends his decision: 'I thought he should play off the front men, while I filled the mid-field with lots of bodies. I came to the conclusion that he didn't have the legs to sustain ninety minutes in the Premiership. He wasn't a ball-winner and, to be fair, maybe we weren't good enough at the time to get the ball to him. He was, however, great in training and there could be no doubting the respect in which he was held, not only by the fans, but by his fellow professionals. I thought in the last five games of the season I'd use him as a substitute and keep him fresh for the final twenty minutes of the game.'

Sheffield Wednesday drifted to the end of the season, winning only once in the last seven matches, and finishing fifteenth. There was no further discussion of a new deal and by the time his four-year contract came to an end in June 1996, it was no longer a question of whether or not he would leave the club, but when, and just how difficult Wednesday would make it with their financial demands. Once again Chris asked if Pleat would release him for nothing at the end of the year, and once again the manager prevaricated. A lesser man would have been tempted to hang up his boots for good, but Chris was never one to be defeated. After all his years in the game, he had come to believe he had nothing to prove to anybody; but Pleat had changed all that, and in his cavalier rejection of the man who had been central to Wednesday's limited successes, he had awoken a burning ambition to succeed all over again elsewhere.

chapter 51

The summer of 1996 was a particularly busy one for Chris Waddle. He was a part of the BBC team that covered Euro '96, handling his coverage of matches with a confidence and fluency that would not have seemed possible a few years earlier. Before England's unfortunate exit at the hands of the Germans, he was able to see Stuart Pearce erase the nightmare of Italy against Spain and then see Gareth Southgate join the roll-call of infamy with his miss against the Germans.

'I really felt for Gareth, and it was me who tried to persuade him to do the Pizza Hut advert that featured him, Stuart and myself. We were all criticised for that in some quarters, but we felt there was no reason not to laugh at ourselves, and of the three of us I think it gave Gareth the most assistance in getting the memory behind him. I had one line and gave it to Stuart. It took us ten hours of filming, and unfortunately we found ourselves laughing too much off camera and finding it difficult to laugh when we were supposed to. Stuart and I reckoned Gareth was being paid by the hour, because we did our parts with about 120 takes whilst he took 145.'

Following close on the heels of England's semi-final exit was

Gazza's wedding. A week after the event, a pale-faced Waddle met up with Mel Stein in Derbyshire. 'You know when you say never again after a drinking session. Well, this time, I really mean it.'

As 30 June 1996 came and went, Chris Waddle was still officially a Sheffield Wednesday player. Yet, as the 1996–97 season kicked off, the possibility of him starting a match for the club that he had served so well and so loyally seemed remote to say the least. The board still seemed reluctant to give him the free transfer that he deserved and no other Premier League club was willing to take a chance by paying a fee for a player who would be thirty-six at Christmas, and who had used the close season to have a long-awaited ankle operation, rather than train to the peak of fitness. Many of the papers reported that his Achilles problem had returned, which may well have put off some potential employers, although in fact he was merely having the ankle 'flushed'.

Many pundits had selected Wednesday as one of the favourites for relegation, along with any combination of newly promoted Leicester, Sunderland and Derby. But to everybody's astonishment, after four matches they were riding high at the top of the table, the only side in the Premiership with a one hundred per cent record. Pleat seized the moment to be magnanimous and finally told Chris, who was on a month-to-month contract, that he could go for nothing. His timing in public relations terms was perfect. A message went out once again through the Press Association that this time he was available on a free transfer and yet, somewhat surprisingly, there was no rush of takers.

Ruud Gullit at Chelsea invited Chris down, but without any promise of a long-term contract. However, not only did Chris not feel fit enough for Premier League football, he also did not fancy the idea of either commuting or sitting on the bench awaiting an injury to Chelsea's expensive imports. At least Gullit had sensed that he still had something to offer as a player – a view that was clearly not shared by any other manager in the Premiership.

Terry Venables, now the supremo at Portsmouth and not yet appointed coach to the Australian national team, also made a call to check on Chris's availability, but once again the distance was a factor in his decision. Somehow or other, everybody seemed to assume that he was ready to move immediately into management and that if he was going to continue playing it would be as a player-coach. A management job did become available when QPR, after an uneasy start to their First Division season, decided to dispense with the services of Ray Wilkins. One of their holding company's directors asked if Chris might be interested, but it went no further, and Stewart Houston got the job, to be joined shortly after by Bruce Rioch. Blackpool did, in fact, invite him to apply for the manager's job, but with their ex-chairman in jail, yet seemingly still in control of the club, it did not seem the most attractive of propositions. He was equally uninspired by approaches from a consortium trying to gain control of Hull City and offers to sign as a player for Walsall, Notts County and Chesterfield.

'I was confident enough to believe that the right opportunity would come along. I was under no financial pressures, and whatever I did had to be right both for me and – of more importance – for my family, although I must say that when Chesterfield reached the semi-final of the FA Cup I wondered if I'd been a bit hasty in turning them down.'

David Pleat now suddenly seemed anxious about Chris's future. After asking Mel Stein whether Chris had received any offers, he told him that Wednesday had decided not to renew his contract at the end of the month. In other words, he was being tossed aside, and if he didn't find another club then he was on his own. There was no mention of the opportunities that had been lost with Sunderland, Newcastle and the MLS. Now it all boiled down to getting an expensive player off their payroll.

Pleat categorically denies that Wednesday's fine start to the season was the sole reason for the club finally allowing him to go on a free transfer. 'Obviously it eased the situation, but I was receiving very abusive letters from the fans who felt that he should be sold. I certainly felt he should be going into coaching sooner rather than later, but it seemed to me that he wanted to step into a big job straight away rather than having an apprenticeship in the lower regions of the league. I was always convinced that he was highly intelligent and tactically sound, but believed he needed to prove that before he moved on to bigger things. It was hard for me, without having played at the top level myself, to say to a great player that I thought he couldn't do it any more at the highest level and that he had no future with the club.'

As it was, his time with Sunderland was to prove Pleat wrong, but at the time Chris was faced with a stark future having had a massive blow to his hard won confidence. Salvation came from an unusual source. Falkirk, in the Scottish First Division, were probably one of the last clubs that Chris would have thought of joining from the Premiership, yet they were the only one to make a firm offer, and a generous one at that. George Fulston, the chairman, and Neil Binney, his co-director, were straight and honest people and the negotiations were speedily concluded. By the middle of September, with Sheffield Wednesday still at the top of the table, Chris Waddle, formerly of Newcastle United, Tottenham Hotspur, Olympique de Marseille and England, made his debut in Scotland for Falkirk. Wednesday, having indicated they would pay him until the end of the month, changed their minds and merely apportioned his salary to the day of departure. Chris could not even be bothered to take the issue up with them. He was pleased to be leaving and actually looking forward to knowing that his name would be first on the team-sheet.

His first match was against Clydebank before a crowd of 4,800. Inevitably it was a winning debut and during the month that Chris spent with the club, they lost only once and began to look real promotion candidates. Although Chris felt himself fit to play at that level, he made it clear to everybody at the club that he was looking to get back into the English league and would take every opportunity in a Falkirk shirt to get himself fully prepared for that re-entry.

He continued his record of scoring for every club with whom he played, but by the end of the month he was yearning for a higher class of football. The directors, the fans and the players all made him and Lorna more than welcome, but travelling up on a Thursday and then having to rely on all sorts of strange train connections or a long drive to get himself home for Sunday was not ideal.

Neil Binney, the Falkirk director who was largely responsible for signing Chris, remembers him with affection: 'I'd been watching Sheffield Wednesday ever since my business brought me down from Scotland to Scunthorpe. Waddle was the star man and I always dreamed that if I had the money and opportunity I'd bring him up to Falkirk. When I heard he was available on a free transfer and made my approach, my wife thought I'd taken leave of my senses. After I'd spoken to Chris on the phone I was confident he'd join us, and after I met him I was certain. He lifted the club and the whole town, even though he was only with us for a month. The lasting image of him is a picture in the *Daily Record*, taken during that first match, which showed kids of ten and old men of eighty literally jumping with joy after Chris had scored. During his time with us, nothing was too much trouble. He'd spend hours signing autographs for the youngsters, mingling in our hospitality suite, and I'm certain that his influence was the launching pad for our successful season. I don't think anybody who saw him play will forget that brief, but glorious, time when Chris Waddle played for Falkirk.'

Now that Chris was no longer a Wednesday player, Pleat seemed to have softened in his attitude and was quite happy for him to use the club's facilities for training. But Chris felt like a stranger going back there and was anxious for something more permanent. Once he had made it clear that he would not be ending his career with Falkirk, there were more offers. Milwall wanted him, but again there was the question of upheaval without any long-term commitment, and once more Venables was on the phone to see what his plans were.

Again, the offer that he would accept came from an unlikely quarter. Bradford City, managed by Chris Kamara, were in nineteenth position in the First Division, having struggled to adjust after their promotion the previous season via the play-offs.

Kamara was bolder than many others would have been in his position. If he signed Chris Waddle and it didn't work out, not only was his job on the line, but the club also had a natural successor on the staff. Whether or not that thought occurred to him, he was clearly prepared to put the future of the club before his personal security, and on 11 October, Chris signed a one-month contract. In a career spanning some fifteen years, Bradford was only his fourth English club. Again there were all sorts of mumblings in the press as to why he had set his sights so low, but as far as Chris was concerned, he was joining a sleeping giant. Even as they struggled, their crowds were well above the likes of Wimbledon and most other First Division teams. The potential was there. And, best of all, he could travel from home each day to training. If the rest of the world outside Bradford saw it as the end of his career, Chris saw it as a challenge and one to which he was determined to rise.

chapter 52

There was no magic wand waved over Valley Parade. By Christmas, with Chris having celebrated his thirty-sixth birthday, Bradford were still occupying one of the relegation spots. Every time they took the lead or threatened to win a match, they seemed to pluck a draw or defeat from the jaws of victory. It was becoming a question of mind over matter. Yet, for all that, Chris was enjoying himself. He had always liked a battle and the fact that this was one against relegation made no difference.

As it was, there was an interesting mix of promising youngsters at the club, together with such seasoned professionals as Gordon Cowans, who had, of course, played with Chris for England. Indeed, it was Cowans who had been substituted for Gazza in that fateful match in Dublin so many years before, when Chris's own long-term England career had, with hindsight, effectively come to an end. The club needed something more, and to Kamara's credit he was able to persuade the chairman to dip into the transfer market again and bring in a foreign squadron consisting of Schwarzer in goal, Sas in defence and Steiner up front.

It was the FA Cup that finally kick-started their season.

Drawn to play Wycombe in the third round, they were fancied to lose, but came through comfortably, and Chris was beginning to feel the old excitement that only the FA Cup could bring. 'Everybody who knew me knew how bitterly disappointed I'd been to miss out on so many winners' medals in the cups over the years. But everybody also assumed that my chance of ever getting a victory at Wembley had gone. They thought I was joking when I said I reckoned I had a chance with Bradford City.'

If they had considered Chris's comments to be nothing more than tongue in cheek, the realism of the situation came home on Saturday 25 January 1997. Chris had thought that his days on the Premier stage were behind him. Just the week before the game there had been an enquiry from Harry Redknapp at West Ham, but Chris had replied that he was flattered by the offer but he felt he just couldn't leave Bradford in their hour of need. They'd been good to him, offering him a chance after his spell at Falkirk, and he felt that then had been the time for any Premier club to come in for him. His loyalty to City was to be rewarded in spades in a very short space of time.

The chance to visit Goodison in an away fourth-round tie against Everton was welcomed as a windfall opportunity. Everton, under Joe Royle, had started their Premiership campaign with a win over champions-elect Newcastle United, tailed off, and then got together a run that had people tipping them as dark horses for the title themselves. By the start of 1997, though, that was behind them, and they were beginning to look a very ordinary side. Just the week before had brought the taunts of the Arsenal crowd of 'Can we play you every week?' as they had tumbled tamely to a 3–1 defeat.

The FA cup seemed to be Everton's best chance of European football, and certainly Chris and his manager expected to have the kitchen sink thrown at them. However, there were one or two who sensed it might be Waddle's day rather than Everton's. David Maddock writing in *The Times* on the morning of the match said: 'Centre stage beckons once more this afternoon .... It will be a brief moment, a reminder of the mesmeric, nonchalant skills that were cultivated in England and blossomed spectacularly in France. There is every chance that Everton will be on the receiving end of his relatively undiminished talents and that is an uneasy prospect for an FA Carling Premiership side that has lost its last five league matches.'

On paper it looked no contest. Everton had the million-pound players – Nicky Barmby (with whom Chris had last chatted at Gazza's wedding), Duncan Ferguson and Andrei Kanchelskis, who was just a few days away from an £8 million move to Italy. City had Lee Duxbury, Andy Kiwomya, Wayne Jacobs and Chris himself, all assembled for virtually nothing. But they also had their foreigners, and although none of them would be moving for £8 million, they were all good players in their own right.

In front of a crowd of just over 30,000, it was just like old times, with a considerable Bradford contingent that swelled not only the numbers but also the noise levels with their incessant singing. At half-time, with the score still goalless, it was those visiting fans who were entitled to be the happier. They had seen Chris put a free-kick just over the bar and then provide Dreyer with another chance which went the same way.

The writing was on the wall, and within four minutes of the restart, Chris put in another teasing cross, which was deflected to Dreyer, who volleyed home from the edge of the area. Within a couple of moments Chris had stamped his own name and class indelibly on the match. Before the match, Kamara had said to his opponent's long-serving keeper Neville Southall, 'Wads is playing, so you'd better stay on your line.'

If the advice was heeded, it was certainly forgotten when, in the fifty-first minute, Chris picked up a loose ball some forty yards from goal and from a seemingly harmless position, with an instant replay of the unsuccessful effort in the World Cup semi-final, coolly lobbed the goalie to put City 2–0 ahead. He celebrated as if it had been his first goal as a debutant, leaping along the half-way line until the rest of the team recovered from their disbelief and buried him beneath an avalanche of bodies.

Everton pulled one back with an own goal, but Chris was not going to let the moment go. He split the beleagured Everton defence with a through ball to Steiner, who calmly slotted it home. There was still time for an Everton consolation goal with virtually the last kick of the match, but it was Bradford who were through and the Toffeemen left to lick their wounds.

Although it was a team victory, Chris Kamara could not resist singling out his veteran star for praise: 'I said beforehand that he would be the best player on the pitch and he was. I am fortunate enough to have him.' He was not to know that within a week of that thrilling victory, there was every possibility he would lose him.

The draw for the fifth round was enticing. A home fixture against Sheffield Wednesday, David Pleat and all, in a game to be televised live on 16 February. Chris had unwittingly set the tone for the match in his comments after the Everton game.

'Why aren't you still in the Premier League, Chris?' one

reporter asked, voicing the question that was on everybody's lips.

'You'd better ask Mr Pleat that,' Chris replied.

That was a signal for every aspect of the media to pursue Chris for an interview that would enable them to bill the forthcoming cup-tie as Waddle versus Pleat. But Chris resisted, despite the cheque books being waved in his face. He had momentarily dropped his guard in the heat of victory, but from now on he would let his football do the talking.

Yet before he could really focus on the match, an opportunity arose that Chris Kamara and his chairman could have envisaged only in their nightmares. They'd reached the fifth round of the FA Cup, a mid-week league win over Port Vale had hauled them out of the relegation spots, and everything revolved around Chris Waddle. It was then that the West Bromich Albion chairman rang his opposite number, asking for permission to speak to Chris about the vacancy at the Hawthorns. WBA, only a place or two above Bradford in the table, could not only be described as yet another sleeping giant, but were also about to float as a public company on the stock market. They needed a big name and Chris fitted the bill. Although he had committed himself to Bradford for the rest of the season, there had always been the understanding that they would not stand in his way if a managerial appointment came along. On Tuesday 4 February, WBA were due to visit Birmingham City, now managed by Trevor Francis. If Chris was not to come back to haunt Pleat at the end of the month, there seemed every possibility that he would be haunting another ex-Sheffield Wednesday manager who had failed to appreciate his talents.

As he travelled to Rotherham on Sunday 2 February for his

interview, he was torn as he had never been before in all his years in football, even when it had come to leaving Tottenham. He had already grown to love Bradford and everybody associated with the club. Kamara was not much older than him, and a friendship had immediately sprung up between the two men. There was also the threat of missing the next round of the cup, of missing his last chance to progress on the way to Wembley. Whatever he decided, the decision would not be an easy one.

chapter 53

The lengthy meeting with Tony Hale, the West Bromich Albion chairman, and his co-director Paul Thompson was educational, if nothing else. By the time Chris joined them shortly after noon, Teletext was already announcing his appointment. If that information came from the club, then they were jumping the gun. They chatted in Thompson's office in Rotherham for some three hours, at the end of which the West Bromich representatives told Chris he was their first choice and the job was available to him if he wanted it. He told them, as he has told every club with which he has been associated, that he did not deal with financial matters himself and asked Paul Thompson to ring Mel Stein.

Thompson told Stein that their financial parameters for the position had already been set and were virtually non-negotiable. Stein and Len Lazarus quickly agreed that they were far from generous, advising Chris accordingly, but the Midland club would not budge by a penny, insisting that if Chris didn't want the job, then they had already satisfied themselves that another big-name manager, with experience, would jump at it.

Chris held his ground, thanked them for their time, and returned to Dore. Lorna respected his decision, although she had been far keener for him to move into management sooner rather than later, accusing him of cowardice when he'd hesitated over even going for the interview.

'You can't play for ever,' she'd said.

'No, but I want to keep on playing as long as I can.'

That had been one of the problems with the WBA offer. They were really not interested in the fact that they would be getting a player of Waddle's ability and were not prepared to pay for it, either. They wanted a manager and felt they were offering generous terms to a man with no managerial credentials.

One person overjoyed to hear the news was Chris Kamara, who had almost resigned himself to playing Sheffield Wednesday without Waddle. Now, he told Chris, he was about to break open the champagne that he'd had on ice. The following morning, Stein received another message from Paul Thompson of WBA: 'I think we were a little too entrenched yesterday. Can we talk some more?' Thompson had already spoken to Chris, having asked the player, as he'd left their meeting, to sleep on the matter despite his rejection of their offer. He didn't know Chris Waddle. Once he had made up his mind, for better or worse, there is no moving him. Some people might call it stubbornness, others perverse loyalty, but that is the man.

'Tell them thanks,' he said. 'I really enjoyed the discussion and I'm flattered that they wanted me, but I've already told Chris Kamara that I'm staying, so I think we'll just leave it.'

Back in training with Bradford, Chris tried to concentrate on the battle against relegation. On 8 February, Bradford travelled to south London to visit the fast-improving, promotion chasing Crystal Palace. Within five minutes Waddle had done it again, scoring his seventh of the season to become City's top scorer.

For the next fifty-seven minutes, Bradford ran Palace ragged, but then Palace grabbed an equaliser, within three minutes were ahead and then rubbed salt into the wound by grabbing a third. It was an unfair score-line, but the headlines were still all about Waddle. 'Waddle's wizardry' was typical and Chris Kamara continued to heap praise upon his head. 'The one quality player on show,' he said. 'There's no one out there can get anywhere near him.'

The First Divison table showed a depressing state of affairs as Bradford slipped ever nearer to the relegation spots, having played more games than their rivals. The fifth-round cup tie against Wednesday was almost light relief. City were the underdogs, nobody expected them to win, and they could go out and enjoy themselves.

The ten-day build-up to the match was all about Waddle and Pleat, as if nobody else was involved. Chris continually resisted the temptation to snipe at his former manager and Pleat similarly refused to allow the game to become a showdown between the two men. Yet in all the pre-match interviews and hype, the name Waddle was on everybody's lips.

The Saturday cup matches gave Bradford every encouragement. Portsmouth beat Leeds, Wrexham beat Birmingham and Chesterfield disposed of Nottingham Forest. If only Bradford could overcome Sheffield Wednesday, then the luck of the draw could give them a relatively smooth path to Wembley. If only . . . .

On the morning of the match, a *Sunday Times* article by Joe Lovejoy carried the headline: 'The magician's final trick.' Chris was quoted as saying, 'I've always had this feeling I'd win the Cup as an old man . . . . I was brought up on the story of Stanley Matthews, and how people said he'd missed out only for him to get a winner's medal at thirty-eight and I've often thought, "That's going to happen to me."'

If it was, then he would have to wait another year. There was a carnival atmosphere within Bradford's packed stadium. The band from Wednesday brought drums and noisy fans, while the home supporters filled the ground with colour and passion. Bradford dominated the first half with their possession and corners, but could not create a clear goal-scoring chance. It was not one of Chris's best forty-five minutes, although one seventy-yard diagonal pass was a reminder of what he could do, as were any number of fierce in-swinging corners. Goalless at half-time, Wednesday came out for the second half clearly believing they could win the game first time around and went on the attack.

The game swung back and forth and with five minutes to go could still have gone either way. Then Pleat sent on David Hirst as substitute. He broke down the left and passed to young Ritchie Humphreys whose shot took a wicked deflection off Nicky Mohan and into the net. There was one brief threat from Chris. He beat two men down the right, twisted his way into the penalty area and, with more time than he realised, hurried his shot and saw the ball fly high and wide. It was over. The impossible dream was at an end. He left the field once again with tears in his eyes, his head hung low. All the season now had to offer was the fight against relegation. But he would face up to that with the same determination and resolution that he had brought to the rest of his career. 'Stanley Matthews was thirty-eight. I have two years to go,' he said ruefully.

Whatever the future held in store, whether as player or manager, whether at Bradford City or anywhere else, the Magician would continue to weave his spell.

epilogue

On Saturday 8 March, Bradford City faced up to relegation rivals Grimsby Town at Valley Parade. A healthy crowd of over 15,000 loyally supported their team, captained by Chris Waddle, in a game that see-sawed dramatically. Within fifteen minutes, Bradford were two goals down. They pulled back to 2–2 after thirty-seven minutes, only to concede the lead again two minutes before the interval. Grimsby restored the two-goal cushion, and although O'Brien made it 3–4 just before the end, there was no time for Bradford to secure even one point. With the win, Grimsby leapfrogged over Bradford into 21st position, leaving the Yorkshire side in the relegation zone. They had played a game more than their victors, who were now one place above them on goal difference and two more than Birmingham, managed by Trevor Francis, who were in twentieth spot, but with a nine-point advantage. With only Southend and Oldham below them, and the latter being revitalised by Neil Warnock, the future looked bleak indeed. However, Chris had known when he'd joined the club that First Division survival would not be easy and was quite prepared to roll up his sleeves for the battle ahead. It was a phone-call from Irving

Scholar on the night of Wednesday 12 March that changed all that.

Having served his time out of the game, Scholar had returned as part of the consortium that had bought a controlling interest in Nottingham Forest. His duties included negotiating the acquisition of players and, having seen his new club crash 2–0 at Highbury the previous Saturday, he realised something drastic was required. Earlier in the week, he had concluded the signing of Van Hoojdonk from Celtic, but with Steve Stone sidelined for the rest of the season, he knew that the Dutch international striker needed someone to provide him with the ammunition to score the goals. His thoughts turned to one of the players he had so admired throughout his career, a player he had already bought once and sold reluctantly – Chris Waddle.

There were very few individuals or clubs that could have enticed Chris away from Bradford. He could not remember ever having been happier at a club, despite their lowly position. Yet Irving Scholar set out to persuade him that he still had a future in the Premier League, and by the end of a lengthy conversation, Chris had agreed to join Forest – provided Scholar and Stein could agree terms. Chris knew that Bradford had agreed to let him go in the event of either a managerial or coaching post being offered to him, or should a Premier League club wish to sign him. In any event, Bradford had agreed not to seek a fee for him. Those had been pre-conditions to his original month-to-month contract, and when he had signed up for the rest of the season, similar terms were agreed. They had been confirmed in a letter Stein had sent to Kamara on 18 November 1996, 'so that there should be no misunderstanding'. Unfortunately, there was to be a misunderstanding.

It took Stein and Scholar all of five minutes to agree terms, at which point Chris tried to call Chris Kamara to break the bad news. The Bradford manager was at Loftus Road watching Reading, their opponents the following Saturday, dispose of QPR, with his mobile phone switched off. It remained switched off all evening, leaving Waddle with no alternative but to go to the ground the following morning, collect his boots and tell him to his face. It is not clear who actually leaked the story to the papers, but it was certainly not Chris or his advisers. The *Mirror* carried the story on Thursday morning, so that by the time Chris got to the ground, the news of his impending transfer seemed to be common knowledge. He spoke to Kamara who accepted he had every right to leave and wished him the best of luck, thanking him for all he had done for the club. However, as a courtesy he suggested that somebody from Forest should phone the Bradford chairman, Geoffrey Richmond, to finalise the arrangements.

By the time Irving Korn, the Forest chairman, did telephone his opposite number, Richmond was in no mood for courtesy calls. He called for a copy of Chris's contract, categorically denied there was any escape clause for him to leave to play elsewhere, and said he was going nowhere. For good measure, he threatened to report Forest for an illegal approach to his player. To be fair to Richmond, not only did he have the best interests of Bradford at heart but he had not personally negotiated either of the Waddle contracts, and it may well be that Stein's letter had slipped his mind, if indeed it had ever been brought to his attention.

Stein was away from his office and had no access to his files, and with the Bradford telephone lines jammed with the angry calls of supporters, all hell broke loose. As the day wore on, it became clear that Richmond would not allow Chris to leave without a fee being paid, and was suggesting a total payment of £500,000 if Forest stayed in the Premier League. It simply wasn't on.

By Friday, it was becoming apparent to Chris that perhaps the Forest managerial team of Stuart Pearce and in particular the general manager, Dave Bassett, did not want him as much as Irving Scholar did. Indeed, Bassett made it clear that Chris could not be guaranteed a place in the team, and it later transpired that if Bassett wanted Chris at all, it was only until the end of the season, while Scholar had offered a contract until June 1998. By the weekend, Bassett was making it increasingly unlikely that Chris would be joining Forest, even if Geoffrey Richmond was prepared to tone down his demands.

As it was, by the end of Friday Chris had another option. A few days before, he'd had yet another call from Peter Reid at Sunderland regarding his availability. Reid now spoke to Richmond, who continued that Chris could only go if a fee was involved, although with Bradford now reminded of the letter of 18 November, his tone was more conciliatory. There seemed to be no way that he would or could let Chris go to Forest without litigation, but the Sunderland interest offered everybody an escape route from what was becoming an increasingly embarrassing situation.

To say Chris was upset was an understatement. He felt that promises made to him had been broken and could not understand why, when the letter confirming the terms of agreement had been brought to Bradford's attention, they did not simply concede gracefully. He took to his bed with a blinding headache, spent a sleepless night sick with anxiety, and told Kamara that he was not well enough to play against Reading the next day. Despite some papers jumping to conclusions that the illness was 'convenient', Chris felt sufficiently unwell to ask for the club doctor, and both Kamara and Richmond accepted the genuineness of his condition.

By Monday morning, Chris had decided that he would not be joining Forest. Obviously Scholar wanted him, but Scholar would not be at the club every day and at his age Chris did not feel that he could work with a management team who were less than one hundred per cent in favour of his arrival. That left Sunderland.

After Reid had spoken to Richmond, who had by now accepted that Chris had played his last game in a Bradford City shirt, Stein agreed terms with Sunderland's finance director David Stonehouse almost as quickly as he had done with Scholar, and by late Monday afternoon the clubs themselves had reached an accommodation. If Sunderland retained their Premier League status, Bradford would receive £75,000, and some time within the next two seasons the teams would play each other in a friendly, with the proceeds going to Bradford.

Stein relayed the news to Chris, who had recovered sufficiently to travel to Monaco to cover the Newcastle UEFA Cup match for the BBC. Chris's delight was tempered by fears for his safety. 'Can't we delay an announcement for a day? There are thousands of Geordies out here and they'll lynch me!' Richmond, however, felt he himself had been unjustly lynched by the media and, in his anxiety to make the deal public, had already given an interview, leaving Chris to take his chances.

On the morning of 19 March, Chris arrived at Roker Park to sign for the club who had rejected him as a teenager and failed in so many efforts to secure his services as a veteran. As he went training with his new team-mates for the first time, there were familiar faces: Paul Stewart, who'd played alongside him at Spurs, Paul Bracewell, who had also made the journey from Tyneside to Weirside, and, of course, Peter Reid himself, who'd been with him on so many England trips.

Inevitably the fixture computer had thrown up its usual dramatic coincidence. Chris Waddle's first game for the club he had supported in his heart since a child would be at home to Nottingham Forest on 22 March. It was a crucial six-pointer. Sunderland had accumulated thirty-two points from thirty-one games. Forest were three places below them, in one of the relegation slots, with twenty-nine points from the same number of games.

Before the match, the club shop stocked up with T-shirts bearing a picture of Chris and the words 'True Colours'. It felt like that, too, as he pulled on the red and white stripes of Sunderland for the very first time, with the number 25 emblazoned on the back. Incredibly it was the first time he had ever played at Roker Park in a competitive match. He'd appeared in one testimonial, but that had not prepared him for the 'Roker Roar' that greeted him as he came out of the tunnel in this, the last season at Roker Park itself. The reception from the fans was magnificent. For Chris, the match had been a long time coming – not just the previous week when he had been the centre of media focus, but over twenty years, the span of his footballing career. The sixteen-year-old who had stood at the Fulwell end and nurtured ambitions to play on the park was now the thirty-six-year-old in the twilight of his footballing days.

He began the match against Forest full of tension. With both teams fighting for their Premiership lives, it was not the sort of match into which he could settle slowly. Sunderland started with a 4–4–2 formation, with Chris wide on the left rather than in his favoured free role, and by half-time he had made little impact on the game. However, in the sixty-first minute Sunderland won a corner on the left, Chris hit a tempting ball to the feet of captain, Kevin Ball, and he hit an unstoppable volley into the net. It wasn't over as far as Chris was concerned, nor, as it transpired, was it the end for Forest. In the eighty-third minute Chris switched to the right and displayed a typical piece of Waddle skill. He dragged the ball along with his left foot and, from what appeared to be a harmless position, he suddenly dropped his shoulder, accelerated between Brian Roy and Stuart Pearce with a deceptive change of pace and shot instinctively. The ball missed the goal by a whisker. Then four minutes from the end, Sunderland failed to clear a Pearce free-kick, and Lyttle seized upon the loose ball to equalise for the visitors.

There was no doubt that a draw was a better result for Forest than for the home side. Peter Reid was left to ponder why Chris had seen so little of the ball, and Chris himself wanted to figure out how the ball could be put to better use on the break. Because of England's friendly international against Mexico on Easter Saturday, they had an extra week to work on things before the match that Chris had so looked forward to, yet so feared – away at St James' Park to Newcastle United. Although Chris had been staying with Lorna's parents rather than in a hotel, without Lorna herself and the children, he still felt homesick. Home was in Dore now. Home was where he could return after training, put his feet up, watch television, take the children to and from school. There was, in some ways, very little difference between the teenage Chris Waddle who had returned so unhappily from his various trials and the married family man of 1997.

He knew it was going to be difficult to return to Tyneside in a Sunderland shirt. Newcastle had made an embarrassing exit from Europe at the hands of Monaco and now a win for the home team was vital if they were to cling to the thin life-line that still attached them to the Premiership title race. Yet before the match, with the help of Peter Reid's calming words, Chris felt incredibly relaxed. As he got off the coach, he was greeted by some chants of 'Judas', which reached their peak after his first few moments on the pitch. It wasn't as if he hadn't played there before in a visitor's kit, for he'd done so with both Tottenham and Sheffield Wednesday. But neither of those sides was the permanent target of the Geordie fans' hatred. Even at matches which didn't involve their deadly rivals from Wearside, the chant of 'We hate Sunderland' would echo from the hard-core travelling supporters. And now one of their own favourite sons was actually playing for those rivals. That had also happened before, with players moving both ways, but nobody with the profile of Chris Waddle had done it since the days of Len Shackleton, who had made the move from Newcastle to Sunderland in February 1948 and who had, coincidentally, come to St James' from Bradford.

There were still a few familiar faces at the ground, although the stadium itself, with its magnificent new stands, had changed out of all recognition since Chris had last played in the black and white stripes. Under the stewardship of Sir John Hall, the new management had dragged the club screaming towards the twenty-first century – and it showed. Peter Beardsley was still there, although he did not get off the substitutes' bench. Chris also met the old club secretary Russell Cushing, now its chief executive, who together with a few of the old security men made sure he felt welcome. Or as welcome as he could feel in the visitors' dressing-room.

Peter Reid had made a few tactical changes. Just before the transfer deadline, he had bought Allan Johnston, a Scot, from the French club, Rennes. Johnston was a naturally right-sided wide player and his acquisition allowed Chris to slot into the hole just behind Paul Stewart up front, who was effectively playing off him. That was something familiar from their Tottenham days, although Stewart had then been accompanied in a two-pronged attack by Paul Walsh.

Before the match, Chris had joked about wearing cotton-wool earplugs and a tin helmet and after thirty-two minutes it seemed as if he might need them both. A few moments before, he'd set Michael Gray up for a volley, but now he picked up the ball in mid-field, making space for himself as he moved towards the Newcastle goal. He held the ball up until he thought Gray had got himself into a shooting position and then sent him away with a clever curling pass. In fact Gray had changed his mind and cut inside several statuesque Newcastle defenders, before hitting the ball low and hard past a helpless Shaka Hislop in the home goal. The silence was deafening. Sunderland had been allocated no tickets and although a few of their fans had inevitably wangled their way into the ground, none were brave enough to participate in any organised celebration.

As it was, honours finished even when Alan Shearer scored an inevitable equaliser thirteen minutes from the end. Any suggestion that Chris might not be up to ninety minutes of Premier League football were quashed as, with David Kelly (another former Newcastle favourite) on for Johnson and Niall Quinn replacing Stewart, Chris gave the Tyneside faithful a reminder of what once had been, carving out chances for both of the substitutes. On this occasion the point was more rewarding for Sunderland. With Liverpool and Manchester United losing unexpectedly at home a victory for Newcastle would have put them back into the title contention, but with only a draw and Arsenal winning at Chelsea, it seemed to have become a three-horse race. The best the Geordies could hope for was a place in Europe, while Sunderland had every reason to believe they would survive for another season in the top echelon.

Gary Lineker, now the anchor man on *Match of the Day*, watched Chris's display with interest and admiration. There is only a month between them in age, yet Lineker is convinced that Chris can still do it at the highest level. 'Obviously you can't be the same player at thirty-six as you are in your twenties, yet a hugely talented footballer like Chris, with his natural gifts, could still pass and create chances. There was no doubt in my mind that he still had things to offer in the Premier.'

Chris continued to prove that to be the case. Two goals down at home to Liverpool on 12 April, he placed a perfect corner for Paul Stewart to head home, and although Sunderland could not find an equaliser, Chris was still running at the end of ninety minutes to give the lie to David Pleat's prognosis of his future.

Mid-week fixtures plunged Sunderland back into the bottom three relegation spots and the match against local rivals Middlesbrough took on a horrible significance. If it had been a difficult week for Sunderland, then it had been even worse for Middlesbrough. They had been fortunate to stay in the FA Cup after a 3–3 draw with Second Division Chesterfield and had lost the Coca-Cola Cup replay against Leicester. A season that had promised them two cups and the retention of their Premier status now threatened to produce nothing except relegation. But Sunderland's record at Middlesbrough was so poor that the last player to score a winning goal for them had been Brian Clough. Chris was determined to change all that, and in a game played at frenetic pace, he seemed the only participant able to put his foot on the ball, to slow down the pace as he stroked the ball around, distributing passes with pin-point accuracy.

When he had signed him Peter Reid had spoken of the options Chris would give him from dead ball situations. He'd proved his worth in that respect in earlier matches and right on the stroke of half-time he was to do it again. Whyte fouled Johnston and Chris moved purposefully over to the right, just outside the penalty area. He looked up and saw young Darren Williams moving in, free of markers. He curled in a perfect free-kick with his left foot, Williams met the ball with his head, still running, and Sunderland had the only goal of the match, moving them out of the bottom three. The goalscorer shrugged off the attention of his team-mates and ran over to hug the provider of the cross. The nineteen-year-old and the thirty-six-year-old embraced, bridging the generation gap, and leaving nobody watching at the Riverside Stadium in any doubt that the skills of Chris Waddle could always survive as long as the beautiful game was played.

FOLESHILL

POSTSCRIPT

Falkirk reached the Scottish FA Cup final by beating Celtic 1–0. However, they lost the final 1–0 to Kilmarnock, on 24 May 1997.

Bradford City escaped the drop from the First Division by beating QPR 3–0 on 4 May 1997.

On Sunday 11 May Sunderland lost 1–0 at Wimbledon and were relegated from the Premier League.